WILLIAM BLAKE

HIS LIFE

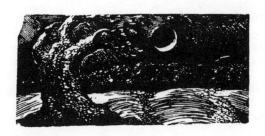

JAMES KING

St. Martin's Press
New York

Also by James King

William Cowper: A Biography
Interior Landscapes: A Life of Paul Nash
The Last Modern: A Life of Herbert Read

co-editor

The Letters and Prose Writings of William Cowper
William Cowper: Selected Letters

Library of Congress Cataloging-in-Publication Data

King, James.
    William Blake—his life / James King.
        p.   cm.
    Includes bibliographical references (p.   ) and index.
    ISBN 0-312-05292-8
    1. Blake, William, 1757–1827—Biography.   2. Poets, English—19th century—Biography.   3. Poets, English—18th century—Biography.
    4. Artists—Great Britain—Biography.   I. Title.
    PR4146.K56   1991
    821'.7—dc20
    [B]   90-8962
                                                                            CIP

First published in Great Britain by George Weidenfeld and Nicolson Limited.

First U.S. Edition: May 1991
10 9 8 7 6 5 4 3 2 1

TO CHRISTINE

Contents

Plates

Frontispiece. *William Blake*. Watercolour. Likely a self-portrait of about 1802. Robert N. Essick, Altadena

Illustrations in the Text
(all by Blake)

xi

Acknowledgements

I wish to thank David V. Erdman, Stanley Gardner, Anthony Goff, William Ober, Dennis M. Read, Aileen Ward and, especially, Robert N. Essick for providing me with information and assistance. I am also mindful of how much I have learned about Blake from my former students: Lil Bloom, Mairi Fulcher, Kelly Kowalchuk, Judith Pearson, Leila Ryan, Karin Steiner and Eleanor Ty. My Select Bibliography also reflects the enormous debt I owe to a number of Blake scholars, in particular to the work of David Bindman, Martin Butlin, Leopold Damrosch Jr, Robert N. Essick, Northrop Frye, Jean H. Hagstrum, Geoffrey Keynes, Morton D. Paley and Irene Tayler. Above all, I have learned a great deal from my friend G. E. Bentley Jr. Next to Alexander Gilchrist, Professor Bentley has been the most innovative and tireless investigator of Blake's phantom existence.

At the planning stage, Juliet Gardiner, my former publisher at Weidenfeld, provided me with many perceptive and much-needed hints. I am much indebted for the valuable editorial guidance given by Hilary Laurie and Peter James. Generous financial assistance was provided by the Social Sciences and Humanities Research Council of Canada and the Killam Foundation of the Canada Council. John Covolo and Donald C. Goellnicht read drafts of this book, and I am grateful to them for many helpful suggestions and comments.

Preface

William Blake, poet and artist, is one of the most important and controversial figures in English cultural history. Above all, he was a man of enormous contradictions, whose intense, unique vision led him to create his own philosophy and mythology. He was a Christian who despised Christianity. He was an extremely private person who retreated from society. But he was tortured by his rejection of the world: he wanted fame – and yet he did not want to be tainted with success.

There are two standard biographies. The first is Alexander Gilchrist's, published posthumously in 1863. Gilchrist began work on his book in about 1855 (he died in 1861), and he was motivated by a deep love of Blake and an affection for the truth about a man who he said 'attracts the more of my sympathy, the better I understand him'. The resulting book is extremely Victorian, however. Gilchrist felt that he had to apologize for his subject, who frequently embarrassed him. Mona Wilson's life of 1927 attempts to integrate Blake the man and artist, but she is too dependent upon Evelyn Underhill's theory of mysticism – very faddish in the 1920s – in explicating Blake's intense inner life. A great number of new facts about Blake's existence have been discovered in the past sixty years, and such findings make a new life of him essential.

Still, much of our knowledge of Blake's early and middle life comes from the recollections of disciples who knew him at the end of his life. The shifting sands of time allowed him to recall incidents which he wanted to remember and in the manner in which he wanted them retold. Accidentally or not, he altered the record. So the facts of Blake's life are at best difficult to reassemble and, at worst, a morass of contradictions.

As a result, most accounts of Blake tend to keep his symbolical world and his private existence separate from each other. This hardly prompts interesting speculation on Blake the man. For example, mothers and fathers in Blake's poetry and illustrations are often forbidding creatures, and sons have enormous contempt for any kind of parental interference – or affection. As a child, Blake experienced a profound sense of alienation from his parents, and his closest familial attachment was to his brother Robert, whose early death was the great trauma of Blake's life.

On a larger scale, Blake felt that England had divorced itself from past greatness. His art and writing are filled with nostalgia for a strong, resolute nation: he desperately wanted England to restore and renew itself. According to him, England had to be infused with a new kind of energy. Blake's aspirations for his country are resolutely centred on renewal, *not* change.

Blake's profound sense of personal and societal estrangement is acutely revealed in his work. He was intrigued but also disturbed by the possibility of exploring the alienated portions of the self. Particularly in mid-life, realizing that satanic impulses did not solely reside in others, he had to confront and expel the Satan within himself. In the resulting pictures and illuminated books, he paid a great deal of attention to mythical characters who are shut off or divorced from some aspect of themselves.

Although Blake's work records the struggle to come to grips with the grim facts of human existence, he sometimes finds solutions evading him. His paintings and illuminated books reflect such indeterminacy – the impossibility of imposing unity on disarray. Still, he resolutely experimented with works of art which might be able to achieve this forbidding task.

Blake attempts to redeem his characters – and himself – from the distortions of their own past and history by allowing them to find their ways back to their true essences (such quests are not always successful, and he is not always quite sure of the correct solution to the dilemmas he presents). In any event, his psychology frequently involves the search for unity, and he demonstrates as well that such searches are arduous and frightening. Although he fervently desires redemption, he knows how difficult it is to unite thought and action. Few writers or artists have been so touched by the deep sense of loss of friends, society and self that Blake endured.

Blake had many other conflicts. He loved Christ the revolutionary and the beneficent God the Father who encouraged his son to redeem fallen mankind; Blake was profoundly hostile to the excessively submissive Jesus, who followed the dictates of a punitive God the Father. Also, Blake's deeply divided feelings about sexuality have been neglected in previous accounts. Although he may have been faithful to his wife, his erotic (sometimes pornographic) imagination has to be examined. Also, he was not always an exemplary figure, and he did have a strong paranoid streak. Intimately aware of dark inner forces which threatened to conquer him, he valiantly battled against them.

My life of Blake also attempts to recreate his literary–artistic milieu. Although he had a tendency to cut himself off from other artists, Blake remained friendly for a long time with, among others, Flaxman, Fuseli and Stothard. In particular, his strange friendship with the eccentric writer William Hayley has to be treated in detail and with new emphases.*

At Felpham, Hayley's retreat in Sussex, Blake was in daily contact from 1800 to 1803 with a man of similar radical sentiments whose reputation (well known in contrast to Blake's obscurity) was in part based on his republican biography of Milton, with whom Blake had an intense love–hate relationship. Hayley's saccharine personality bothered Blake because he discerned a satanic personality hiding beneath a tranquil, gentle surface. Yet Blake was forced to recognize the authenticity of Hayley's iconoclasm, and the older man became a rival, a competitor to be overthrown. Blake meditated upon his envy and jealousy in *Vala* (begun in 1797), but his anger was so intense that the poem led merely to chaos, and he abandoned it. He then turned to the illuminated book *Milton*, where, in a bitter act of sibling rivalry, he redeemed his spiritual father, Milton – and himself – by surpassing Hayley's earlier, sympathetic reconstruction of Milton's life.

Blake dramatizes his inner struggles in pictures as well as in words – something no other major writer has ever attempted. In Blake's view, art is expressive – not mimetic: it is concerned not with the imitation of nature but with the manifestation of imaginative forms from the artist's imagination. In the process, art becomes for Blake an expression of personality and is thus deeply autobiographical.

This biography, which I have written for those interested in reading an account of Blake's life which shows the relationship between his existence and his art, is thus the story of the growth of a poet–artist's mind, but it is also one in which I have sought to capture the fullness of his divided personality. I have tried to reveal the desperate, often

---

* Almost half of Blake's extant letters are to Hayley; a substantial amount of his remaining correspondence was written while he was living at Felpham under Hayley's patronage.

self-imposed loneliness of much of Blake's existence and to dramatize the admirable courage with which he faced life. I have also sought to show the selfless, dedicated Christian prophet, and to evoke the damaged, envious and demonic person who sometimes preferred chaos to order.

WILLIAM
BLAKE

1

Infant Joy and Sorrow

1757–1767

FROM 1684 the parish church of St James's, Piccadilly dominated its surroundings. Almost twenty-five years before, Charles II had given Henry Jermyn permission to develop St James's Fields, and, in turn, Jermyn had invited Christopher Wren to build his only London church constructed on an entirely new site. The exterior was unduly modest, the interior sumptuous. The limewood reredos is by Grinling Gibbons, and John Evelyn was moved to claim that there was 'no altar anywhere in England, nor has there been any abroad more handsomely adorned'. John Blow and Henry Purcell tested the organ by Renatus Harris given to the parish by Queen Mary in 1691. Lord Foppington, in Vanbrugh's *The Relapse*, when asked which church he most obliged with his presence, replied: 'Oh! St James's, there's much the best company!'

The spire of St James's looked down on a neighbourhood where the fashionable, the rich, the famous, the middling, the poor and the destitute existed side by side. A newspaper account of 1748 describes such a cityscape: 'If we look into the Streets, what a Medley of Neighbourhood do we see! Here lies a Personage of high Distinction; next Door a Butcher with his stinking Shambles! A Tallow-chandler shall front my Lady's nice *Venetian* Window; and two or three brawny naked curriers in their Pits shall face a fine Lady in her back Closet, and disturb her spiritual Thoughts.'[1]

Although the quality of living conditions in London improved enormously throughout the eighteenth century, St James's, like other London parishes, was infested with a variety of urban blights, such as the abuses stemming from the availability, even in the 1750s, of cheap gin. Thirty years later, Horace Walpole reflected that 'as yet there are more persons killed by drinking than by ball or bayonet'.[2] Pregnant women addicted to this spirit often gave birth to weak, sickly children who looked 'shrivel'd and old as though they had numbered many years'.[3] Mechanics, artisans and labourers who drifted to London in search of employment routinely deserted their wives and children when they discovered that the metropolis did not offer them a lucrative style of life. The abandoned wives frequently had to pawn their beds and wedding-rings, and their children were dressed in rags. In feeble attempts to raise funds, these women invested in the State Lottery or the fraudulent and illegal private lotteries called 'Little Goes'. There were other diversions: cards, dice, draughts, baitings of bears, badgers and bulls, cock-matches and games with the intriguing names of bumble-puppy and Mississippi Fables.

In contrast to a uniformly poor district such as Stepney, Piccadilly contained an uneasy mix of opulence and destitution. There were beguiling shops, open until ten in the evening, one selling crystal flasks, another displaying pyramids of pineapples, figs, grapes and oranges; in one china shop, tableware was laid out as though a lavish dinner party was in progress. These emporiums of wealth existed in an environment where masses of ordure were left in the road and where open cellars and stone steps projected into and blocked the same streets. There was usually an assortment of mad dogs, beggars and bullock-carts. Profanity was commonplace, and the streets were poorly illuminated.

Behind or above the alluring, brightly lit windows were the usually cramped, dark and poky living quarters of the shopkeepers. Built on a cramped corner site, 28 Broad Street, with its entrance on Marshall Street, was four storeys high, with a basement. In this setting, on 28 November 1757, William Blake was born; he was baptized on Sunday, 11 December, in St James's Church. William was the third son of Catherine and James Blake, a hosier and haberdasher.

By birth, William was a child whose social status hovered between the 'middle sorts' and the 'working trades', as Defoe dubbed them. He was certainly of what Henry Fielding called 'that very large and powerful body which forms the fourth estate in the community and has long been dignified by the name of the Mob'. From the outset, Blake was, like so many others, an outcast from the refined, aristocratic mode of existence of eighteenth-century culture. As boy and man, he was a citizen of the Other London.

James, William's father, was bound as a draper's apprentice to one Francis Smith on 14 July 1737. James went with his father, also James, to the great hall of the Company of Drapers for this ceremony, where his father paid a consideration of £60 and a fee of 1s 2d. The boy would have been about fourteen, and the premium paid by his father was on the high side of average. James and his father were from Rotherhithe, a grimy offshoot of the City, across London Bridge on the south side of the Thames (Swift located Lemuel Gulliver's birth there). Seven years later, when his apprenticeship was over, James moved to a more central location at 5 Glasshouse Street, also a scruffy, disagreeable environment. According to a report of 1720, 'the houses were meanly built, neither are its Inhabitants much to be boasted of'.[4]

By 1749, James was registered as a hosier in his own right. By the time he reached his mid-twenties, he had spent twelve years working from dawn to dusk, earning between £30 and £40 a year, a sum which allowed him to live in London precariously above the poverty line. In compensation for his long hours of work and relatively low wages, James would have formed close friendships with other apprentices and journeymen in his trade. These men shared a comradeship of work-songs, horse-play, coats of arms, regalia, slang and parades; most of their meetings were held in taverns. Out of such experiences came an increasing sense of deprivation, of being outsiders to plainly visible wealth. In 1751, for example, the workers employed by a hatmaker of St Olave's, Southwark, struck against him until he raised their wages: on 21 July, thirty dissidents arrived at his house demanding to know the name of an informant. The hatmaker refused the request and, but for the intervention of his neighbour, his house would have been burned.[5]

On 15 October 1752, James married Catherine Harmitage, whose family lived at 28 Broad Street, Golden Square. Nothing else is known of Catherine's ancestry. The ceremony took place just off Hanover Square at St George's Chapel, which had been built by John James in 1721–4. This area was fashionable in the early 1710s, but by the mid-1750s the chapel had acquired the unsavoury reputation of performing hasty, informal marriage ceremonies – fifteen took place the day James and Catherine were married.

Catherine was about thirty at the time of her marriage, the groom being a year younger. The couple lived in Glasshouse Street for a year before moving to the bride's family home on Broad Street. Their first child, also James, was born on 10 July, almost nine months after they married. A second son, John, arrived on 12 May 1755; this boy probably died young. After William came another John on 20 March 1760. Richard was born on 19 June 1762 – he apparently died as an infant. The poet's only sister, Catherine Elizabeth, was born on 7 January 1764. All these children were baptized at St James's. Three years later, on 4 August, William's favourite sibling, Robert, was born. Significantly, the youngest Blake child was not baptized at St James's, and the register of subscribers who supported the ministry of the Grafton Street Baptist Church lists a 'Blake' who contributed there from 1769 to 1772.[6]

James Blake probably became a Baptist in the mid-1760s. Such a conversion was not uncommon. Many members of the mercantile, artisan and working classes had long been convinced that the hierarchal authority of the Church of England was intended to keep them firmly in their places. Also, they yearned to feel more directly the beneficent love of God. Thus they dissented from the Church of England and joined groups such as the Baptists, Quakers and Methodists. These religions were of the heart: the individual cultivated the divinity within himself. These were creeds of strongly expressed passions, in which regulations and rules took second place to feeling. By 1769, the earlier, 'Old' wave of dissent was linked to the mercantile classes, the comfortable 'middling' group. The 'New' Dissent, much more the religion of outsiders, was associated with political reform. Whether sympathetic to the 'Old' or 'New' Dissent, James was in touch with sentiments to which he would have been exposed as an apprentice and journeyman. Such religious belief often went hand in hand with political millenarianism, as in the stirring words of the Shakers' Jane Wardley: 'And when Christ appears again, and the true church rises in full and transcendent glory, then all anti-Christian denominations – the priests, the church, the pope – will be swept away.'[7]

In particular, the 'New' Dissent had a strong political axe to grind, coming into existence as it did because of the sense of outrage which had become pronounced among the working and artisan classes. This group witnessed the concentration of wealth in the hands of a small minority and increasingly realized that the King, Parliament and institutionalized religion were in league with the privileged few. This outrage led to antinomian sentiments, whereby the civil laws of a corrupt nation should be subverted because they were not in accord

'I found him beneath a Tree'

with the moral Law of the Christ who drove the money changers from the Temple.*

The artisan, shopkeeping culture into which Blake was born was one in which children were seen as slowly evolving individuals, not as little people who eventually became larger-sized adults. Throughout the century, there had been a slow but steady move in this direction: familial love was openly displayed, hierarchical authority was questioned, and gestures of love were freely bestowed on children by parents. The religious beliefs of both the 'Old' and 'New' Dissent, whereby the individual found within himself the warm feelings of a benign Saviour, obviously spilled over into corresponding emotions about family members.

The intriguing particles of information which have survived about the Blake household show that both father and mother communicated their feelings of devotion and attachment to their children. John was the favourite of both parents, and when William protested about this, he was told that he would eventually 'beg his bread' at John's door.

---

* 'Antinomianism in the strict sense is the doctrine that, for Christians, Christ's crucifixion has abolished the Mosaic law.... Near the heart of [this type] of Christian doctrine, then, is a belief of great subversive potential. If all the laws of Deuteronomy are null for believers, why shall we not do whatever we wish?' (Michael Ferber, *The Social Vision of William Blake* (Princeton University Press, 1985), pp. 117–18.) No direct link between Blake and the antinomian sects has yet been established.

William often 'remonstrated' against John's special status and was ordered to be 'quiet'.[8] His position as the 'third' child deeply disturbed him: he saw himself as inconsequential, as a mandrake infant who is carelessly picked up to join two other siblings.*

Favourites frequently have no friends, and William was later to refer to John as 'the evil one'.[9] Eventually, John borrowed money from his parents, became a baker, lost money through a combination of sloth and recklessness, threw himself on the mercy of his brothers, and, finally, joined the army, where he died. As a youngster, James, William's eldest brother, talked of seeing Abraham and Moses. Later, these visionary qualities vanished, and James developed a contempt for his 'erratic' younger brother, who began to see visions himself.

If William was not the favourite, he was certainly coddled by his father, 'always more ready to encourage than to chide'.[10] As soon as the young boy developed a taste for collecting prints, the same 'indulgent parent soon supplied him with money to buy'[11] them; he also gave him plaster casts of various antique statuary. By the mid-1760s, James seems to have won a measure of worldly success, which is strongly corroborated by his ability to gratify William's fascination with prints.

William was definitely not the easiest of children to deal with, although he was often 'easily persuaded' of the rights and opinions of others.[12] From the outset, he displayed a daring impetuosity and 'vigorous temper'.[13] He disliked any kind of regulations and rules, so much so that James decided not to send him to school. And William so 'hated a Blow' that he inveighed against any form of chastisement. As a result, 'his Father thought it most prudent to withhold from him the liability of receiving punishment'.[14]

Like his elder brother, William experienced visions between the ages of eight and ten. At Peckham Rye, near Dulwich Hill, he saw a tree filled with angels, 'bright angelic wings bespangling every bough like stars'.[15] When he returned home, his father was not pleased to hear what he considered to be a confabulation and would have broken his own rule about corporal punishment but for his wife's timely intervention.

In mid-century, it was still possible to leave the urban confines of London quickly behind and on such excursions the young boy

---

* 'As Blake was aware, the root of the poisonous mandrake was often said to resemble human beings and, according to legend, it screamed when plucked, as in *Romeo and Juliet*: 'Shrieks like mandrakes, torn out of the earth.'

experienced sharply felt epiphanic moments. One summer morning, he saw angels walking among some haymakers at work.[16] The boy was also outspoken: when he heard a traveller tell of some exotic foreign place, he exclaimed, 'Do you call *that* splendid? . . . I should call a city splendid in which the houses were of gold, the pavement of silver, the gates ornamented with precious stones.'[17] There is also a legend that at the age of four William screamed when he saw God 'put his head to the window'.[18]

Members of shopkeeping families often worked together to reduce expenses. Catherine Blake, following a time-honoured tradition, almost undoubtedly served in James's shop. So did the children. But William's exuberant personality surfaced early when he showed himself 'totally destitute of the dexterity of a London shopman'.[19] He drew designs on 'the backs of all the shop bills, and made sketches on the counter'.[20] Finally, he 'was sent away from the counter as a booby'.[21]

William Blake the child simply did not have the temperament of a favourite: he was obviously opinionated, questioning, rebellious, and sometimes obdurate and saucy. He had the penetrating eyes and high forehead evident in all the portraits of Blake the man. His single-mindedness and imagination were recognized by his mother and father. Although the speaker in 'The School Boy' from *Songs of Experience* laments how dreadful it is to go to school on a summer morning –

> O! it drives all joy away;
> Under a cruel eye outworn,
> The little ones spend the day,
> In sighing and dismay[22]

– William's parents readily agreed that their son should not endure such privation. The boy who did not want to attend school probably received his earliest instruction in reading and writing from his mother. Thus the speaker in the same lyric castigates parents far different from Blake's:

> O! father & mother, if buds are nip'd,
> And blossoms blown away,
> And if the tender plants are strip'd
> Of their joy in the springing day,
> By sorrow and cares dismay,
>
> How shall the summer arise in joy.
> Or the summer fruits appear?[23]

7

William's own sense of the tenderness which parents can bestow is found in the twin poems 'The Little Boy Lost' and 'The Little Boy Found' from *Songs of Innocence*. In the first, the child, separated from his father, is 'wet with dew' and the mire is deep; he weeps. God appears 'like his father in white' in the companion poem and leads the child to his mother, who in 'sorrow pale, thro' the lonely dale / Her little boy weeping sought'.[24] Significantly, the little boy is cut off from his father because the parent walks too fast, his brusque behaviour leading directly to the boy's unhappy experience. In 'On Another's Sorrow' the father is a compassionate figure: 'Can a father see his child / Weep, nor be with sorrow fill'd?'[25]

Nevertheless, if Blake was moved by the power of parental love, he had an even stronger perception of how it can damage or destroy a child. In 'The Little Girl Found', Lyca's parents simply do not understand the visionary world which she enters:

> Tired and woe-begone,
> Hoarse with making moan:
> Arm in arm seven days,
> They trac'd the desart ways.
>
> Seven nights they sleep,
> Among shadows deep:
> And dream they see their child
> Starv'd in desart wild.

Eventually, they are led to the place where Lyca lives among 'tygers wild'. Henceforth they dwell apart from her, having learned that there is nothing to fear from the 'wolvish howl' or the 'lions' growl' emanating from the palace where Lyca dwells.[26]

In 'A Little Boy Lost', also from *Experience*, the child who dares to challenge authority is 'burn'd ... in a holy place,/ Where many had been burn'd before'. He asks:

> And Father, how can I love you,
> Or any of my brothers more?
> I love you like the little bird
> That picks up crumbs around the door.[27]

Here Blake questions the nature of father-and-son relationships. The child does not love the father with an affection 'freely given': he is immured in an uneasy dependency on the older man. In this poem, it

Tiriel Supporting the Dying Myratana and Cursing his Sons

is a priest who seizes the child, but the father is a silent, passive witness of the child's death. Both parents weep in vain, deferring to the minister's patriarchal authority.

Blake's strongest statement about his contempt for parental supremacy is found in the poem *Tiriel*. In a manner redolent of Lear, the aged King, Tiriel, after the death of his wife, finds himself spurned by his children. He himself has enslaved one of his brothers, Zazel, and his other brother Ijim does not recognize him. He finds no solace with his senile parents, Har and Heva. Throughout the poem, Tiriel moves restlessly from place to place cursing his children and being cursed in turn by them.

The text is filled with unnatural relationships: Tiriel is a cruel, wrathful father; Tiriel and his brothers loathe each other; children scorn their parents. Tiriel's eldest son tells him that he is 'obdurate as the devouring pit' and Hela, one of his daughters, screams at him: 'thou cruel man ... thou wantest eyes'.[28]

William's poems about fathers reflect his own unease with James. At the simplest level, he realized at a very early age just how different he was from his father. He was not the ideal child that John or the

'Infant Joy'   'Infant Sorrow'

more compliant James were. So William felt guilty, his guilt leading to anger at the person who caused him so much discomfort. His own father and fathers in general became the targets of his resentment. But it should not be forgotten that he frequently depicts fathers as warm, caring figures.

Not unexpectedly, a similar pattern of conflicting emotions is present in Blake's depiction of maternal figures. In his illumination to his poem 'The Echoing Green', mothers gently mind their restless children, and in 'The Little Black Boy' the mother tenderly teaches her son under a tree. However, the mother who brings the child into existence in 'To Tirzah' is condemned for such a depraved act:

> Though Mother of my Mortal part,
> With cruelty didst mould my Heart,
> And with false self-deceiving tears,
> Didst bind my Nostrils, Eyes & Ears.
>
> Didst close my Tongue in senseless clay
> And me to Mortal Life betray.[29]

Blake perceives the mother's role in a double-sided way: she can offer comfort and joy, or she can be seen as a demon who, having behaved in an evil way by bringing the child into existence, smothers him. William, who never endured the physical tortures described in his chimney-sweep poems, felt that he underwent corresponding mental agonies.

Blake's reticence (noted by friends and acquaintances) as an adult in speaking of his parents is prompted by a desire to present himself as a self-originating genius, a person whose mortal genesis is cloudy and unspecified. In so doing, Blake characterizes himself as a prodigy whose dazzling intellect and accomplishments are drawn directly from himself or some internal divinity. Like Christ, his miraculous attainments are due not to mortal parents but to inner strengths springing directly from a supernatural source. Consistently, Blake looked at the phenomena of birth and creation with a jaundiced eye, as in *Jerusalem* where a foetus is compared to a malignant tumour: 'Then all the Males combined into One Male & every one / Became a ravening eating Cancer growing in the Female / A Polypus of Roots of Reasoning Doubt, Despair & Death.'[30] He insists that conception, which seems to be a beneficent deed, subjects the person born to suffering.

In an attempt to make himself into a truly valorous personality, Blake presented himself as his own best creation. In so doing, he could examine the possibilities of paradise latent within himself and point in the direction of a new kind of spiritual renewal. For such a person, then, parents and all other authority figures were an impediment, as expressed in this lyric in his Notebook:

> The Angel that presided o'er my birth
> Said, 'Little creature formd of Joy & Mirth,
> Go live without the help of any King on Earth.'[31]

Although Blake rebelled against the notions of mother and father and against his own mother and father, he tried to overcome the anxiety caused by such defiance by simply doing away with the figures against whom he should naturally have revolted.

Blake's characterization of himself as a *Wunderkind* did mean, however, that he felt cut off from those from whom he could have derived comfort and warmth. This was a heavy psychic price, and a sense of deprivation is a predominant theme in much of Blake's writings: he feels distant from relatives, friends, colleagues. As a loner, he also looks from the outside at political and religious institutions and finds them wanting. Blake the poet and artist gained a great deal of leverage from this vantage point, but he also suffered deeply because of self-imposed estrangement.

As a child, many of the contradictions in Blake's personality were evident: he craved recognition, esteem and love, and yet, at the same time, he wanted to be left alone to cultivate the forces of genius within himself. His reluctance to be dependent on others was overcome in the single most important relationship of his life, that with his brother Robert, who was born when William was nine years old.

The difference in their ages meant that William could act in a paternal as well as fraternal way towards his young brother. Soon he realized that Robert was the only other member of the family who shared his own special view of the world – or William may have only identified that potential within Robert. In any event, Robert became the:

> affectionate companion of William, they sympathized in their pursuits & sentiments, like plants planted side by side, by a stream they grew together, & entwined the luxuriant Tendrils of their Expanding minds. They associated and excelled together, & like all true lovers delighted in & enhanced each other's beauties.[32]

The metaphor of 'lovers' is not too strong. There may well have been more than a hint of the narcissism of twins in the relationship of the brothers: William needed to see himself reflected in a child who looked and acted very much like himself. But beyond any such mirroring was genuine affection and love. At the age of nine, the fiery, lonely little boy finally had a companion on whom he could bestow the fullness of the generosity and affection which made up a large part of his personality.

2

The Young Antiquarian

1768–1778

A LTHOUGH by the late 1760s his family was financially stable (his father was now of 'substantial Worth'),[1] William was a witness to the plight of those who were not – and who vehemently proclaimed their anger. If he were at all inclined to be rebellious, he could observe and become sympathetic to the outcasts with whom his prosperous father might, by now, have been at odds.

On 18 April 1768 the *Annual Register* carried this news item: 'Yesterday a 1/2 penny loaf, adorned with mourning Crape, was hung up at several parts of the Royal Exchange, with an inscription, containing some reflections touching the high price of bread....'[2] Three weeks later, during a protest at the House of Lords, some cried out that 'bread and beer were too dear & that it was as well to be hanged as starved'.[3]* Almost a year later in March 1769, merchants loyal to the Crown attempted to present a petition of support directly to the King. This led to the 'Battle of Temple Bar' in which a 'desperate mob ... insulted, pelted and maltreated the principal conductors, so that several coaches were obliged to withdraw, some to return back, others to proceed by

---

*The poor were threatened by lack of bread, or they were forced to pay unreasonable prices for it, or it was of poor quality. Dissent against the government was often focused on the unavailability of this staple, and the shortage of bread is referred to many times in Blake's verse. A nation's refusal to take heed of its citizens' basic needs is, according to Blake, indicative of pervasive indifference.

bye-ways, and those who arrived at St James's were so daubed with dirt, and shattered, that both masters and drivers were in the utmost peril of their lives'.[4] All the shops in the neighbourhood, including that of Blake's father, had to be shut.

Another series of incidents with which the Blake family would have been familiar were the fights between two types of journeymen: single-hand weavers (the 'cutters') and engine-weavers, whose machines could do as much in one day as six of the other group. The masters took the opportunity to reduce the price of work and so a three-cornered dispute ensued. On 10 August 1768, a band of Spitalfields weavers broke into the house of one master, Nathaniel Farr, shredded the silk in two looms and killed seventeen-year-old Edward Fitch, an employee.[5] The 'cutters' banded together and collected money to build up a strike fund, to which masters were expected to contribute. Those who did not pay up could expect reprisals: Lewis Chauvet's premises on Crispin Street in Spitalfields Market were besieged by 1500 weavers led by John Valline. Seventy-six looms were 'cut' because of Chauvet's earlier refusal to contribute. He avoided further damage only when he agreed to hand over £2 2s in beer money and promised to pay his subscription in the future. The journeymen's violent behaviour soon led to vigorous counterattacks by the authorities. At the Dolphin Ale-House in New Cock Lane, two 'cutters' were shot dead during a raid. In December 1769, Valline was hanged before a large crowd of weavers at Bethnal Green.

Blake's later, vehement defence of the oppressed may derive in part from his realization that his father, who had emerged from origins not dissimilar to those of the 'cutters' but had attained a measure of security, rejected the aims of the agitators of the 1770s.

As he became more aware of the rising tide of social activism, young Blake's intellect was blossoming. Like many poets, Blake later claimed that his earliest verse was written at a precocious age: in his mid-twenties, he let it be known that some of his *Poetical Sketches*, published in 1783, were 'commenced in his twelfth' year.[6] This poetry shows a remarkable knowledge of Milton, Shakespeare, Spenser and Collins as well as the Old and New Testaments.

At the age of fourteen, Blake wrote this 'Song':

> How sweet I roam'd from field to field,
> And tasted all the summer's pride,

'Till I the prince of love beheld,
    Who in the sunny beams did glide!

He shew'd me lilies for my hair,
    And blushing roses for my brow;
He led me through his gardens fair,
    Where all his golden pleasures grow.

With sweet May dews my wings were wet,
    And Phoebus fir'd my vocal rage;
He caught me in his silken net,
    And shut me in his golden cage.

He loves to sit and hear me sing,
    Then, laughing, sports and plays with me;
Then stretches out my golden wing,
    And mocks my loss of liberty.[7]

Despite the use of some catch-phrases from Elizabethan and mid-eighteenth-century verse, the evocation of a pastoral landscape is fresh, the power of the poem deriving in part from the young versifier's sensuous response to nature.

This small lyric is also concerned with oppression, a condition of existence about which this precocious adolescent was particularly troubled. The speaker, a female bird, is passive – she accepts the blandishments of the 'prince of love' and, as a result, she is seized and imprisoned in a 'golden cage'. The way out of such impasses, the poem implies, is to taste the summer's pride in isolation.

Increasingly, the boy felt cut off from his parents and immediate surroundings. Years later, he recalled: 'I thought my pursuits of Art a kind of Criminal Dissipation & neglect of the main chance which I hid my face for not being able to abandon.' Guiltily, he saw himself clinging to a 'Passion which is forbidden by Law & Religion'.[8] Nevertheless, William was intrepid: 'I read Burke's Treatise when very Young; at the same time I read Locke on Human Understanding & Bacon's Advancement of Learning.'[9] One book with which he would have been familiar was John Bunyan's *Pilgrim's Progress*, the first part of which was published in 1678 (second part, 1684). Bunyan's early existence bears some resemblance to Blake's: he was the son of a brazier and, after learning to read and write at a village school, was set to learn his father's trade.

Bunyan's book was the great foundation-text of the working-class movement and for many young dissenters this spiritual adventure story was their book of books.[10] For one thing, Bunyan's allegorical depiction of Christian's flight from the City of Destruction to the Celestial City is vividly written. Also, Christian's confrontations are startling and filled with tension. The foul Apollyon, for example, was 'clothed with scales, like a fish (and they are his pride), he had wings like a dragon, feet like a bear, and out of his belly came fire and smoke'.[11] Bunyan had a keen visual sense, and nothing is left to chance in the portrayal of the Slough of Despond, Vanity Fair and the Valley of the Shadow of Death. Yet these are intellectual concepts which are being brought to life. Above all, *Pilgrim's Progress* is a story of oppression being mastered, a manual of how to overcome forces which seem impossibly daunting. Christian's enemies include the aristocratic Lord Luxurious, the Lord Carnal Delight and Lord Lechery. This book, saturated with class-conflict, was the most widely known literary text among artisans and labourers.

Although there is at the heart of *Pilgrim's Progress* a passive acceptance of the horrors of earthly existence which would have been repugnant to Blake, he learned a great deal from Bunyan. He would have been stirred by Bunyan's incredible ability to picture his allegorical world – the union of the visual and verbal is consistently masterful. He would also have seen the story of Christian as a narrative dealing with how despotic forces could be overcome. He would have been impressed by how the events in the story have a straightforward spiritual meaning. Although Blake sometimes railed against allegory, he often writes in an allegorical manner.

Bunyan envisages a spiritual world which has been lost by the greed and corruption of the aristocracy and bourgeoisie. Much of Blake's writing is about the possibility of restoring that which has been taken or of repairing that which was once beautiful. Blake's tentative adherence to the antinomianism of working-class religious movements derives from an intimate acquaintance with their doctrines readily at hand on the London streets and from a concept of liberty he imbibed from writers such as Bunyan, whose literary child he was. Much later, in the midst of a crisis, Blake asserted that his was a 'Divided Existence', but, he very much hoped, he would be able 'to travel on in the Strength of the Lord God, as Poor Pilgrim says'.[12]

At the same time as Blake was poring over a wide variety of books, his interest in the visual was struggling into being. The young man's talent for drawing showed itself 'as spontaneously as it was premature'[13] and initially was encouraged in secret by his mother.[14] He was fascinated with the prints, drawings and paintings on which he

Christian Begins his Pilgrimage

could feast his eyes at Abraham Langford's auction rooms in Covent Garden and at Christie's in Pall Mall. Since the collections of the rich were notoriously difficult to enter and since there were virtually no public exhibitions, the auction houses and print shops were the best places for a young eye to train itself. Early on, Blake was enthralled by the classical style of High Renaissance art, a predilection then considered eccentric. Heedless of whether or not he was in a small minority, and, with money given to him by his father, he purchased prints by Raphael, Michelangelo, Durer and Giulio Romano. Years later, he boasted: 'I am happy I cannot say that Rafael Ever was from my Earliest Childhood hidden from Me. I Saw & I Knew immediately the difference between Rafael and Rubens.'[15] It was said that 'Langford favoured him by knocking down the lots he bought so quickly, that he obtained them at a rate suited to the pocket savings of a lad.'[16] The celebrated auctioneer called Blake his 'Little Connoisseur' but others 'harassed' him for his interest in artists deemed outré. Young Blake made up his own mind about such matters, enduring ostracism by other collectors in the process.

In about 1768 John Boydell moved his print shop to 90 Cheapside (at the corner of Ironmonger Lane). There, the former engraver specialized in reproductive prints, particularly of historical subjects. Capitalizing on the rising vogue for print-collecting among the middle class, Boydell commissioned paintings which could then be engraved: although he sold the resulting oil paintings and watercolours, his real profits arose from the marketing of the engravings. From 1770 onwards, much of his business was concentrated on the vast export market in France and Germany.

Boydell became one of the most important patrons of English art in the eighteenth century, since he eagerly sought native painters and engravers who could produce work for his increasingly lucrative market. The young collector Blake probably visited this shop, where he would have been inspired by the splendid new opportunities now awaiting the person who dedicated himself to the life of artist or engraver.

At the age of ten, William's interest in drawing and copying led him to take lessons at Henry Pars' academy near Beaufort Buildings in the Strand. Through its founder, William Shipley, this drawing school was closely related to the Society for the Encouragement of the Arts, Manufactures and Commerce, of which Shipley had been a founding member in 1754. This institution, therefore, laid emphasis on both the practical and fine arts. Pars, who took over the school in about 1761, ran it along the lines envisaged by its originator. Although some academies then used life models, Pars' instruction stuck to the copying of prints and antique casts. After gaining some proficiency, the better students were allowed to work in the Duke of Richmond's celebrated gallery of casts. Thomas Jones, a student there in 1761–2, ruefully observed that he was 'reduced to the humiliating Situation of copying drawings of Ears, Eyes, Mouths and Noses among a group of little boys of half my age who had the start of me by two or three years'.[17] Blake would have been a member of such an assemblage, but he was not one of the children who won prizes offered to students at the school by the Society of Arts.

When William turned fourteen, a profession had to be found for him. The young man's print-collecting and drawing pointed in the direction of the arts. At first, the family considered apprenticing him to 'a painter of Eminence', the necessary applications being made. However, a large fee was required, and with 'characteristic generosity'

William told his father that he would not allow a great deal of money to be spent on himself at the expense of his brothers and sister. The young man suggested that he take up engraving, a calling which required a much lower premium. So one legend states.[18] Another possibility is that William was not attracted to the 'polite art' of painting and preferred engraving. He was, after all, an ardent collector of prints.

Once William had determined to become an engraver, the family approached William Wynne Ryland, the fashionable stipple engraver to George III. At the boy's instigation, the negotiations failed. After leaving Ryland's studio, he turned to James: 'Father, I do not like the man's face: *it looks as if he will live to be hanged!*'[19] Ryland's print-selling business was in serious financial trouble, and he went bankrupt in December 1771. Certainly, Ryland was hanged in 1783 for forging a cheque.* Ryland, whose premises were on Russell Street in Covent Garden, would have charged the Blakes at least £100. James may have known of Ryland's financial instability and hesitated to use him. Instead of Ryland, William and his father settled on James Basire.

In 1771, Basire was a well-known forty-seven-year-old failure, whose fee of £52 10s was decidedly in the middle range. As a younger man, Basire had been one of the most distinguished line engravers of his day, numbering William Hogarth and Benjamin West among his clients. Now, the choicest assignments were going to those who practised the modish English style of engraving, which had developed techniques which disdained the appearance of lines and sought instead to give the impression of surfaces and masses. Such engravers, Blake felt, favoured 'Fine Tints' over 'Fine Forms'.[20] Since Ryland was of the newer persuasion, Blake, whose collecting interests favoured the masters of line engraving, would obviously have been more comfortable with Basire. At the outset, Blake cast his lot with an out-of-fashion segment within his chosen profession.

According to the standard form for indenture, the master taught his pupils the 'Art and Mystery' of his calling. These 'Secrets' initiated the students into what was then still considered a clandestine profession, one still linked to recondite pseudosciences. Basire himself was renowned for the 'correctness of his drawing and the fidelity of his burin'.[21] His workshop was small and, perforce, intimate. He usually had only two apprentices, and his pupils were therefore thoroughly

---

*Blake recounted this story to Frederick Tatham towards the end of his life, and thus his knowledge of Ryland's fate might well have assisted his recollection.

indoctrinated in all aspects of the engraving process. Unlike other masters, Basire did not encourage specialization.

Basire required his students to pay careful attention to scale, outline and 'minute particulars'. Blake, who later claimed that 'Singular & Particular Detail is the Foundation of the Sublime',[22] remained a faithful disciple of his master. In addition to teaching Blake the secrets of his profession, Basire had texts sent to him for engraving which introduced Blake to intriguing topics: archaeology, mythology, Gothicism, early British history, comparative religion. Thus the young man's earlier readings in the English classics were supplemented by the texts readily available in Basire's shop.

The boy had moved more into the mainstream of literary and artistic London. One day, Oliver Goldsmith walked into Basire's. William 'mightily admired the great author's finely marked head as he gazed up at it, and thought to himself how much *he* should like to have such a head when he grew to be a man'.[23] This occurred in about 1773, when he was sixteen. However much he enjoyed the labour and admired his master, the sometimes surly teenager eventually, after two 'smooth' years, quarrelled with two new apprentices, probably James Parker and one of Basire's sons. As he recalled, the 'harmony' of the engraving shop was disrupted by the new arrivals; according to Blake, Basire declared that he was 'too simple' whereas the other two lads were 'too cunning'.[24]* Thus he 'was sent out to make drawings'.[25] Obviously, Basire wanted his talented but irascible student out of the way.

It was to Westminster Abbey that Blake was dispatched. There, in shadowy seclusion, he made sketches of the tombs in preparation for the two large collections of engravings commissioned from Basire by the Society of Antiquaries: Richard Gough's *Sepulchral Monuments in Great Britain* and *Vetusta Monumenta*. Blake was delighted to have been set loose to copy there: 'he drew in every point he could catch, frequently standing on the monument, and viewing the figures from the top.'[26] Just as he preferred Basire's method of engraving to the more faddish one, William found in Westminster Abbey 'the simple and plain road to the style of art at which he aimed, unentangled in the intricate windings of modern practice'.[27] A blind adherence to technological innovation was for him a form of idiocy.

* Malkin *implies* that Blake and Basire were in league against the two wayward apprentices. He states (G. E. Bentley, Jr, *Blake Records* (Oxford: The Clarendon Press, 1969), p. 422; henceforth, *BR*): 'Blake, not chusing to take part with his master against his fellow apprentices, was sent out to make drawings.'

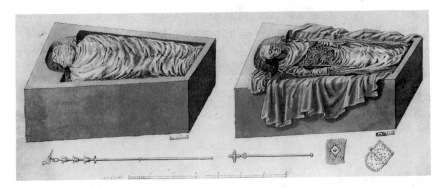

The Body of Edward I in his Coffin

Blake went to great lengths to find subjects to engrave. On 12 May 1774 a private company of antiquaries was granted permission to open the tomb of Edward I in the Abbey. Blake took advantage of the occasion to make some drawings of this macabre event, of which Sir Joseph Ayloffe was also a witness. He described how Edward's face 'was of a dark-brown, or chocolate colour, approaching to black; and so were the hands and fingers. The chin and lips were entire, but without any beard ... some globular substance, possibly the fleshy part of the eye-balls, was moveable in their sockets under the envelope.'[28] Such an eerie experience may have triggered the lines 'Fancy returns, and now she thinks of bones, / And grinning skulls, and corruptible death, / Wrap'd in his shroud' in 'Fair Elenor' from the *Poetical Sketches*.[29]

Blake's verse demonstrates a knowledge of the graveyard poetry which became increasingly fashionable throughout the century. In *Westminster Abbey: An Elegiac Poem* (1784), Thomas Maurice mixes antiquarianism, sepulchral statuary and a fascination with the presence of death as he evokes:

> Majestic monuments of pious toil,
> Whose tow'rs sublime in Gothic Grandeur soar,
>   Where Death sits brooding o'er his noblest spoils,
> And strews with royal dust the sacred floor.[30]

Many years later, Samuel Palmer asserted that Blake experienced 'his earliest and most sacred recollections' at Westminster Abbey.[31] These memories possibly included the illuminated manuscripts which were on display in the Westminster Chancery House Library. Certainly,

Blake drew the effigies of Henry III and of Queen Eleanor, the wife of Edward I. He completed a sideview of the tomb of the Countess of Aveline, and he also copied from wall-paintings around the Abbey. There he had further visions. One day in its gloomy recesses the:

> aisles and galleries of the old building (or sanctuary) suddenly filled with a great procession of monks and priests, choristers and censer-bearers, and his entranced ear heard the chant of plain-song and chorale, while the vaulted roof trembled to the sound of organ music.[32]

During services, the vergers routinely locked Blake alone with the 'solemn memorials of far off centuries'. A boy with his imagination would have no difficulty in conjuring up such a vision or one involving the appearance of Christ and his Apostles. The 'Spirit of the past' had literally become his 'familiar companion'.[33]

Throughout his life, Blake knew that his visions were of his own devising. At the home of the wealthy patrons, Mr and Mrs Charles Aders, he told of one such experience:

> 'The other evening,' said Blake, in his usual quiet way, 'taking a walk, I came to a meadow, and at the farther corner of it I saw a fold of lambs. Coming nearer, the ground blushed with flowers; and the wattled cote and its woolly tenants were of an exquisite pastoral beauty. But I looked again, and it proved to be no living flock, but beautiful sculpture.'

A lady who was listening to this anecdote interrupted him: 'I beg pardon, Mr Blake, but *may* I ask *where* you saw this?' '*Here*, madam,' answered Blake, touching his forehead.[34]

As it was the custom for apprentices to live with their masters, William moved in 1772 from his parents' home to Basire's residence at 31 Great Queen Street, Lincoln's Inn Fields. Blake's anxiety about parental oppression would have been considerably lightened by a change of domicile. His visits to Broad Street were now limited to the evening or a Sunday. Much of his attention on these occasions would have been devoted to Robert, to whom he gave instructions in drawing.

In young manhood Blake kept his distance from his parents. Vestiges of adolescent rebellion remained intact, as in 'A Little Girl Lost' where even a loving father imposes guilt:

> To her father white
> Came the maiden bright:
> But his loving look,
> Like the holy book,
> All her tender limbs with terror shook.[35]

Blake loved his father, but he did not want to be compelled to bestow affection. His own particular form of defiance led him to claim that 'Patriarchal pride' is cruel, exclusive and destructive. In a sketch for *Vala*, the son Orc looks with scarcely concealed jealousy on the amorous embrace of his parents, Los and Enitharmon. But in another section of the same poem Los beholds the 'ruddy boy / Embracing his bright mother & beheld malignant fires / In his young eyes'.[36] In an interesting twist, it is the jealous Los who nails the fourteen-year-old Orc down upon a Promethean rock. According to Blake, parental love is an 'Appetite Craving'.[37] In later life, Blake was obsessed, as he told Samuel Palmer, with the parable of the Prodigal Son: he repeated part of the story, 'but at the words, "When he was yet a great way off, his father saw him," could go no further; his voice faltered, and he was in tears'.[38]

What Blake attempts to eradicate from his own psychology is any responsibility for his sense of guilt. He believes that, if a young person feels shame, that is the parent's fault. For Blake, boy and man, a love imposed is hateful: he wants to decide whom he is going to love. Since it is impossible for children to select their parents, that type of affection remains repugnant to him. The price for such tenacious feelings was the tremendous guilt which remained with Blake all his life, as evidenced in his reaction to the parable of the Prodigal Son. Much more acceptable to him was fraternal love, where there is an element of choice.

William picked Robert, upon whom he bestowed affection withheld from his mother, father and other siblings. There is a fine irony here. Blake chose a favourite brother towards whom he could act in a paternal way. He was Robert's teacher, mentor, guide. In this manner, he was able to displace his parents – particularly his father. And, of course, Blake helped to shape Robert's character, notwithstanding that such moulding on the part of parents was a special target of his venom. Blake's cultivation of Robert was his most sustained and successful piece of Oedipal insubordination.

As his twenty-first birthday approached, Blake was an isolated, opinionated young man. He was obsessed with an ideal, primitive past. He wanted to return to a simpler way of engraving. He hankered after a birthright which excluded obligations to parental figures. Above all he felt deprived, as if he and other members of his class were separated from a glorious inheritance. He became increasingly suspicious that governmental and religious institutions had squandered that legacy, and he thought that the clues to the restoration of himself and his society lay in that past. At this stage in his life, it is no wonder that Blake became a devoted antiquarian. In his view, early British history was the story of how freedom-loving patriots overcame 'The Cruelties used by Kings & Priests'.[39]

In 1773, at the age of sixteen, Blake made a trial engraving, employing the dot-and-lozenge techniques (wherein dots or short lines are incised into the shade created by intersecting sets of parallel lines) taught by Basire. When he reworked this piece, he called it *Joseph of Arimathea among the Rocks of Albion*. Blake's design is after a print attributed to Beatrizet from Michelangelo's fresco of the *Crucifixion of St Peter* in the Pauline Chapel, which has been said to be a self-portrait by Michelangelo. In his inscription to the second state of his engraving Blake wrote that Joseph was 'One of the Gothic Artists who Built the Cathedrals in what we call the Dark Ages; Wandering about in sheep skins & goat skins of whom the World was not worthy; such were the Christians in all Ages.'[40] The classic foot, the muscular arms and legs, and the larger-than-life qualities of Joseph attest to Blake's early skill as an engraver. Even then he was aware that the act of copying was essential in order to learn the language of art.

If there is an autobiographical touch in Michelangelo's St Peter, there is definitely one in Blake's depiction of Joseph, who in his engraving is an heroic but lonely figure placed at the margin of the sea with huge rock formations behind him. The folded arms convey a sense of entrapment, as does Joseph's clothing, which appears to weigh him down. Blake was perhaps commenting on the long years of discipline and servitude which awaited him near the onset of his apprenticeship. Joseph's isolation stems from his fiercely independent nature. His slightly hunched posture suggests that he must look inwards to discover truth. Increasingly, Blake had to do the same.

According to legend, Joseph of Arimathea was sent by St Paul to preach the gospel in England, where he founded the first church at Glastonbury. Although the inhabitants of England were a barbarous lot, he used his considerable powers of rhetoric to convert many souls. Joseph's secluded sojourn on a bleak Druidic island ultimately came

Joseph of Arimathea

to fruition, and Blake's engraving thus contains a touch of optimism. He hoped that England could be revitalized by a return to a glorious past in which Boadicea could overcome the Romans, the barons overpower King John, and Queen Emma vanquish her cruel son Edward the Confessor. He fervently believed that the political, artistic and parental tyrannies which had 'stain'd fair Albion's breast with her own children's gore'[41] could be vanquished.

3

Conservative Revolutionary

1778–1784

As an apprentice, Blake witnessed the onslaught of the new industrial ethic which was sweeping England. Richard Arkwright's 'Waterframe' spinning machine was put into operation in 1769, and Arkwright inaugurated his first factory at Cromford, Derbyshire two years later. Josiah Wedgwood started 'Etruria', his new pottery works, in 1769.

Blake cast his lot with the older generation of engravers. His suspicions about Britain's wholehearted embrace of the Industrial Revolution were coupled with an admiration for the Americans' attempt to free themselves from the shackles of English imperialism. The events in America were part of a pervasive questioning of inherited authority in other places, such as Poland, Greece and Holland. Blake's attention was focused on America and such events as the Boston tea party in December 1773 and the ensuing clashes at Lexington and Concord in 1775. Although the American Revolution may have been a revolt by middle-class entrepreneurs against the competing mercantile dictates of empire, this is not how Blake viewed this confrontation. He saw the Americans as a group who said no to the dictates of a social and governmental system of oppression. He would have been stirred by Washington's words: 'Unhappy it is . . . to reflect that a Brother's Sword has been sheathed in a Brother's breast, and that the once happy and peaceful plains of America are either to be drenched with blood or

Inhabited by Slaves. Sad alternative. But can a virtuous Man hesitate in his Choice?'[1]

From the 1760s opposition in London to the war in America was widespread. 'Wilkites' were routinely elected to Parliament from London and Middlesex, and John Wilkes came to personify opposition to George III's tyranny. Although Wilkes was a bit of a demagogue, he took on – in his flamboyant way – the Hanoverian regime. He bitterly attacked it in the *North Briton* and successfully fought an attempt to unseat him in Parliament. Wilkes argued that George III's policy towards America was metaphoric of a similar intolerance of freedom in domestic affairs. For many of Blake's class, the American struggle was a secular apocalypse, a staging ground for the eventual restoration of religious and political liberty in England. In about 1780, Blake drew 'Albion the ancient Man' who 'rose from where he labourd at the Mill with Slaves / Giving himself for the Nations he danc'd the dance of Eternal Death'.[2] Like Milton's Samson, Albion must sacrifice himself in order to redeem others. In fact, he must endure death on behalf of the 'Nations' (America); only when this task is accomplished can his own country be fully rejuvenated.

In many ways Blake was a conservative revolutionary: he valued the past and wanted its values to be restored. One of his first responses to the American insurrection and its heroes was to examine those figures in British history who exemplified corresponding moral courage. *The Landing of Brutus in England, Lear and Cordelia in Prison, St Augustine Converting King Ethelbert of Kent, The Ordeal of Queen Emma* and *The Penance of Jane Shore* are among a series of watercolours of about 1779. In an ambitious manner, reminiscent of the artist–engraver Hogarth – who had been trained a rung lower down on the social ladder than Blake as a silver-plate engraver and who became rich and famous by publishing his own series of prints – Blake intended to transfer these paintings into a small collection of engravings, 'The History of England'.[3] The common denominator in these illustrations is a concern with how a resolute, self-motivated individual can determine the course of history. More particularly, in the cases of Cordelia, Queen Emma and Jane Shore, Blake highlights the plights of courageous women who dared to question oppressive legal authority.

Jane Shore, who died in about 1527, had been the mistress of Edward IV. When he died in 1483, the Protector – the future Richard III – confined her to the Tower, confiscated her possessions and accused her of being a harlot. The Ecclesiastical Court ordered her to do public penance at St Paul's, where she was brought wrapped in a white sheet,

The Dance of Albion

holding a wax taper in her hand. 'She behaved with so much modesty and decency, that such as respected her Beauty more than her fault, never were in greater admiration of her, than now.'[4]

In a picture from the same series, *The Death of Earl Godwin*, Blake shows the final moment of a bloodthirsty villain. According to legend, Godwin had been responsible for the murder of Alfred, the brother of Edward the Confessor. While dining some months afterwards with the monarch, he swore: 'I pray God that this morsel I am going to eat may choak me at this moment, if I had any hand in the death of that Prince.'[5] As Blake shows, the piece of food 'stuck in his Throat and choaked him immediately, to the great astonishment of the Standers-by'.[6]

At about the same time that he was meditating upon the lessons to be drawn from England's past, Blake produced a parallel series of watercolours which are concerned with more recent British history: the plague of 1665 and the fire of 1666. In reality, these urban landscapes return Blake to what he knew best: the London of the 1780s. He is predicting new calamities for a nation which has failed to live up to its noble past and which seeks to impose its imperial will on the other side of the Atlantic. The tiny figure of the bell-ringer in the background to *Pestilence* adds a small haunting touch to the grim deaths taking place in the central area of the picture: time has run out.

Royal oppression is a predominant theme in 'Gwin, King of Norway', 'King Edward the Third', the Prologues to 'King Edward the Fourth' and 'King John' and 'A War Song to Englishmen' from *Poetical Sketches*, his first volume of verse. A heavy-handed irony pervades the 'War Song':

> Soldiers, prepare! Our cause is Heaven's cause;
> Soldiers, prepare! Be worthy of our cause:
> Prepare to meet our fathers in the sky:
> Prepare, O troops, that are to fall to-day!
> Prepare, prepare.[7]

Unlike Shakespeare, Blake evinces little or no ambivalence in his depiction of monarchs. In 'Gwin', Gordred the giant, aroused by the monarch's 'cruel' treatment of his subjects –

> The Nobles of the land did feed
> Upon the hungry Poor;
> They tear the poor man's lamb, and drive
> The needy from their door![8]

Pestilence: The Great Plague of London

– ultimately prevails, splitting the head of Gwin.

Although, in figures such as Orc and Los, Blake would tell similar stories of headstrong opponents of authority, he would become more and more aware of just how difficult such struggles are.

The clear republicanism of the poetry and paintings of the late 1770s is not reflected in Blake's decision to enrol as a student at the Royal Academy in Somerset House, the Strand, on 8 October 1779. That resolve displays residual conflicts in this earnest young man: he seemed to be diametrically opposed to the celebration of empire seen in the paintings of Benjamin West, a prominent Academician, and yet he pursued wordly success at the institution which nurtured such artists. Moreover, the Royal Academy discriminated against engravers: only 'Painters, Sculptors, or Architects' were acceptable. Francesco Bartolozzi, the first engraver to become an Academician, was granted that status on his merits as a painter. Only in 1770 were engravers allowed to become Associate Members. Such limited distinction was granted only because some Academy members were anxious for the financial rewards which engravings of their work could give them. Nevertheless, many renowned engravers refused such scraps from the Academy's table.

Blake shared some of the prejudices of the Academicians: he did not wish to remain a mere copier. As he said, 'No other Artist can reach the original Spirit [in an engraving] as well as the Painter himself.'[9] He claimed, 'from early Youth [he] cultivated the two arts, Painting & Engraving'.[10]

Before the inauguration of the Academy in 1768, there existed organizations of artists such as the Free Society of Artists, the Incorporated Society of Artists of Great Britain, and the St Martin's Lane Academy. On the Continent, such groups survived under royal patronage and such a benediction – and protection – was asked of George III, the founders of the Academy being anxious to foster a national school of art. This goal was to be accomplished in several ways: a school for the sound training of the young, an annual exhibition by members and non-members, the establishment of a library, and the setting up of professorships in anatomy, perspective, architecture, painting and geometry. Thirty-six of the forty Academicians were named in the Instrument of Foundation. From the start, it was very much a closed shop, directly linked to bureaucratic power.

Sir Joshua Reynolds was the first President of the Academy, an office he held almost continually until his death in 1792. The Academy's meetings during its first eleven years were held on the south side of Pall Mall, and it was there that Blake attended classes. Rules, such as the following, would have been repugnant to him: 'There shall be Weekly, set out in the Great Room, One or more Plaister Figures by the Keeper, for the Students to draw after, and no Student shall presume to move the said Figures out of the Places where they have been set by the Keeper, without his leave first obtained for that Purpose.'[11]

In the summer of 1779, Blake, in accordance with printed regulations, must have submitted a drawing and testimonial from a recognized artist to George Michael Moser, the Keeper, who was in charge of the Schools. Blake's admission allowed him to work for three months as a Probationer in the Antique Schools. Specifically, he was required to make an outline drawing at least two feet high of an anatomical figure; this had to be accompanied by lists of muscles and tendons.

Despite its serious purposes, the Schools was a place of high jinks, the students 'playing at leap frog, knocking off the hand of Michaelangiolo's beautiful Fawn, spouting water, breaking the fingers of the Apollo, pelting one another with modeller's clay and crusts of bread, roasting potatoes in the stove, teizing the Keeper by imitating cats'.[12]

Richard Wilson, who was appointed Librarian in 1776, once remarked to a boisterous young man: 'Don't paw the leaves, sirrah ... have you got eyes in your fingers, boy?'[13] The straitlaced Keeper was also short-tempered. He was once insulted by a student, who was forced to make a public apology. G. B. Cipriani, one of the Visitors who attended the Schools to offer advice, also quarrelled with Moser, who received this admonishment: 'resolved that the Visitor shall be considered as Master of the Living-Academy; and that neither the Keeper nor any other Academician shall presume to enter the Room whilst the Visitor is setting the Model'.[14]

Moser, an enameller, medallist and goldsmith from Schaffhausen and once the manager and treasurer of St Martin's Lane Academy, had served as drawing master to the young George III. In 1780, he was pleasantly dumbfounded when Queen Charlotte, on a visit to Somerset House, sought him out for an hour's chat in German. Subsequently, he could hardly contain himself when describing this event.

Two difficult persons were thrown into immediate conflict the day Moser came upon Blake poring over prints by Raphael and Michelangelo. Decisively, the seventy-four-year-old Swiss upbraided him: 'You should not Study these old Hard, Stiff & Dry Unfinished Works of Art. Stay a little & I will shew you what you should Study.' These parental words of wisdom were softened by the invitation, but Blake seethed inwardly when portfolios of engravings by LeBrun and Rubens were opened for him to admire – and thus mend the errors of his bad taste. Finally, Blake could not contain himself: 'These things that you call Finishd are not Even Begun; how can they then, be Finishd? The Man who does not know The Beginning, never can know the End of Art.'[15] Like Reynolds, Moser was advocating a pictorial style of representation which was eclectic. Blake wanted a simpler, less refined and more intense mode of representation. He clung resolutely to his admiration for a type of art for which he had earlier been 'harassed'. For Blake, Reynolds's grand style led not to sublimity but to bathos.

Such feelings on Blake's part were reinforced when he showed some designs to Reynolds, who instructed him to 'work with less extravagance and more simplicity, and to correct his drawing'. Ever after, Blake was indignant in recalling that encounter.[16] He also became increasingly irritated with the Academy exercises of drawing from antique casts and live models: 'But now his peculiar notions began to intercept him in his career.' Drawing from life was particularly hateful. The results looked, he maintained, 'more like death ... smelling of mortality'.[17]

One person connected with the Royal Academy whom Blake greatly admired was the Irishman James Barry, who had been elected an Academician in February 1773. Like West, Barry was committed to historical painting: he showed *King Lear and Cordelia* at Pall Mall in 1774 and *The Death of General Wolfe* there in 1776. After that, Barry, a loner, turned to printmaking, which increasingly absorbed his attention. He avoided commercial high finish by gouging his copper plates: for example, huge areas of undisciplined crosshatching underline the theme of emotional turbulence in his *King Lear* engraving.

Early in his career, Barry had decided that history painting should be one of the main ways 'of every people desirous of gaining honour by the arts. These are tests by which the national character will be tried in all ages, and by which it has been, and is now, tried by the natives of other countries.'[18] In the late 1770s, Blake obviously held similar opinions, and he identified with this outsider, who was a well-known supporter of American radicalism. In attending the Royal Academy Schools, Blake may have for a time envisaged a career for himself identical to Barry's.

Barry had returned from Italy in 1771, determined to create pictures on the scale of those in the Sistine Chapel and Raphael's *Stanze*. Later, Blake wrote: 'While Sir Joshua was rolling in Riches, Barry was Poor & Unemployd except by his own Energy.'[19] In 1799, Barry was expelled from the Academy because he had attacked fellow members in *A Letter to the Dilettanti Society*. Blake's identification with Barry the outcast is loudly signalled when he roars his disapproval with the way in which the Society of Arts treated Barry's offer of 1777 to decorate its Great Room:

> Who will Dare to Say that Polite Art is Encouraged, or Either Wished or Tolerated in a Nation where The Society for the Encouragement of Art Suffrd Barry to Give them his Labour for Nothing? A Society Composed of the Flower of the English Nobility & Gentry – A Society Suffering an Artist to Starve while he Supported Really what They under pretence of Encouraging were Endeavouring to Depress. – Barry told me that while he Did that Work – he Lived on Bread & Apples.[20]

Barry provided young Blake with a dire object lesson in how the establishment treated someone who tried to work within it. Another early influence was John Hamilton Mortimer, the President of the rival

Society of Artists, who did not join the Royal Academy until just before his death in 1779 and whose history paintings contain veiled references to his republican sympathies.

Although Moser's and Reynolds's desires for an art of compromise was anathema to Blake, he stayed involved at the Royal Academy Schools until at least May 1780, when he exhibited *The Death of Earl Godwin* there. This work was on display in the Ante-room, which was devoted to flower-pieces, miniatures and watercolour landscapes, some by Gainsborough. This was the Academy's first exhibition at Somerset House; it included canvases by Reynolds, Sandby, de Loutherbourg, Kauffmann, Zoffany and Fuseli. Subsequently, Blake showed *A Breach in the City* and *War* there in May 1784. Despite his stated disdain for the Academy, Blake repeatedly exhibited there (April 1785, May 1800, May 1808). Tenuously, he clung to the hope of fame.

Blake's stay at the Royal Academy Schools was probably brief and unrewarding, not apparently giving him the opportunity to meet like-minded young artists. Such contacts eventually came through his engraving, although George Cumberland, a painter and etcher who worked for the Royal Exchange Assurance Company, had been impressed by Blake's entry in the Royal Academy exhibition of 1780: 'though there is nothing to be said of the colouring, there may be discovered a good design, and much character'.[21] In about 1780, Blake began to spend evenings in drawing and designing in the company of Cumberland, Thomas Stothard, William Sharp and John Flaxman.[22] Like Blake, Sharp was an engraver: he also had a reputation for taking 'voluntary excursions into the regions of the preternatural'.[23] Through one Trotter, an engraver who took lessons from him, Blake met Stothard, who in turn introduced him to Flaxman.

George, a cousin of the dramatist Richard Cumberland, was the son of a London money-scrivener who had died when George was nineteen. His passing meant that his ambitious eldest son, who had enrolled the year before at the Royal Academy Schools, had until 1784 to earn his living at the insurance company, an occupation the headstrong, impulsive young man found repulsive: 'Who knows but in time I may come to be plodding, avaricious, and mean, a man of the world, a submissive Hypocrite.'[24] Upon receiving an inheritance of £300 a year from a family friend, Cumberland retired from business and lived as a gentleman of modest means. He travelled extensively in Europe and farmed, coming to London to collect his quarterly dividends.

Cumberland's moderate wealth allowed him to cultivate his interest in new methods of printing and engraving; it also allowed him to collect classical and Italian art. His preoccupation with inventing extended to experiments with mail delivery, life-rafts, jet propulsion and mine-safety and to writing on a number of social causes: the reformation of prostitutes, methods of teaching the blind to read, and free trade.[25] Despite his relative prosperity, Cumberland retained a firm commitment to justice for the poor and oppressed. He also disregarded convention by living openly with Elizabeth Cooper, the wife of his London landlord. Polymath and dilettante, Cumberland was an interested witness to the art world of his time.

By 1780, Thomas Stothard, who had been brought up in Yorkshire, was well on his way to being a prolific, much sought-after illustrator. Shortly after his father's death in 1770, the fifteen-year-old boy was apprenticed to a designer of silk brocades, a trade then in decline. Two years before the expiration of the indenture, his master died, Thomas remaining on with the man's widow. Early on, husband and wife had encouraged him to draw and paint, and Thomas was rescued from a humdrum existence when Harrison, the proprietor of the *Novelist's Magazine*, called upon the widow to place an order. Deeply impressed by the Stothard sketches he saw on the fireplace, he gave Thomas a book and told him to make a design from any subject which appealed to him: 'The book (a novel) was read, and instead of one, *three* designs were executed and ready for the gentleman; who, true to his time and word, called again. The drawings were examined and approved; half-a-guinea was put into his hand; and Stothard's future lot was decided.'[26]

A measure of Stothard's consuming ambition can be discerned from his businesslike conduct on the day of his wedding, immediately after which he accompanied his bride home:

> and then very quietly walked down to the Academy, to draw from the Antique till three o'clock, the hour at which it then closed. There he sat, by the side of a fellow-student named Scott, with whom he was intimate, and, after drawing the usual time, at length said to his friend, 'I am now going home to meet a family party. Do come and dine with me, for I have this day taken to myself a wife.'[27]

The gentle, retiring John Flaxman entered the Royal Academy Schools when he was fourteen in 1769; in that year, he was awarded one of the Academy's silver medals. Before that, the boy had been intrigued by the plaster casts and models which his father made in his shop in the Strand for sculptors such as Roubiliac and Scheemakers and the porcelain manufacturer Josiah Wedgwood. Flaxman endured a solitary, withdrawn childhood: he was never able to remedy the curvature of the spine with which he was born. Although 'unhappily formed by nature', as his friend C. R. Cockerell recalled, the contrast between his ungainly body and serene face made it appear when he laughed as 'if he were mocking himself'.[28]

Soon after George Romney's return from Italy in 1775, Flaxman met the painter at his father's shop. This relationship was crucial to Flaxman: 'I was a little boy, and as he frequently found me employed in modelling, he would stand by me a long while together giving me encouragement in a manner so obliging and affectionate that he won my heart, and confirmed my determination in the pursuit of sculpture.'[29] From 1775 until 1787 the ever good-natured Flaxman subsisted in a hand-to-mouth way as a designer of wax models for the cameo wares of Wedgwood. Impressed in the mid-1770s by some of Stothard's designs in the *Novelist's Magazine*, he asked his father to contrive an introduction.

Eventually, Blake's friendships with Flaxman and Stothard went through various kinds of turmoil, leading Blake to say, somewhat improbably and untruthfully: 'I found them blind; I taught them how to see / And now they know neither themselves nor me.'[30] In the late 1780s, Blake, Cumberland, Flaxman and Stothard, on the verges of vastly different kinds of careers, formed a loosely knit circle.

Blake remained a disgruntled observer of – never an active participant in – English political life. His closest brush with active radicalism came when he was momentarily caught up in the Gordon Riots. Lord George Gordon, the flamboyant twenty-nine-year-old third son of the Duke of Gordon, was the ringleader of a group opposing Parliament's decision to remove civil restrictions from Catholics. On 2 June 1780, he arrived at the House of Commons with four huge marching columns of supporters to present his anti-Catholic petition. When Parliament proved unbudging, violence was unleashed that evening. Many members of Blake's own artisan class, fearful of losing their jobs to Irish black-leggers, were avid followers of Gordon, who was suspicious that the Government's toleration of papists was based on a desire to pave the way for sending Catholic soldiers to fight against the Americans.

On 6 June, four days later, at the height of the ensuing burning and looting of Catholic churches and businesses, Blake involuntarily participated.[31] By that time the rioters had wreaked a great deal of devastation in the artist's neighbourhood. Then flushed with success and gin, they became more rambunctious. That night Blake was walking:

> in a route chosen by one of the mobs at large, whose course lay from Justice Hyde's house near Leicester Fields, for the destruction of which less than an hour had sufficed, through Long Acre, past the quiet house of Blake's old master, engraver Basire, in Great Queen Street, Lincoln's Inn Fields, and down Holborn, bound for Newgate. Suddenly, he encountered the advancing wave of triumphant Blackguardism, and was forced (for from such a great surging mob there is no disentanglement) to go along in the very front rank, and witness the storm and burning of the fortress-like prison, and release of its three hundred inmates.[32]

Another bystander, George Crabbe the poet, 'never saw anything so dreadful'. The rioters broke the gates and climbed up the prison's exterior. 'They broke the roof, tore away the rafters.' Earlier, the Bavarian Embassy in Warwick Street was stripped, its windows smashed; Broad Street, where Blake was born, had also been a scene of carnage.

Four months later, Blake was mixed up in a milder, comical political incident when he went sailing up the Medway with Stothard and James Parker, with whom he had been apprenticed at Basire. The three went ashore as various bits of landscape caught their fancy. On such a foray, they 'were suddenly surprised by the appearance of some soldiers, who very unceremoniously made them prisoners, under the suspicion of their being spies for the French government'.[33] The young men protested to no avail; the soldiers brought the artists' provisions ashore and a tent was formed of their sails. The hapless trio was detained and placed under guard until 'intelligence could be received from certain members of the Royal Academy' to certify that they were not spies for France. On liberation, the three men spent a 'merry hour' with the commanding officer.[34]

Both episodes exemplify the turbulence of the early 1780s. There was the distinct possibility that Lord North's Government would increasingly employ repressive measures to ensure stability. They did not want 'King Mob' to gain the upper hand. A bitter rivalry between England and France still persisted centred on overseas expansion, and the Government's paranoia about a possible invasion led to the droll incident on the Medway. In each episode, Blake absorbed first-hand the political climate.

In 1781, the twenty-four-year-old Blake became aware of 'where lisps

the maiden's tongue'.[35] Although he was short of stature – five feet
five inches tall – he was muscular, broad shouldered and well made.
His penetrating, gleaming eyes immediately captured the attention
of anyone who met him.[36] Next to them, his yellow-brown hair was
his most striking feature: it was 'curled with the utmost crisp-
ness & luxuriance. His locks instead of falling down stood up like
a curling flame, and looked at a distance like radiations.'[37] His small
nose gave his face 'an expression of fiery energy, as of a high-mettled
steed'.[38]

The course of first love did not run smooth. Polly Wood, the object
of his affections, allowed him to 'keep company' with her. However,
she did not wish to marry him, and Blake became jealous of her other
beaux. When he complained that she had walked out with one of
these men, she gave him a scornful look while upbraiding him: 'Are
you a fool?' As Blake later claimed, 'That cured me of jealousy.'[39]
When he had first met her, Blake had incorrectly thought Polly 'no
trifler'.

Despondent after Polly's rejection, Blake escaped central London by
going to stay near relatives of his father in Battersea, where the rich
soil yielded a multitude of vegetables, including the asparagus sold in
'Battersea bundles'. There were even gypsies in Battersea Park, where
pigeon and sparrow shooting was practised. While there, Blake roomed
with William Boucher or Butcher, a market gardener. He told William's
daughter, Catherine Sophia, who had previously worked as a maid
servant, of his broken heart. Unlike Polly, Catherine, a vivacious, pretty
brunette, was deeply attracted to the engraver and commiserated with
him. Her manner was so 'tender and affectionate' that he was quickly
'won'. In his typically abrupt manner, he asked her: 'Do you pity
me?' 'Yes, indeed I do' she straightforwardly responded, in a manner
reminiscent of Desdemona. 'Then I love you,' he rejoined.[40] The break
with Polly left Blake physically sick and mentally depressed – and led
him into Catherine's arms. This was love on the rebound. Later, Blake
attacked pity as vice masquerading as virtue.

An important clue to the nature of the relationship between William
and Catherine may be found in 'William Bond', which begins: 'I
wonder whether the Girls are mad / And I wonder whether they mean
to kill.' Bond has mysteriously taken to his bed, where he is comforted
by Mary Green and Jane, his sister. Selflessly, Mary tells him:

> O William, if thou dost another Love,
> Dost another Love better than poor Mary,

> Go & Take that other to be thy Wife
> And Mary Green shall her Servant be.

Bond admits he loves another, whom he wishes to marry. He even adds insult to injury by comparing Mary's melancholy paleness to his beloved's dazzling brightness. Becoming ill herself, Mary eventually finds herself lying in a bed on the right of Bond, who realizes the errors of his ways:

> I thought Love livd in the hot sun shine,
> But O, he lives in the Moony light;
> I thought to find Love in the heat of day
> But sweet Love is the Comforter of Night.[41]

In his marriage to Catherine, Blake too chose agape over eros.

William Bond settles for a relationship in which he can be mothered, but, as Blake knew full well, such a choice leads to repression and, eventually, rage. Such feelings are reflected in 'The Crystal Cabinet':

> The Maiden caught me in the Wild
> Where I was dancing merrily.
> She put me into her Cabinet
> And Lockd me up with a golden Key.[42]

Like her future husband, Catherine was impetuous in affairs of the heart. Previously, when her mother had asked her if any man had taken her 'fancy', she replied in the negative. She fell in love with Blake immediately when introduced to him. In fact, Catherine was 'so near fainting that she left his presence until she had recovered'.[43]

It is possible, but not certain, that James Blake objected to his son marrying Catherine. Understandably, William may have wanted to set his finances on a more even footing before beginning wedded life. For a variety of reasons, then, the Marriage Allegation and Bond are dated one year after the couple met: 13 August 1782. The marriage took place five days later at the recently rebuilt parish church of St Mary, Battersea. The James Blake who was one of the witnesses of the ceremony was probably the poet's father, having now abandoned such objections as he may have had. Catherine signed the register with an X. This does not necessarily denote illiteracy, merely that writing was a precarious skill for her.

At the time of their marriage, the couple moved to 23 Green Street, Leicester Fields, where they were lodgers in a few rooms for two years. William Woollett the engraver lived in the same street, and Joshua Reynolds was round the corner. The building of the street, part of the

Grosvenor Estate, extending from North Audley Street to Park Lane, had begun in the 1720s but was not completed until the 1760s. By the time the Blakes settled there, Green Street was unfashionable, but its square was tranquil. In the summer of 1771, James Northcote, who was living with Sir Joshua Reynolds, was touched by the easeful blend of city and country he found there: 'I often hear the cock crow and have seen a hen and chicken strut as composedly through the street as they would at Plymouth.'[44]

Despite his obvious devotion to Catherine, the person who remained at the centre of Blake's existence was his brother Robert, who was admitted to the Royal Academy Schools at the age of fourteen on 2 April 1782, to study as an engraver. One day, in the midst of an argument, Catherine spoke sharply to Robert. Up to this point, Blake had been a silent observer of the dispute. Suddenly, he rose up and shouted at her: 'Kneel down and beg Robert's pardon directly, or you may never see my face again!' Catherine, feeling that she was in the right, was thrown by this haughty request, but, not wishing to alienate her husband whose command was '*meant*', she knelt down and meekly begged Robert's forgiveness: '*Robert, I beg your pardon, I am in the wrong.*' Gallantly, Robert came to her rescue: 'Young woman, you lie! *I* am in the wrong!'[45]

The newly-wed Blake grappled to gain recognition. He must have devoted part of each day to his drawing, sketching, painting and versifying; he also tried to gain a foothold in the precarious world of book illustration. His commissions included *The Royal Universal Family Bible* (design and engraving, 1781) and the 1780 reissue of William Enfield's *The Speaker*, J. Olivier's *Fencing Familiarized* (1780), Henry Emlyn's *A Proposition for a New Order in Architecture* (1781) and Edward Kimpton's *A New and Complete Universal History of the Holy Bible* (c. 1781). (The later (1793) illustrations to John Gay's *Fables* are among his finest work.) Blake's frequently unkempt appearance might have been mainly due to the chemicals he handled on a daily basis, and the inking, wiping and smoking which were an essential part of his profession.[46]

His search for employment was strongly linked to Stothard: eight plates engraved after him appeared in the *Novelist's Magazine* in 1782–3, nine plates in Ritson's *English Songs* in 1783 and five plates in the *Wit's Magazine* a year later; also one plate after him for John Bonnycastle's *An Introduction to Mensuration, and Practical Geometry* (1782). Generously, the painter was using his own burgeoning pop-

'The Butterfly and the Snail'

ularity to assist his engraver friend. Years later, Blake boasted that Stothard achieved his reputation as a draughtsman from 'those little prints which I engraved after him five & twenty Years ago'.[47] There is some truth in this assertion: Stothard's monochrome wash designs perfectly suited the engraver's stylus.

Flaxman was also attempting to promote Blake, about whom he had spoken to George Romney. Romney, who greatly admired history painting rather than the face-painting upon which his own reputation had been built, thought Blake's historical drawings ranked with those of Michelangelo.[48] The sculptor also lamented the fact that Blake was struggling in his attempts to establish himself as an engraver. In 1784 or 1785, Flaxman, who had been commissioned by Josiah Wedgwood to decorate Etruria Hall in Staffordshire, engaged Blake to assist him. Blake's now-lost contribution – after a design by his friend – was either a painting on canvas or an early version of his fresco technique; the painting was completed in London, shipped to Staffordshire and fixed to the ceiling.[49] Flaxman also called Blake to the notice of John Hawkins, a

'Cornish Gentleman' who ordered several (now lost) drawings from him. This early patron, who was later Sheriff of Sussex, even endeavoured to raise a subscription to send Blake to Italy to complete his studies. It was Flaxman in 1787 who was to go to Italy, Blake remaining behind, brokenhearted that he could not see first-hand the Roman and Florentine art he adored. In 1804, he wistfully hoped that he was 'worthy of [Hawkins's] former kindness'.[50] As Blake recognized, Italy, in the last thirty years of the eighteenth century, was the true centre for the training of English artists. There, he could have learned to be a history painter. That disappointment continued to haunt him.

Despite Flaxman's obvious good intentions, Blake later asserted that his friend had 'blasted'[51] his character to Thomas Macklin, for whom Blake engraved three plates in 1782–3. One of these commissions reportedly brought £80, a large sum for the young artist. Blake also claimed that Macklin had 'told [him] at the time'[52] of Flaxman's harsh words. The sculptor, trying to justify any potential personality conflicts with the difficult Blake to an employer who paid well, had probably warned Macklin to go easy. Tactlessly, Macklin repeated this confidence to Blake, who incorrectly assumed that Flaxman was acting against him.

Indefatigable in endeavouring to draw Blake to the attention of those who might assist him, Flaxman introduced him to his own mentor, the Revd Anthony Stephen Mathew. His circle, the second into which Blake drifted, met at 27 Rathbone Place, Soho. Mathew, born in 1733, had been educated at Eton and Peterhouse, Cambridge. Ordained a deacon in 1760, he became joint-lecturer of St Martin's-in-the-Fields in about 1764; in that year, he moved to Rathbone Place to oversee the construction of the Percy Chapel, which opened in 1766.

When he was fourteen in 1769, Flaxman met Mathew, who introduced him to his wife Harriet, a vivacious person anxious to make her own mark in literary and artistic London. She was also not above helping young lovers, as when she assisted Flaxman in his courtship of Nancy Denman in 1780. Nancy wanted to marry John, but her father objected on the grounds of the sculptor's dim financial prospects. Despite a paternal injunction, John and Nancy went for long walks on Sundays and exchanged messages through understanding friends, one of whom was Harriet Mathew, who made a 'general offer of her services'[53] on behalf of thwarted love. So confiding was John to this older woman that Nancy became irritated and chided her lover to practise discretion. As a memorial to their kindness during his successful courtship, Flaxman decorated the back parlour of the Mathews' home, where their library was housed, with putty and sand models of 'figures in niches, in the Gothic manner'.[54]

Although Mrs Mathew's salon was rumoured to have received the likes of Elizabeth Montagu, Hester Chapone and Anna Letitia Barbauld, the only surviving evidence of a celebrated literary figure having been in attendance there is contained in James Boswell's diary for 10 April 1779: 'Breakfast with Mrs. Matthew [sic]. Marriage, she said, must have its Bass, tenor, treble; i.e., esteem, affection, passion.'[55] What is certain is that Blake, at Flaxman's instigation, was one of a group of artists and musicians, including the painter Edward Oram, who were warmly welcomed at Rathbone Place. In 1784, at one of Mrs Mathew's 'delightful conversaziones', J. T. Smith met William Blake: 'There I have often heard him read and sing several of his poems. He was listened to by the company with profound silence, and allowed by most of the visitors to possess original and extraordinary merit.'[56] Before he permanently removed himself from the Mathews' set, Blake frequently performed songs from the *Poetical Sketches* and, very probably, *Innocence*. These occasions must have been moving for, when he performed, Blake's face became suffused with 'expression & animation'.[57]

When Blake needed financial assistance in 1783 to publish some of those songs in *Poetical Sketches*, Mrs Mathew asked her husband to share the cost of publication with the ever generous Flaxman. The lady provided even more money when, a year later, she advanced funds for Blake to go into partnership with James Parker.*

Nevertheless, shortly thereafter, Blake's 'unbending deportment' or 'manly firmness of opinion' led him to curtail his visits and, ultimately, his friendship with the Mathews.[58] He could force himself to accept aid for only short periods of time. Then his independence would reassert itself, and he would become vehemently angry at those who bestowed kindness or pity.

Blake habitually became furious at himself for having allowed himself to be the object of care or concern, no matter how loving or generous such assistance was. Such deep ambivalences continually crippled him: his worldly ambitions and his resolute independence could be precariously conjoined only for short periods of time. On the

---

* According to J. T. Smith, Mrs Mathew 'enabled' Blake 'to continue in partnership, as a Printseller, with his fellow-pupil, Parker ...' (*BR*, p. 457). The wording is confusing. Mrs Mathew may have helped Blake to open the printshop in 1784; if she helped to keep the venture afloat, her assistance would have come in 1785.

other hand, the sheer power of much of his genius was unleashed because he was the outsider, craving recognition and yet never able to receive it graciously.

Blake's vehement dislike of the blue-stocking gatherings at the Mathews' was one of the principal sources of *An Island in the Moon*, where satire, comedy, vituperation and adolescent castigation are mixed together. In that burlesque (probably written in 1785), Blake portrayed members of the Mathews' circle, including himself and Flaxman; other characters are derived from gossip about well-known figures.

At the beginning of *An Island*, Suction the Epicurean, Sipsop the Pythagorean and Quid the Cynic are set to examine the nature of truth, but their conversation soon degenerates into explosive nonsense. In a manner reminiscent of *Tristram Shandy*, all the speakers in this unfinished piece of closet drama, a mixture of random conversations interspersed with songs, are dedicated to their own hobby-horses: they speak at – not to – each other. And this seems to be precisely Blake's point about the self-defeating nature of salon *conversazione*, wherein each participant expressed only his own obsessions.

The name of one character, Mr Jacko, is taken from General Jackoo, the renowned performing monkey, who first appeared in England at Philip Astley's Westminster Bridge Circus in April 1785; the personalities of Jacko and his wife are drawn from the dandyish, monkey-faced miniature painter Richard Cosway (sometimes referred to as 'little Jack-a Dang') and his Irish–Italian wife Maria, whom Cosway had met when her father, Charles Hadfield, was the proprietor of a hotel on the outskirts of Florence. The beautiful Miss Hadfield had accepted Cosway because, unlike her other suitors, he was *'Toujours riant, toujours gai'*.[59] Cosway, who was seventeen years older than Blake, came from lowly origins, had taught at Pars' school and in 1771 had become a full Academician. When Miss Gittipin says, 'I do believe he'll go in partnership with his master,'[60] she may be referring to his close friendship with his most influential patron, the Prince of Wales. The Cosways, a fashionable and glamorous couple, kept a black servant at their apartments in Schomberg House, Pall Mall. In *An Island*, 'black servants lodge' at the Jacko residence 'which has Six and twenty rooms'.[61]

Obtuse Angle is possibly based on the neo-Platonist Thomas Taylor, who at some point instructed Blake in geometry. The description of Inflammable Gass the Windfinder might have come from hearsay about Joseph Priestley, who did not live in London in the 1780s.

Steelyard the Lawgiver, who morbidly sits at his table making extracts from Hervey's *Meditations among the Tombs* and Young's *Night Thoughts*, is a playful portrait of John Flaxman and his enthusiasm for apocalyptic, ruminative religion, particularly Swedenborgianism.

At this time, Flaxman supplemented his income by acting as a collector of the watch-rate for the Parish of St Anne's. In that capacity, he was to be seen 'with an ink-bottle in his button-hole, collecting the rate'.[62] (Steelyard holds a miserable, lowly parish job, which requires him to 'stand & bear every fool's insult'.[63] There is little real merriment at his house.) John and Ann Flaxman lived a frugal life on Wardour Street from 1782 to 1787, when they went to Italy, and this was a style of existence not markedly different from that of another struggling couple, William and Catherine Blake.

Mrs Mathew, a minister's wife, is mirrored in Mrs Sigtagatist:

> O, said Mrs Sigtagatist, if it was not for church & chapels I should not have livd so long – there was I up in a Morning at four o clock when I was a Girl. I would run like the dickens till I was all in a heat. I would stand till I was ready to sink into the earth. Ah, Mr Huffcap would kick the bottom of the Pulpit out, with Passion, would tear off the sleeve of his Gown, & set his wig on fire & throw it at the people. He'd cry & stamp & kick & sweat and all for the good of their souls.[64]

When Mrs Nannicantipot interrupts to pronounce Mr Huffcap a villain, Mrs Sigtagatist rounds on her: 'You Ignorant jade, I wish I could see you hit any of the ministers. You deserve to have your ears boxed, you do!'[65]

The outspoken Quid is probably a self-portrait: 'I think that Homer is bombast & Shakespeare is too wild & Milton has no feelings.'[66] Here Blake shows a capacity to poke fun at himself. And Quid is seen in other moods, as when he poignantly sings 'The Little Boy Lost', later to be one of the songs of *Innocence*. In a scatological piece of buffoonery, Quid and Suction have fun at the expense of the recently deceased Samuel Johnson:

> Quid – O ho, Said Doctor Johnson
> To Scipio Africanus,
> If you don't own me a Philosopher
> I'll kick your Roman Anus.

> Suction – A ha, To Doctor Johnson
> Said Scipio Africanus,
> Lift up my Roman Petticoat
> And kiss my Roman Anus.[67]

And Quid proudly proclaims his independence of coteries, when, at the very end of *Island*, he recalls his appearance at a salon. There he addresses a woman who may be based on Catherine:

> Oh I was at Mrs Sicknaken's & I was speaking of my abilities but their nasty hearts, poor devils, are eat up with envy – they envy me my abilities & all the Women envy your abilities. My dear, they háte people who are of higher abilities than their nasty filthy Selves but do you outface them & then Strangers will see you have an opinion.[68]

If this passage contains condescending, husbandly advice to Catherine about 'improving' herself, one of the songs, sung by Obtuse Angle at Quid's insistence, presents marriage as a snare:

> Hail Matrimony, made of love,
> To thy wide gates how great a drove
> On purpose to be yok'd do come.
> Widows & maids & Youths also
> That lightly trip on beauty's toe
> Or sit on beauty's bum.
>
> Hail fingerfooted lovely Creatures,
> The females of our human Natures,
> Formd to suckle all Mankind.
> Tis you that come in time of need
> Without you we shoud never Breed
> Or any Comfort find.[69]

The conversation and song at Rathbone Place inspired *Island*, which bears a close resemblance to Samuel Foote's slapdash antiplay, *Tea in the Haymarket*. Or Blake could have been aware of Christopher Smart's vaudeville piece of the 1750s: *Mrs. Midnight's Entertainment*.[70] Menippean satire – in which poetry and prose are conjoined to attack intellectual error – would have been known to Blake through the writings of the Scriblerus Club of Pope, Gay, Swift, Arbuthnot and Parnell. Pope's *Dunciad* was its most famous product in that genre, which stretches back to the *Satyricon* of Petronius. Also behind *Island* are the ghosts of Erasmus, More, Ariosto, Rabelais, Cervantes, Rochester. The play testifies to Blake's fecund precociousness: he is able to blend a multiplicity of sources so that he can show himself as the inheritor of the tradition of satire of the eighteenth century, as a commentator on the fascination with Lunardi and his hot-air balloons and on puce as the new fashion colour, and as a stranger who has, against his best instincts, been caught up in such nonsense.

A. S. Mathew's Preface to the *Poetical Sketches* is insipid, very much the timid utterance of a patron anxious to present his protégé to a potentially sceptical audience: 'The following Sketches were the production of untutored youth, commenced in his twelfth, and occasionally resumed by the author till his twentieth year; since which time, his talents have been wholly directed to the attainment of excellence in his profession, he has been deprived of the leisure requisite to such a revisal of these sheets, as might have rendered them less unfit to meet the public eye.'[71] There is a bit of condescension here, certainly enough to explain why the frequently hot-headed Blake would have been offended.

Poetical Sketches are bland only when juxtaposed to *An Island*. Just as *Island* shows an intimate knowledge of the literary traditions of the first part of the eighteenth century, *Sketches* displays an acute awareness of the poets of mid-century: Collins, Gray, Smart, the Wartons. These were writers who were often concerned with their inability to write, their unsuccessful searches for a new poetical language, their Hamlet-like indecisivenesses. Parody is one of Blake's devices in 'To the Muses' where, like William Collins, the speaker laments his lack of inspiration:

> Whether on chrystal rocks ye rove,
> Beneath the bosom of the sea
> Wand'ring in many a coral grove,
> Fair Nine, forsaking Poetry!
>
> How have you left the antient love
> That bards of old enjoy'd in you!
> The languid strings do scarcely move!
> The sound is forc'd, the notes are few![72]

Blake's answer to such complaints is that by their very nature they are self-defeating. A poet must be aware of other poets, but he must create his own voice from within himself. In 1783, this was a comparatively easy observation – it would not be so later on.

In many ways, *Poetical Sketches* must be seen as a prospectus piece in which a determined, sometimes impudent young man boldly charts his future. Poets often use pastoral poems, in which they display their knowledge of that tradition and their original contributions to it, as overtures to their careers. Also, Blake shows his intimate knowledge of the Gothic, Shakespeare's history plays, the Old Testament. Religious feelings can be discerned in these poems, but Christian sentiments are subdued. Blake's hatred of excessive rationality, later to be exemplified by the villainous Urizen, is evident in his portrait of Winter:

> Lo! now the direful monster, whose skin clings
> To his strong bones, strides o'er the groaning rocks:
> He withers all in silence, and his hand
> Unclothes the earth, and freezes up frail life.[73]

In the invocation to the prose piece, 'Samson', the speaker asks the 'white-robed Angel' to guide his timorous hand 'to write as on a lofty rock with iron pens the words of truth, that all who pass may read'.[74] Covertly, Blake is alluding to the etching needles and fine-point gravers of his trade.*

The poems are literally poetical sketches in which the visual is injected into the verbal. Above all, Blake in *Poetical Sketches* demonstrates his ability to write in clear, radiant language, as in 'To Morning', inspired in part by the Song of Songs:

> O holy virgin! clad in purest white,
> Unlock heav'n's golden gates, and issue forth;
> Awake the dawn that sleeps in heaven; let light
> Rise from the chambers of the east, and bring
> The honied dew that cometh on waking day.
> O radiant morning, salute the sun,
> Rouz'd like a huntsman to the chace; and, with
> Thy buskin'd feet, appear upon our hills.[75]

Afterwards, Blake blended the heady experiments of *An Island* with the more moderate pastoralism and political concerns of *Sketches*. He would also strive, in his illuminated verse, to unite the verbal and the visual, so that his strong poetic metaphors could be enhanced by deliberately primitive-looking illustrations. In 1783, he was trying, with increasing success, to discover his own voice.

---

*Possibly this is an anticipation of his illuminated printing, but his references to 'Illuminating the Manuscript' in *Island* seem to be by way of mocking George Cumberland, who claimed, incorrectly, to have discovered a 'New Mode of Printing' in 1784. See Robert N. Essick, *William Blake: Printmaker* (Princeton: Princeton University Press, 1980), p. 113.

4

Brothers of Eternity

1784–1787

By 1784, Blake realized that his attempt to launch himself as an engraver–artist through the Royal Academy had not met with much success; also, he was becoming antagonistic to the Mathews. An opportunity to deepen his commitment to engraving presented itself when his father died in July 1784. James, evidently buried from his brother's house in Hog Lane, near Soho Square, and interned at Bunhill Fields, probably left his son a small inheritance, perhaps £100.

In fact, Blake had become increasingly worried that his pursuit of art was little more than a waste of time. Such guilt might have propelled him into his partnership with James Parker, a fellow apprentice at Basire's, when the two founded a print-selling business, next door to Blake's birthplace in Broad Street. Parker, seven years older than Blake, had begun his apprenticeship in 1773, at the unusual age of twenty-three.

This joint venture was undertaken in the days when 'a Print shop was a rare bird in London'.[1] Earlier in the century, prints had been marketed by booksellers, but by mid-century print-selling had developed into an independent trade. As in emporiums such as Boydell's, the staple items of the Blake–Parker shop would obviously have been a stock of prints, many of which were reproductions of paintings and sculptures. Such merchants usually also sold instruction manuals for amateur artists and calligraphers, architectural and writing books, maps, atlases, watch cases, children's books and novelty prints for peep shows.[2] Blake and Parker were trying to cash in on what they perceived as a growth industry. Two plates Parker engraved in 1783 – *The Fall of Agandecca* and *Fainasollis Borbar & Fingal* – testify to a shared passion with Blake for historical prints and the Ossianic. One of Blake's motives in setting up shop was certainly his desire to launch his own series of prints concerning the history of England. However, two stipple plates of 1784 from designs by Stothard, *Zephyrus & Flora* and *Callisto*, seem to be all that he did for the shop.

Catherine Blake assisted in the shop, while her husband 'busied himself with his graver and pencil'.[3] Blake might have acquired his rolling press worth about £40 at this time.[4] Since the stock to run a print-selling shop cost about £50, the purchase of the press would have been Blake's contribution to the partnership. Quite soon after setting up shop, Blake quarrelled with Parker, who remained in Broad Street until 1794, presumably retaining the stock he had purchased and Blake removing the press with him.

Why did Blake abandon Broad Street so quickly? He may have consented to live at 27 Broad Street next to No. 28, which housed his mother, his brothers James and Robert and his sister Catherine, only because his father was no longer there. Still, he would have felt uncomfortable living next door to his place of birth and any unpleasant associations which it conjured up. James Blake, living his 'yard & a half life', might well have been pestering his brother 'with timid sentences of bread & cheese advice'.[5]* John Blake, who set up a bakery across the street from his brothers, was no doubt a nuisance. And Blake might well have felt the presence of Parker and his wife in the same house with himself and Catherine intolerable. Also, he might have been frustrated by initial lack of success in the print business. For what were a variety of reasons, William and Catherine had moved to Poland Street by Christmas 1785.

This street, and, earlier, a nearby inn, were named in commemoration of the victory of John Sobieski, King of Poland, over the Turks in 1683. The houses and the street were built by the early 1700s. Charles Burney lived at No. 50 from 1760 until 1770. His daughter Frances later characterized the street as a spot 'left in the lurch'. In Burney's time, the Duke of Chandos, Lady Augusta Bridges and the Cherokee King were his neighbours. Gavin Hamilton, the painter, settled there in 1779, after his return from Italy. Blake's new

---

*These harsh words are probably Blake's, as reported to Frederick Tatham.

house was exceedingly narrow. Behind the back garden was a timber yard. A few doors down, at No. 22, was the King's Arms, where in 1781 on Blake's twenty-fourth birthday 'the ANCIENT ORDER OF DRUIDS was revived'.[6] By 1785, there were probably still some supporters of such rites in attendance at the pub.

At about this time, Blake came upon a man beating a woman in the street. His response was quick and vigorous: the small, powerfully built engraver 'coming up in full swing of passion fell with such counter violence of reckless and raging rebuke upon the poor ruffian, that he recoiled and collapsed, with ineffectual cudgel'. The bully had been convinced 'that the very devil himself had flown upon him'. Even more startling for the ruffian was the 'overflow of execration' that came from Blake's mouth – it was the 'fluent tongue of Blake which had proved too strong for the fellow's arm'.[7]

Some of the gloom of 1785 was relieved by William's instruction of 'Bob', whose sunny disposition, in contrast to his brother's, made him 'much beloved by all his companions'.[8] By this time, Robert was also intrigued by key moments in British history, as his sketches in his Notebook of Druids, knights and Gothic churches reveal. And Blake still hoped for some recognition from the Royal Academy, where he submitted four drawings to the exhibition which opened on 27 April. Three depict the story of Joseph from Genesis (*Joseph's Brethren Bowing before Him, Joseph Ordering Simeon to be Bound* and *Joseph Making Himself Known to his Brethren*).

Blake's interest in this story might have been aroused when he engraved Raphael's *Joseph and His Brethren* for *The Protestants Family Bible* (1780–1). On a more personal level, Blake identified with Joseph, who is sold by his jealous brothers and then, years later, acts magnanimously towards them. Perhaps he hoped that his recalcitrant siblings would eventually recognize his talents. Or he might have seen the story of Joseph and his brothers as a fable about his fellow artists, who, motivated by envy, cast him asunder. Eventually, he may have hoped, they would, like Joseph's brothers, repent the folly of their ways. In Genesis, Joseph's father Jacob rebukes his visionary abilities, and Blake may be commenting on James's conduct of years earlier, when he wanted to thrash William at the time the young boy told him what he had seen at Peckham Rye.

Joseph Making Himself Known to his Brethren strongly emphasizes Joseph's fraternal feelings for Benjamin, his youngest brother. Here, Blake's sentiments about Robert surface. Despite his training at the

Joseph Making Himself Known to his Brethren

Academy and his elder brother's pursuit of fame there, Robert's surviving work is altogether more dreamy, primitive and visionary than
William's of the same period, almost as if he were pursuing his elder
brother's private beliefs while William sought public recognition.

The other – now missing – watercolour submitted to the Academy
was *The Bard, from Gray*. In Blake's later tempera (c.1809), King
Edward and Queen Eleanor are prostrate with fear as they hear the
bard's declamation. The power of art to overcome political oppression
is dramatized in that confrontation. One of Blake's exchanges with the
austere Reynolds may have taken place at this time. 'Well, Mr Blake,
I hear you despise our art of oil painting.' Blake retorted: 'No, Sir
Joshua, I don't despise it; but I like fresco better.'[9]

Throughout his life, Blake was an incessant labourer. Catherine Blake
claimed that her husband never appeared idle, except in conversation
or while reading.[10] Once, he approvingly underlined this aphorism by
Lavater: 'He, who can at all times sacrifice pleasure to duty, approaches
sublimity.'[11] Strangely, there is little sign of activity from 1785 to
1787. As opposed to the fifty-seven book and magazine illustrations

from 1780 to 1784, only twenty-two survive from the five years on Poland Street.*

Blake certainly viewed the worldly successes of two other engravers, William Woollett and Robert Strange, as evidence of corruption:

> What is Calld the English Style of Engraving such as proceeded from the Toilettes of Woolett & Strange ... can never Produce Character & Expression. I knew the Men intimately from their Intimacy with Basire my Master & knew them both to be heavy lumps of Cunning & Ignorance.[12]

Those who purchase such work prefer 'Ignorance & Imbecility' to 'Genius & Animation'.[13] Blake's own style of engraving was not dissimilar to that of these two. Here, he is expressing his fury that these men, led on by money, had kept engraving a form of copywork. He now made some sort of break with Stothard: after completing an engraving after him on 16 April 1785 he never worked from his designs again.

Like Woollett and Strange, Blake felt the impulse to give in to the power of materialism, but he realized that the love of money might deprive him of his independence as an artist. By 1787, he did not know the precise form his ambitions would take, although he was intrigued by the possibilities of stereotype printing. He was in limbo, his somewhat half-hearted attempts at worldly success having led nowhere. He was also immured in self-doubt.

A constant, wearying sense of subjugation is evident in some of his drawings and watercolours from the mid-1780s, as in the hunched-over body postures of *The Mourners*, or in the two drawings of Ugolino, whose sad plight, commemorated by Dante, had fascinated artists as varied as Reynolds, Fuseli and Flaxman. A Guelph leader in thirteenth-century Pisa, Ugolino, along with his sons and grandsons, was incarcerated by the Ghibelline Archbishop in 1288. The following year, Guido da Montefeltro, the new commander of the Pisan forces, threw the keys of the prison into the Arno, leaving the prisoners to starve. Isolation is also delineated in Blake's scenes from *Robinson Crusoe* and a small pencil drawing of a solitary pastoral figure looking despairingly over a pool of water. Another important subject is *The Complaint of Job*, which exists in various states. These initial depictions of Job emphasize the theme of solitude, the price the enlightened artist must pay to

---

* Blake probably received no remuneration in 1786 for either plates engraved earlier (*Sepulchral Monuments*) or plates reprinted (the Kimpton Bible illustrations were reissued in *The Complete Works of Flavius Josephus*).

practise his art. A similar preoccupation is obvious in the portrayal of Ezekiel, who, commanded by God neither to mourn nor to weep, is confronted with his wife's death that very evening.

In the winter of 1787, Blake tended Robert when he fell ill, probably of consumption. He watched 'continually day and night by his bedside, without sleep'.[14] Bob's strength seeped away, and the beautiful young man died. At that moment, William beheld 'the released spirit ascend heavenward through the matter-of-fact ceiling, "clapping its hands for joy"'.[15] Immediately afterwards, William, exhausted, slept for three days and nights; he probably was not present at the funeral on 11 February and the interment at Bunhill Fields. His depression was replaced by crushing sorrow.

Without doubt, his young brother's death was the single most important event in William Blake's life. William was deprived not only of a brother. In a sense, Robert had been William's child, whom he had tutored to be, like himself, an artist. Robert had been integral to his existence, and his passing deprived William of a part of himself. His attachment to Robert may have been extremely self-centred, but

Ezekiel

55

Robert was the person upon whom he had been able to bestow a full measure of love and devotion. Now that person was gone. It is a measure of Blake's emotional health that his creativity found release, the rite of mourning unleashing new visionary potential. When Robert died, Blake inherited his Notebook. There the surviving brother felt free to write down his most private thoughts. In this way, he linked the death of his brother to his own life as an artist.

Later, Blake claimed, the secret of stereotype printing was imparted to him in a dream: 'In a vision of the night, the form of Robert stood before him, and revealed the wished-for secret, directing him to the technical mode by which could be produced a fac-simile of song and design.'[16] The harrowing experience of death moved Blake out of the slumber in which he had previously been enveloped. It led immediately to the discovery of a form of printing which had previously eluded him.

Up to now, Blake had shown little interest in Christianity: religious belief is presented in a vague, undifferentiated way in *Poetical Sketches* and comparatively few of Blake's early drawings or watercolours are derived from the New Testament. Now deeply stricken, he became devoutly Christian. The quest for the Christ within himself was aroused by a corresponding search for the spirit of his dead brother. For the first – and last – time Blake flirted briefly with organized Christianity when he joined the Swedenborgians.

His sorrow was so devastating that he tried to keep in touch with his brother through adherence to a religious creed and through a sudden dramatic change in his entire conception of himself as an artist. He would become a poet–painter–engraver. The fraternity of man would be one of his major themes. Blake would soon turn to the world of childhood innocence, a pursuit in part kindled by his remembrances of himself at nine when Robert had been born. Having been thrown into the world of bitter experience, he would examine the happy state of innocence. As Blake himself affirmed in 1800, it would be difficult to overestimate the influence of Robert's death on his subsequent existence: 'Thirteen years ago, I lost a brother & with his spirit I converse daily & hourly in the Spirit. & See him in my remembrance in the regions of my Imagination. I hear his advice & even now write from his Dictate.'[17] So idealized was Blake's relationship with Robert that he would seek to re-establish similar bonds with other men. Eventually, he became dissatisfied with such friendships, which could not match his memories of his younger brother.

5

A Rural Pen

1787–1789

R OBERT Blake's death brought an immediate change in his elder
brother's life: he became deeply attracted to the visionary poetics
of Emanuel Swedenborg, and he discovered a method of printing which
could capture the forms of his imagination. In a state of increased
anxiety, he was attempting to find ways of harnessing his energies so
that which was lost could be restored to him.

Blake's interest in Emanuel Swedenborg and his beliefs was probably
triggered by John Flaxman, who in 1784 joined the Theosophical
Society or New Jerusalem Church, founded to promote in London the
beliefs of the Swedish mystic who had died in 1772. Blake's initial
disdain for Flaxman's attendance at the Society's meetings at the
Middle Temple can be seen in the portrayal of Steelyard the Lawgiver
in *An Island in the Moon*. Blake's fellow engraver, William Sharp, had
become a member of the Theosophical Society by 1787. At some point,
the dandyish Richard Cosway also converted, claiming that he could
raise the dead, that the Virgin Mary had sat to him, and that he had
spoken with God and Christ.

Swedenborg had been a renowned scientist who had published on
anatomy, geometry, physiology and metallurgy when, in his early
fifties, he experienced a series of dreams which convinced him that he
had made contact with the hidden spiritual world. For Swedenborg,
the natural and spiritual 'are so distinct, that they have nothing in

common with each other; but nevertheless are so created, that they communicate, yea are joined together, by Correspondences'.[1] Swedenborg also maintained that God invests man with apparent life but that only God really lives. He also condemned predestination: 'All who are born Men, in whatever Religion they may be principled, are capable of being saved.'[2] The portion of the Swedish mystic's doctrine which especially attracted Blake was his assertion that the appearance of ordinary objects was a veil behind which their true essences were concealed. For Swedenborg, an object and its spiritual meaning are united, but it is necessary to learn how to 'read' the correspondences. Apprenticeship was mandatory. Natural man could only comprehend the Bible in its literal sense; the spiritual portion of the Bible was closed off from the uninitiated.

Swedenborgian doctrine is extremely Platonic. However, unlike the neo-Platonists, Swedenborg insisted that an object's meaning and its physical existence are linked. He does not emphasize, as does a neo-Platonist such as Joshua Reynolds, an ideal form towards which actual forms aspire. In particular, Swedenborg was deeply suspicious of the Egyptians: he felt that they had substituted magic for religion and that their art objects had become mere idols, instead of icons which pointed the way to their own inner meanings. Enoch, the biblical sage who had heard of the world of correspondences from the mouths of angels, was, for Swedenborg, a true messenger of God. Significantly, the New Jerusalem Church was also millennial. The Revd Jacob Duché, who preached Swedenborgian doctrine at his church in Lambeth, wrote in 1785 to a relative in America: 'The New Church from above, the Jerusalem of the Revelation, is come down upon earth. Look henceforward for an Internal Millennium.'[3]

Robert Hindmarsh was the head of a faction of Swedenborgians who insisted on a more conventional mode of worship. In 1787 they were granted a licence for public worship, and in January 1788 the New Jerusalem Church held its first service in a chapel in Great East Cheap. William and Catherine attended a General Conference – actually a recruitment meeting – of this group at a public house on Easter Monday, 13 April 1789.* Why did Blake and his wife choose

---

* According to Benjamin Malkin (BR, 440), Blake joined this sect through the agency of the Revd Joseph Proud, a Baptist minister who became a Swedenborgian in 1790, was ordained in 1791, and soon afterwards opened a church in Birmingham. In 1797, he opened a church in Hatton Garden, where Flaxman was at one time a member of his congregation. Either Proud's invitation came *after* Blake had for all intents abandoned Swedenborgianism or Proud interested Blake in this group at the time he too was contemplating switching allegiances.

this sect? Why did they affix their names to this claim?: 'We whose Names are hereunto subscribed, do each of us approve of the Theological Writings of Emanuel Swedenborg, believing that the Doctrines contained therein are genuine Truths, revealed from Heaven, and that the New Jerusalem Church ought to be established, distinct and separate from the Old Church.'[4]

The Church of England's link with Establishment values obviously made it suspect for Blake. Although he might have been intrigued by some aspects of the 'Old' or 'New' Dissent, this was the route earlier taken by his father. Swedenborg had never wanted to start a church. In fact, he had been antithetical to such a scheme. Initially, the members of the New Jerusalem Church were conjoined together in a makeshift alliance which ignored many of the bureaucratic features of institutionalized religion. This would have appealed to Blake. The abolitionist stance of Swedenborg and his followers would also have met with his approval. Moreover, the New Jerusalem Church was attracting the attention of the artisan class. Crucially, Swedenborg's claim to have found a connection between the earthly and the divine moved Blake, who desperately wished to believe that his brother still lived. He wanted to be reassured that death had not been the end of Robert's existence and so, briefly, he enrolled in a sect which emphasized that possibility in a manner which was acceptable to him.

In 1785, Blake had playfully commented on Cumberland's attempts to produce a kind of engraved printing which could bypass movable type: 'I would have all the writing Engraved instead of Printed & at every other leaf a high finished print all in three Volumes folio, & sell them a hundred pounds a piece.'[5] Such a goal had long been a desideratum. Could engravers find a method which would make them no longer at the beck and call of publishers, printers and other middlemen? In 1725, William Ged had experimented with such a procedure, but he met firm resistance in the printing trade. Alexander Tilloch in 1781–2 perfected such a technique in Glasgow, taking out a patent in 1784 for 'printing books from plates instead of movable type'.[6] By 1787 Tilloch was in London, where Blake knew him. However, Tilloch's process still required conventional typesetting in the preparation of the plate. Another way of combining handwritten text with a plate had been available since 1758 in a book translated from the French, *Valuable Secrets Concerning Arts and Trades*, where the procedure was to draw on the copper plate with a compound impermeable to acid. Upon immersion, the acid would eat away the rest of the copper 'so that the work [appeared] like a basso relievo'.[7] A problem remained: the lettering came out in reverse.

Robert's appearance in the dream impelled William the next morning to send Catherine 'out with half a crown ... and of that laid out 1s. 10d. on the simple materials necessary for setting in practice the new revelation'.[8] J.T. Smith claimed that Blake's breakthrough consisted of 'writing his poetry, and drawing his marginal subjects of embellishments in outline upon the copper-plate with an impervious liquid, and then eating the plain parts or lights away with aquafortis considerably below them, so that the outlines were left as a stereotype'.[9] Previously, the usual intaglio method required the engraver to etch a plate, ink it, wipe its surface clear so that ink remained only in the incised lines, and then press the plate firmly against a piece of paper. Blake's new technique used a plate on which the inked illustration and text stood out in relief, that is, he inverted the process of intaglio printing, so that the ridges – rather than the incised lines – of the plate were printed. Since the age of fourteen, Blake had routinely worked in reverse, and it is likely that he wrote in this way on to his plates.

Blake's 'discovery' of relief etching was, in a limited sense, a technological advancement, but it was an experiment in which he attempted to skirt the ordinary means of production of the 1780s. The book and engraving trades were moving more and more in the direction of specialization, which Blake abhorred. Every aspect of book production and marketing would now be under his control. Blake found a method which allowed him to 'Create' his own system rather than being 'enslav'd by another Man's'.[10] The resulting 'primitive & original ways of Execution'[11] went directly against the delicate tonal transitions and elegance of late-eighteenth-century taste. Yet again this is revolution in reverse.

In the mid-1780s Blake might have been invited to the splendid Pall Mall premises of James Edwards, the wealthy bookseller, who in 1786 purchased for £213 the Bedford Hours, an illuminated manuscript, from the Duchess of Portland. Edwards was a good friend of the publisher Joseph Johnson, for whom Blake had worked from 1780, and Edwards was anxious for scholars, students and persons of taste to examine his wares.[12] Created by Flemish artists between 1430 and 1450, the richly coloured Bedford Hours could have inspired Blake in pursuit of an equivalent system of illumination.

Whether or not Blake was influenced by the Bedford Hours or another series of medieval illuminations, colour had begun to dominate the book market. Hand-coloured copies of Blake's illustrations in the

Wit's Magazine were on sale in 1784, and over eighty per cent of his illuminated books were printed in colour, usually in a warm earth tone. When he hand-coloured the printed books, Blake 'limmed' or 'washed' them as he did his watercolour drawings. He did not like the contemporary use of gum as a fixative – he preferred size made of carpenter's glue, the method used by the Italian Renaissance artists he admired.[13]

Pastoral landscape remained a preoccupation of Blake's in the late 1780s. This might seem a strange choice for a man who lived in the heart of London. However, in Blake's boyhood and young manhood, it was possible by a short walk to reach stretches of open country. And earlier Blake had withdrawn to the relative tranquillity of Battersea.

Blake's fascination with the countryside might also have been piqued by his knowledge of the generosity of the overseers of his parish, St James's, Piccadilly, in sending workhouse children to wet nurses and temporary foster mothers in the rustic parish of Wimbledon. This practice, begun in the 1760s, was undertaken in order to reduce the appalling mortality rate which children in the parish workhouses suffered. Often such children stayed at Wimbledon for six years before returning to the workhouse in Poland Street where, one contemporary account declared, 'Examples of Vice and Profligacy being continually before their Eyes, very little Good could be expected to arise to the Children.'[14] In Blake's mind, there might have been a contrast between the dangerous illnesses of the inner city and the serenity of Wimbledon.

Especially in the Renaissance, the pastoral – as in *As You Like It* – had been employed as a suitable backdrop for metaphysical, often neo-Platonic, speculations about man's place in a fallen universe. In the *Poetical Sketches*, Blake had used such a setting because similar landscapes were integral to the mid-eighteenth-century poets he was both copying and parodying: Gray, Collins and the Wartons. Also, the countryside had become a popular locale for book illustrators, such as Thomas Stothard in *The Children in the Wood* and in his frontispiece to Thomas Tickell's *Kensington Gardens*.

A bit earlier, Blake had made a series of 'Good Farmer' drawings in which a Christ-like figure is implored for assistance. Those pictures may have been inspired by Matthew 9: 38: 'Pray ye therefore the Lord of the Harvest.' In these relatively tranquil pieces, the fraternity of Christ with his followers is emphasized. In his first experiments in illuminated printing, Blake examines Christianity in a similarly quiet setting.

The two versions of *There is No Natural Religion* are probably Blake's earliest attempts in his new stereotype printing. In Version A, Blake takes certain propositions found in the writings of John Locke, the deists and the *philosophes*, and summarizes them in seven brief aphoristic quotes, such as 'Man's desires are limited by his perceptions. None can desire what he has not perciev'd.'[15] The accompanying picture shows a naked boy seeking to embrace a swan. In a literal sense, the child craves what he perceives, but the exuberance of the boy, his heightened sense of himself as he experiences an overwhelming urge to be in touch with the animal, runs contrary to the text. As a unit, these illustrations provide metaphors for the dull language of philosophy; they also undercut, in a sarcastic way, its sentiments. In this series of plates, the text and illustration, which take up equal parts of the page, are united by vines or trees.

In the conjunction of text and illustration, Version B of *No Natural Religion* is slightly more sophisticated in technique than its predecessor. The statement 'If any could desire what he is incapable of possessing, despair must be his eternal lot'[16] is counterpointed to a naked man, a chain on his right ankle, who, presumably in despair, is tearing his hair. The bald emotionless statement is patently ridiculed by the illustration: reason is a pale concept when juxtaposed to the emotional posture of the suffering man. As the book concludes, the aphorisms catch up with the emotional resonance in the illustrations: 'He who sees the Infinite in all things sees God'; '... God becomes as we are, that we may be as he is.'[17] The ringing endorsement of Christianity in Version B is in its frontispiece, where Christ raises Lazarus from the dead. This picture dramatically affirms the ineffectualness of 'natural religion'. And here the viewer sees how central death and resurrection had become in Blake's aesthetics.

The frontispiece to *All Religions are One*, like the corresponding illustration to Version B of *Natural Religion*, is markedly Christological: a naked John the Baptist is 'The Voice of one crying in the Wilderness'. Jesus, whose coming was foretold by the Baptist, is the summation of all religious belief – in that sense, all religions are said to be one. In contrast to the often impersonal statements in both versions of *Natural Religion*, the assertions in the remainder of the text are uttered in a virile voice: 'The Religions of all Nations are derived from each Nation's different reception of the Poetic Genius which is every where call'd the Spirit of Prophecy.'[18]

Poets and artists are in touch with the essential truths of existence and seek to give verbal or pictorial expression to them. They are carrying out divine, prophetic missions. As he became more intimately aware of his own role as seer, Blake proclaimed Christ as the prototype of the artist.

Blake's increasing mastery of relief printing is evident in *Songs of Innocence* of 1789, which is much more refined than his three previous journeyman attempts in the same medium. Blake had sung some of these poems at Mrs Mathew's – versions of 'Holy Thursday', 'Nurse's Song' and 'The Little Boy Lost' are included in the manuscript of the unfinished *An Island in the Moon*. The conjoining of text and illustration in this sequence is inspired by such compilations as Joseph Ritson's *English Songs*, for which Blake had engraved seven plates in 1783.

In the 'Introduction' the child is so touched by the piper's piping and singing that he asks him to write the poems down. In response to that heartfelt request, the verses are given permanent form:

> And I made a rural pen,
> And I stain'd the water clear,
> And I wrote my happy songs
> Every child may joy to hear.[19]

Many of the poems display the loving care bestowed upon babies and children. 'Sweet dreams form a shade'[20] over the baby in 'A Cradle Song'; a newborn baby names itself Joy; the nurse is indulgent when the children ask for more time to play: 'Well, well, go & play till the light fades away / And then go home to bed.'[21] Even institutional charity is praised in 'Holy Thursday', the time each year when the Charity School children gathered at St Paul's.

Darker forces are described in 'A Dream', 'Night' and 'On Another's Sorrow', but good comes even out of apparent evil. And there is a bittersweet aura to poems such as 'The School Boy':

> How can the bird that is born for joy,
> Sit in a cage and sing?
> How can a child when fears annoy,
> But droop his tender wing,
> And forget his youthful spring?[22]

Even grim social oppression can *apparently* be overlooked, as in 'The Chimney Sweeper', Blake probably knowing that in 1788 Parliament passed legislation which insisted that 'climbing boys' could not be apprenticed before the age of eight, that they be washed once a week and that they not be forced to go up an ignited chimney.

When my mother died I was very young,
And my father sold me while yet my tongue,
Could scarcely cry weep weep weep weep!
So your chimneys I sweep & in soot I sleep.

There's little Tom Dacre, who cried when his head
That curl'd like a lamb's back, was shav'd, so I said,
'Hush Tom, never mind it, for when your head's bare,
You know that the soot cannot spoil your white hair.'

And so he was quiet, & that very night,
As Tom was a sleeping he had such a sight,
That thousands of sweepers, Dick, Joe, Ned & Jack
Were all of them lock'd up in coffins of black,

And by came an Angel, who had a bright key,
And he open'd the coffins & set them all free.
Then down a green plain leaping, laughing they run
And wash in a river and shine in the Sun.

Then naked & white, all their bags left behind,
They rise upon clouds, and sport in the wind.
And the Angel told Tom, if he'd be a good boy,
He'd have God for his father & never want joy.

And so Tom awoke and we rose in the dark
And got with our bags & our brushes to work.
Tho' the morning was cold, Tom was happy & warm,
So if all do their duty, they need not fear harm.[23]

The chimney sweep endures the oppression which has been visited upon him. Even though he is able to revel in Tom's dream of an existence freed from the tyranny of a society which uses him as a slave, he tolerates the lot assigned to him and, in a somewhat condescending manner, tells Tom Dacre that he should do likewise. He himself lacks the power to imagine a destiny different from his own, and he readily accedes to the oppressive authority of the angel. There is a great deal of incongruity between what the sweep accepts and what Tom imagines, but that irony is not turned against the sweep.

Only in 'The Little Boy Lost' is a frightening force – darkness – depicted, but the triangular gleam which the child moves towards assures the viewer of a happy ending. Other illustrations depict children being watched over, being led to safety, playing tranquilly. These pictures are reinforced by those in which the shepherds, like the 'good farmer', protect their flocks.

For Blake *Innocence* is an idealized landscape, in which children are nurtured. In some poems, the conclusions are disturbing, as when the black boy imagines a time when he and the white boy will be brothers.

> I'll shade him from the heat till he can bear,
> To lean in joy upon our father's knee.
> And then I'll stand and stroke his silver hair,
> And be like him and he will then love me.[24]

But this is not true reciprocity. Why should the little black boy be worthy of love only when he becomes 'like' the white boy? But, in general, children in *Innocence* are shown to have tremendous powers of self-healing, even though their optimism might not always be justified. As a group, the poems show the love which can be bestowed upon children and their eager responses to it. Nevertheless, Blake remained decidedly uneasy about parents and parent-substitutes such as nurses.

Since William had himself acted as a father to Robert, he had to believe in the power of some parents to act virtuously and this conviction gives *Innocence* much of its vigour. There is no irony in the presentation of 'God our father dear' in 'The Divine Image' and no condescension in the authoritative, patriarchal 'Voice of the Ancient Bard':

> Youth of delight, come hither:
> And see the opening morn,
> Image of truth new born.
> Doubt is fled & clouds of reason,
> Dark disputes & artful teazing.

In a kindly way, the Bard will guide the children through folly's maze and the 'tangled roots' which may 'perplex' their ways.[25] The world of childhood may not be permanent – and it may be threatened or contain real evil – but it is removed from the concerns of adulthood. Sadly, however, Blake realizes that idyllic innocence must ultimately be supplanted by adult experience.

Blake did not engrave the poem *Tiriel* (c.1789), but there is a series of watercolours depicting portions of the text. A grim view of parental love, as we have seen, is central to that poem, which is also about despotism. But in some of the illustrations the vale of Har is presented as a place of sensuous dreams. Such is the landscape of *The Book of Thel*, probably completed shortly after *Innocence.*

Thel, one of the daughters of Mne Seraphim, is lonely in her angelic state of innocence. Like Samuel Johnson's Rasselas, she wants to leave her Happy Valley behind. In particular, she is convinced that hers is an insubstantial existence, like 'a reflection in a glass, like shadows in the water. / Like dreams of infants, like a smile upon an infant's face ...'[26] In an attempt to make herself more real, she interrogates the lily of the valley, the 'tender' cloud, the worm and the 'matron clay'. All these creatures cheerfully accept their places in the cycle of existence. The cloud is certainly aware of the Law of Correspondences when he says:

> O maid, I tell thee, when I pass away,
> It is to tenfold life, to love, to peace, and raptures holy:
> Unseen descending, weigh my light wings upon balmy flowers;
> And court the fair-eyed dew, to take me to her shining tent.[27]

After Thel completes her catechizing, she is invited to fulfil her destiny by entering the house of 'matron clay', having been assured that she has nothing to dread. Soon after entering in and seeing 'the secrets of the land unknown' where 'the fibrous roots / Of every heart on earth infixes deep its restless twists', Thel comes upon her own grave, sits down and listens to a series of paradoxical, unanswerable queries, such as 'Why a tender curb upon the youthful burning boy? / Why a little curtain of flesh on the bed of our desire?'[28] Terrified, she shrieks and flees back to the vale of Har.

Thel is about the dangers of becoming adult. It is also concerned with the fear of one's own sexuality, this theme being visually encapsulated in the title-page illustration where the male aggressively pursues his female counterpart. As with many Blakean characters, her own coming into being is a source of anxiety to Thel. Does one want to exist? Is life really a gift? Here, these questions are being asked in a much more secular manner than in *Innocence*, Blake having begun in *Thel* and in *Tiriel* to create his own mythology.

Thel obviously reflects Blake's own dilemmas in 1789 and argues in favour of pursuing adulthood, despite accompanying disadvantages. For the past two years, Blake had moved steadily towards his own unique form of art. Did he wish to accept the lonely consequences attendant on his new system of printing? Was he committed to this new form begotten of suffering? Was he able to transcend the immense pain which had been inflicted upon him by Robert's death? The maturational crisis of Thel is one Blake himself experienced as he approached thirty-three, the age at which Christ died. Was he willing to undergo similar ostracism and deprivation? Was he willing to be a voice preaching in the wilderness?

6

Prophet from Albion

1789–1791

I N the autumn of 1790, William and Catherine crossed the Thames
to Lambeth and moved to 13 Hercules Buildings, one of twenty-six
attached houses which occupied more than half the street. Up to the
eighteenth century, Lambeth had been a marshland, favoured for duck
hunting, traversed by a few roads raised against floods. In Blake's time,
this section of London remained little more than a series of houses
built along roads bordering meadows and swamp. Positioned between
the centre of London and his boyhood haunts, this place had a pastoral
air, as if Blake had chosen to dwell where the urban and suburban
could be, in a sort of compromise, blended.

The houses in Hercules Buildings, lying diagonally between the
Westminster Bridge New Road and Lambeth Road, were irregularly
sized – one to three storeys high. Blake's home was on the east
side of the street. The three-storey, eight- or ten-room house had a
wainscoted parlour, low windows and a narrow strip of garden at the
rear. A vine grew in the garden, which he refused to prune: 'the
affranchised tree consequently bore a luxuriant crop of leaves, and
plenty of infinitesimal grapes which never ripened.'[1] Philip Astley,
whose circus was three streets away, owned a house in the garden of
No. 15.

At the crossing of the New Road and Hercules Buildings were three
pleasure gardens: the Temple of Flora, the Apollo Gardens and the

Flora Tea Gardens. The grounds of the Temple contained cascades, alcoves and statuary, and the Temple itself had been designed after the rotunda at Ranelagh. The hot house had fountains and a transparency of Flora. When Blake moved to Lambeth, the Temple had an excellent reputation, but in 1796 the proprietor was imprisoned for keeping a bawdy house. The Apollo had a domed concert-room with a large organ; in 1790 the nightly music and puppet shows (*fantoccini*) were halted, the owner went bankrupt, and the moated temple eventually fell into decay. 'Genteel' paintings remained on display at the Tea Gardens, a place where 'democratic shopmen ... might be heard railing against King and Church'.[2]

The Royal Asylum for Female Orphans, a 'house of refuge' where the Hercules Tavern once stood, was near by, as was the Lambeth Charity School. The renowned Swedenborgian divine, Jacob Duché, was secretary and chaplain at the Asylum from 1779 to 1792,[3] and in 1779 Blake had been among the subscribers to Duché's *Discourses on Several Subjects*, for which Sharp engraved the frontispiece. Since Blake was still favourably disposed to Swedenborgianism in 1790, Duché's presence in Lambeth might have been an inducement for moving there. From the back of Hercules Buildings, Lambeth Palace was clearly visible.

Lambeth offered many pastoral comforts, and William and Catherine supposedly felt free enough to create their own Eden by walking about their garden in the nude. Thomas Butts, Blake's patron, called one day and found them seated in their summer-house reciting passages from *Paradise Lost*. 'Come in!' called Blake, 'it's only Adam and Eve you know!' Blake's neighbours were only a bit scandalized by such behaviour, for they seemed to have known 'sufficient of the single-minded artist not wholly to misconstrue such phenomena'.[4]

Gilchrist came upon this anecdote while researching his biography, but the story was later denied by Blake's disciples, Samuel Palmer and John Linnell, and also by Butts' grandson, 'who distinctly remember[ed] hearing his grandfather declare that there was no truth in it'.[5] There might be a germ of truth in the incident as recounted by Gilchrist, but two conflicting interests are at work. Palmer and Linnell wanted to make Blake respectable whereas Gilchrist wanted to uncover the eccentric side of Blake's personality.

A similar note of caution has to be sounded about the supposed ghost at the top of the staircase at Hercules Buildings. One day, a friend asked Blake if he had ever seen or had any experience of such a phenomenon.

'Never but once,' was the reply. And it befel thus. Standing one evening at his garden-door in Lambeth, and chancing to look up, he saw a horrible grim figure, 'scaly, speckled, very awful,' stalking downstairs towards him. More frightened than ever before or after, he took to his heels, and ran out of the house.[6]

Blake may have thought that he beheld a ghost, or he might have been having fun at the expense of the credulous.

His irascibility found a suitable outlet when one day, standing at a window which looked on to Astley's, he noticed a boy hobbling along with a log attached to his foot, 'as if put on a Horse or Ass to prevent their straying'. Blake asked Catherine what was happening. She told him that the child was obviously being punished for some misdemeanour. Blake's 'blood boiled & his indignation surpassed his forbearance'. He rushed to the Astley house, demanding that the boy be set free. No Englishman should have to suffer an indignity 'inexcusable even towards a Slave'. Blake's anger prevailing, the boy was released. However, when Astley returned home, he was furious at what had transpired and quickly made his way to No. 13. The two men almost came to blows, but the argument finally ended in 'mutual forgiveness & mutual respect'.[7] In the midst of such gossipy accounts, the death of Blake's mother on about 7 September 1792 goes unnoticed in the surviving records of the Lambeth years.

What was strange about Blake's choice of Hercules Buildings was the proximity to Lambeth Palace, the Archbishop of Canterbury's official residence. Although the land had been purchased in 1190–7, a chapel was not constructed until the thirteenth century. Here, in 1378, John Wycliffe was examined for 'propositions, clearly heretical and depraved'. Three years later, Wat Tyler's rebels overran the Palace. London apprentices had attacked it in 1640, and the Gordon Rioters had surrounded it. Starting in the fifteenth century, the Palace had been a place of conspicuous charity: the Lambeth Dole was handed over to the poor three times a week, a practice which continued until 1842.

From his back garden, Blake's view was blocked by a building which symbolized the oppressive power of the established Church. Its proximity – less than a half-mile south-west – must have weighed deeply on him, reminding him of just how mighty the enemies of America and Albion were. On the other hand, he must have identified with Wycliffe, Tyler and the followers of George Gordon, the building providing a specific focus for the political animus which began to consume him. Through words and pictures, he tried to tear down the palace and all that it represented.

At first, Lambeth offered Blake the financial security which had previously evaded him. During their stay at Hercules Buildings, the couple 'kept a servant, but finding (as Mrs. Blake declared . . .) the more service the more inconvenience',[8] they dismissed her. In fact, Blake may well have chosen Lambeth because of its somewhat lower cost of living. What he hoped to do in 1790 was to find a balance between his occupations as his own publisher and as commercial engraver.

Blake's comparative affluence in the early 1790s is underscored by the value of possessions stolen from him. One day, when Catherine and he were away, thieves broke in and stole plate worth £60 and clothes valued at £40. Blake was even able to lend £40 on another occasion to a 'free-thinking Speculator' who claimed that he did not have enough money to feed his children. The next day Blake was flummoxed to discover that the man's wife, 'who was a dressy & what is called a pretty woman, had squandered some large portion of the money, upon her worthless sides'.[9] This unnamed lady even had the gall to ask Catherine's opinion of an ornate dress she purchased the day after Blake had given her husband the money.

It may be more the stuff of legend than of fact that Blake had a number of wealthy pupils and that he was 'recommended & nearly obtained an Appointment to teach Drawing to the Royal Family'.

> Blake stood aghast; not indeed from any republican humours, not from any disaffection to his superiors, but because he would have been drawn into a class of Society, superior to his previous pursuits & habits; he would have been expected to have lived in comparative respectability, not to say splendour, a mode of life, as he thought, derogatory to the simplicity of his designs & deportment.[10]

The semblance of financial stability, which bred rumours of possible royal pupils, was based on Blake's success as an engraver, and much of this good fortune was due to his complex, entwined dealings with Henry Fuseli and Joseph Johnson, friendships which became central at this time.

Johnson first published an engraving by Blake in 1780: a plate for Enfield's *The Speaker*. Further assignments followed in 1782 and 1783. After a hiatus of five years, he engraved for Johnson Fuseli's portrait of Democritus, for the Swiss artist's translation of Lavater's *Aphorisms on Man*. In 1790–1, Blake undertook approximately thirty-four engravings, including those for Salzmann's *Elements of Morality*, which led to a favourable notice in Johnson's periodical, the *Analytical Review*: 'The [anonymous] prints are far superior, both with respect to design and engraving, to any we have ever seen in books designed for children; and that prints, judiciously introduced, are particularly calculated to enforce a moral tale, must be obvious to every one who has had any experience in education.'[11]

Blake's relationship with Joseph Johnson only changed from occasional employee to friend under the aegis of Fuseli, whom Blake came to know well in 1787, when Flaxman went to Italy and, he observed, 'Fuseli was giv'n to me for a season.'[12] Since Fuseli had taken rooms on Broad Street from 1779 to 1782, they may possibly have met at that time.

Both Flaxman and Fuseli 'were in the habit of declaring with unwonted emphasis, that "the time would come" when the finest [of Blake's designs] "would be as much sought after and treasured in the portfolios" of men discerning in art, "as those of Michael Angelo now" '.[13] Although Fuseli pointed out that Blake was '*d —— d good to steal from!*'[14] and there is a similar anecdote about Fuseli exclaiming, in admiration for a design Blake showed him, 'Blake, I shall invent that myself,'[15] the relationship worked the other way. Blake, sixteen years younger, learned from the older man, who was well on the way to secure fame by 1787. Despite their bad tempers, the two stayed friends, as Flaxman recalled:

Flaxman: 'How do you get on with Fuseli? I can't stand his foul-mouthed swearing. Does he swear at you?'

Blake: 'He does.'

Flaxman: 'And what do you do?'

Blake: 'What do I do? Why – I swear again! and he says astonished, "*vy, Blake, you are svaring!*" but he leaves off himself.'[16]

The Swiss-born artist, baptized Johann Heinrich Füssli, had, under familial pressure, taken holy orders in 1761, although he never officiated as a priest. From the age of eight, art had been his real interest. With the intention of acting as a liaison between the German literati and their English counterparts, he arrived in England at the age of twenty-three in 1764. Encouraged by Reynolds, he had gone to Italy in 1770, where he remained for eight years. Although diminutive in stature (he was barely five feet tall), he had an unshakeable sense of his own worth. He was able to cultivate several modes at once – canvases which are extremely neo-classical were painted at the same time as he was labouring on psychologically inspired, Gothic pictures such as *The Nightmare*. Fuseli was fascinated by the other side of existence, the visionary world hovering at the edge of everyday reality – and it is his eerie poeticism which fascinates and disturbs the viewer. Unlike Blake, Fuseli's sublime is excessively dependent on the exaggerated, often grotesque lines of Italian mannerism; like Blake, he wanted to be another Michelangelo. Fuseli's eroticism is plainly evident in many of his canvases, whereas Blake's sexuality is usually much more covertly expressed.

Fuseli's mercurial personality led him to master a variety of styles. He also had a keen political sense against which he balanced his idiosyncrasies. He was elected an Associate of the Royal Academy in 1788 and, in the face of Reynolds's objections, a full Academician in 1790. With his eye resolutely on the main chance, he attempted to improve the market for engravings of his work by opening a Milton Gallery in Pall Mall in 1799. That same year, he became Professor of Painting at the Academy, eventually becoming Keeper in 1804.

The Blake–Fuseli friendship was cemented when Blake engraved the frontispiece to the Swiss artist's edition of his close friend Lavater's *Aphorisms*. Blake annotated his own copy of that book, leading Fuseli to declare that Blake's own character could be discerned in those jottings.[17]* Although Blake's attempt to emulate the sublime of horror was inspired by Fuseli, the Swiss did not share with him any interest

---

*For example, although Blake proclaims the equality of all men, this does not stop him from judging his fellow men astringently in this set of marginalia. He flatly contradicts Lavater when he asserts, 'Severity of judgment is a great virtue' (*The Complete Poetry and Prose of William Blake*, ed. David V. Endman (Berkeley and Los Angeles: University of California Press, 1982), p. 585; henceforth, *Writings*.) In particular, he loathes sneerers, crawlers and nibblers. In contrast, one should 'solicit boldly'. And he distrusts Lavater's naivety, as when the Swiss philosopher declares: 'Every thing may be mimicked by hypocrisy, but humility and love united.' Blake condescendingly remonstrates: 'all this may be mimicked very well. This Aphorism certainly was an oversight for what are all crawlers but mimickers of humility and love?' (ibid., p. 586).

In the late 1780s, Blake ws torn between attempting to gain public recognition for his work – and the desire to live in penurious isolation. On the one hand, he rejects Lavater's advice that a 'scarcer smile' is more publicly acceptable than 'frequent laughing': 'I hate scarce smiles. I love laughing' (ibid., p. 585). On the other hand, Blake grudgingly has to admit the truth of Lavater's claim that only the 'fool separates his object from all surrounding ones': this makes him 'uneasy because [he] once thought otherwise but now know it is Truth' (ibid., p. 599). Blake's solitude and his steadfast belief in himself is captured in two instances where he merely underlined the latter portions of two statements:

The richer you are, the more calmly you bear the reproach of poverty: THE MORE GENIUS YOU HAVE, THE MORE EASILY YOU BEAR THE IMPUTATION OF MEDIOCRITY. (ibid., p. 593)

Who in the same given time can produce more than any others, has *vigour*; who can produce more and better, has *talents*; who CAN PRODUCE WHAT NONE ELSE CAN, HAS GENIUS. (ibid., p. 585)

in Christianity: 'I am no anti-Christian, no un-Christian, but a decided non-Christian.'[18] The religious differences between the two men are underscored when Blake asserts, in a Swedenborgian mode, that 'our Lord is the word of God & every thing on earth is the word of God & in its essence is God'.[19]

Blake's sense that he had to win some sort of public recognition increased his attendance at the shop of Joseph Johnson, who had migrated to London from Liverpool in 1754 at the age of fourteen, at which time he began his apprenticeship in the book trade. From August 1770, he was established in St Paul's Churchyard. In addition to publishing controversial works by Wollstonecraft, Priestley, Paine, Malthus and Beckford, Johnson was a committed Unitarian and many tracts by fellow members of that religion carry his imprint; he had a keen interest in scientific treatises and some significant medical publications bear his name. Also, he cultivated authors from his native city.

Blake was much younger than Johnson, and, yet again, as in the case of his presence six years before at Rathbone Place, he lingered on the fringes of Johnson's circle. His shop was a meeting place, where argument, chatter and intrigue were intermixed. Johnson gave 'plain but hospitable' dinners in his living quarters 'in a little, quaintly shaped upstairs room, with walls not at right angles, where his guests must have been somewhat straitened for space'.[20] William Godwin, who frequented Johnson's, has left little conclusive evidence in his diary of Blake's presence at Johnson's salon. Blake certainly was there on 4 April 1797, the company including Fuseli, Grignion an engraver, Dr John Anderson and Arthur Aikin, a nephew of Mrs Barbauld, the renowned Blue Stocking. He had been there earlier in June 1794 with the engraver Bartolozzi, the portrait-painter Rigaud and the retired soldier John Stedman.[21]

In any event, Blake was always uncomfortable with polite chat. At times, he would simply utter opinions at marked variance from those of his companions. Or he said 'things on purpose to puzzle and provoke those who teased him'.[22] He could also be perversely obstinate, as when Thomas Taylor was teaching him geometry. They had reached the fifth proposition:

> which proves that any two angles at the base of an isosceles triangle must be equal. Taylor was going thro the demonstration, but was interrupted by Blake, exclaiming, 'ah never mind that – what's the use of

going to prove it, why I see with my eyes that it is so, & do not require any proof to make it clearer.'

The two men had another comical exchange:

'Pray, Mr. Taylor, did you ever find yourself, as it were, standing close beside the vast and luminous orb of the moon?'
  'Not that I remember, Mr. Blake: did you ever?'
  'Yes, frequently; and I have felt an almost irresistible desire to throw myself into it headlong.'
  'I think, Mr. Blake, you had better not; for if you were to do so, you most probably would never come out of it again.'[23]

Blake knew the gossip of the Johnson circle, but he was not an active participant in its activities.

Through Johnson, Blake must have become more aware of revolutionary politics. For example, his friendship with the radical Unitarian William Frend, who was expelled from Cambridge in 1793, probably began at this time; through William Sharp, Blake would have known of the activities of the Society for Constitutional Reform, which vigorously promoted Paine's *The Rights of Man*. Late in life Blake called himself a 'Liberty Boy', 'jokingly urg[ing] in self-defence that the shape of his forehead made him a republican'.[24] He might well have worn the white hat of liberty. George Cumberland certainly did this.

In the 1790s, there was widespread fear in England of French (insurrectionist) ideas. Such apprehension was made worse by England's declaration of war against France in 1793. Much of the strength of Pitt's regime was derived from crisis. Hysteria was rampant. Even in the light of these circumstances, the legend that Blake warned Tom Paine in 1792 that his life was in danger ('You must not go home, or you are a dead man!')[25] is open to serious doubt. Although Paine had been indicted for seditious utterance, the government was not anxious to try this case before a London jury, which might find in Paine's favour. In any event, Paine went to France to attend the opening of the French Convention, not to avoid arrest. Much more believable are stories about religious conflicts between Blake and Paine. Despite republican sentiments, Blake remained resolutely anti-deist and 'rebuked the profanity' of the author of *The Rights of Man*: 'In one of their conversations, Paine said that religion was a law & a tye to all able minds. Blake on the other hand said what he was always asserting, that the religion of Jesus, was a perfect law of Liberty.'[26] Blake would also have sharply disapproved of Joseph Johnson's Unitarianism, especially that sect's insistence that Christ was not divine. Also questionable is the depth of Blake's sympathies with Mary Wollstonecraft.

Blake probably received the commission for the five plates for *Original Stories from Real Life: with Conversations. Calculated to Regulate the Affections and Form the Mind to Truth and Goodness* because of the public praise given to the engravings in *Elements of Morality*. In Wollstonecraft's heavily didactic novel, Mrs Mason, a governess, seeks to inculcate high moral virtue in her two charges, Mary and Caroline, by exposing them to the dire realities of daily life in the 1790s. Wollstonecraft's book, as the title indicates, is excessively moralistic, and Blake might have seen the sentiments therein as too heavy-handed to be of any use. Johnson was evidently pleased enough by such assignments, for he engaged him – and Blake had begun work – as one of the engravers for the soon abandoned Cowper–Fuseli edition of Milton, which was meant to rival a competing undertaking of Boydell's. The failure of this venture prevented Blake from becoming involved in what seemed then, in spite of his experience with Parker, to be the crest of a demand for large-scale, illustrated books.

Johnson reiterated his confidence in Blake in a letter of July 1791 to one of his most distinguished authors, Erasmus Darwin, and Blake eventually engraved ten plates for *The Botanic Garden*.[27] And there were other signs of success: the architect Willey Reveley asked him to engrave some of the drawings of William Pars, Henry Pars's brother, for *The Antiquities of Athens*. And Blake, always a dilatory letter writer, was busy enough in November 1791 *not* to respond to a plea from Nancy Flaxman: she and John, now living in Italy, were sufficiently worried about him to ask John's sister Maria to 'call on Mr Blake & beg of him to answer your Brother's Letter directly'.[28]

Ultimately, the activism of the Johnson circle would have irritated Blake, whose concern for social justice was much more linked to inner awareness and transformation than action. The common ground of Blake and Johnson can be found in *The French Revolution*, but even here there may have been a marked difference in opinion. Apart from *Poetical Sketches*, *The French Revolution* is Blake's only poem in conventional typography. The title page is dated 1791 where the book is described as 'A Poem in Seven Books'. The Advertisement adds: 'The remaining Books of this Poem are finished, and will be published in their Order.'[29] However, it was never published: all that remains is a single set of page proofs of the First Book. Plans for the completion of the text might have been well advanced, but all further evidence of the poem has disappeared. The intriguing question is: why was Book the First not published as planned? The most likely explanation is that Johnson, despite his manifest sympathy with the notion of social upheaval, was an extremely cautious man. Although he printed the first volume of Paine's *The Rights of Man* in February 1791, he decided against issuing it and Paine had to find another publisher. Within that year, publishers were jailed for selling Paine; by the next year, governmental clamp-downs had modified considerably and Johnson issued Barlow's *Conspiracy of Kings*.

Initially, Johnson's natural prudence may have inclined him to suppress a book with a provocative title, despite the fact that Blake's poem contains no reference to England. The book was never advertised in the *Analytical Review*, and it was not registered at Stationers' Hall. Blake tended to be cagey about placing himself in potentially threatening situations and there is the possibility that he withdrew from the project when he saw what was happening to Paine. Also, Blake might have felt that he was betraying his new method of illuminated printing in pursuit of public success which might, paradoxically, brand him an outlaw.

Although Blake did not engrave Book the First of *The French Revolution*, it is a text which displays its author's acute visual awareness, the scenes being composed as a static series of friezes or tableaux. Blake's text, perhaps influenced by Joel Barlow's *The Vision of Columbus*, depicts the earliest stages of the Revolution, before the fall of the Bastille. On 22 June 1789, the Third Estate finally declared itself a National Assembly; three days later, in the tennis-court oath, the Assembly became openly defiant of the King, who gave in to some of its demands and yet clung to the use of mercenaries at Paris and Versailles, although these forces were not used to defend the Bastille, which fell on 14 July. King Louis also dismissed Necker, the Finance Minister, who had become a symbol of popular resistance to tyranny.

Blake is more concerned with the lessons of history than actual historical events: for example, he locates events in Paris which actually took place at Versailles. The poem opens with a portrayal of Louis as the epitome of the ineffectual monarch, as the representative of a corrupt regime which is slowly dying:

> The dead brood over Europe, the cloud and vision
> descends over chearful France;
> O cloud well appointed! Sick, sick: the Prince on his
> couch, wreath'd in dim

> And appalling mist; his strong hand outstretch'd, from
> his shoulder down the bone
> Runs aching cold into the scepter too heavy for mortal
> grasp. No more
> To be swayed by visible hand, nor in cruelty bruise, the
> mild flourishing mountains.[30]

The disease of the King has infiltrated the landscape. One of those who clings to the old order is the fictional Duke of Burgundy, whom Blake paints in a series of vivid reds:

> Then the ancientest Peer, Duke of Burgundy, rose
> from the Monarch's right hand, red as wines
> From his mountains, an odor of war, like a ripe
> vineyard, rose from his garments,
> And the chamber became as a clouded sky; o'er the
> council he stretch'd his red limbs,
> Cloth'd in flames of crimson, as a ripe vineyard
> stretches over sheaves of corn,
> The fierce Duke hung over the council; around him
> crowd, weeping in his burning robe,
> A bright cloud of infant souls; his words fall like
> purple autumn on the sheaves.[31]

The vibrancy of the Duke of Burgundy, despite the colour scheme, is false: he is a man of blood, a corrupt, selfish politician who will do anything to maintain power.

The narrative moves swiftly from one imaginative tower at the Bastille to another. In the one called *Order* sits 'an old man, whose white beard cover'd the stone floor like weeds / On margin of the sea'. He was once a preacher in Paris who, urged by his conscience, 'taught wonders to darken'd souls'.[32]

In a manner reminiscent of *The French Revolution*, Blake tries in *America* (1793) and *Europe* (1794) to capture the essence of historical events. In these, the only two illuminated books which he actually labelled 'prophecies', he portrayed the military conflicts in America and Europe as harbingers of a revolution which he hoped would finally reach England. These writings are decidedly nationalistic: when would England finally take heed of the American past or the European present? *America* and *Europe* are thus meant to be prophetic of a new English order. Blake's commitment to the destiny of his own nation had found a new outlet.

America dramatizes the strife between the English forces of George III and the Americans led by George Washington by showing how the King's minion, Albion's Angel, victimizes the colonists with a virulent pestilence. When the plague is driven back towards England by Orc, a 'hairy youth', Urizen intervenes and freezes the action of the poem. Although Blake uses historical characters in his text, the struggle in the poem is encapsulated by two mythological figures of his devising: Orc, large, winged and Promethean, and Urizen, the tyrant-god of snow and ice. The young, virile and passionate radical stands in direct contrast to the paternal god of reason. Although the forces of rationality are victorious at the conclusion of *America*, Blake foresees the triumph of revolution in England: 'But the five gates were consum'd, & their bolts and hinges melted / And the fierce flames burnt round the heavens, & round the abodes of men.'[33]

The clash between Orc and Albion's Angel continues in *Europe*, where Blake introduces Los and Enitharmon, the father and mother of Orc. A much more vulnerable person than Orc, Los has insurrectionist tendencies but is tinged with pity for Urizen. He is not a central character in *Europe*, but Enitharmon is: she is a corrupt person who uses her dazzling beauty in a less obvious way than Urizen or Albion's Angel to seduce and thus dominate her opponents. However, the hegemony of these three cracks apart at the end of this 'prophecy':

> The sun glow'd fiery red!
> The furious terrors flew around!
> On golden chariots raging, with red wheels dropping
>   with blood;
> The Lions lash their wrathful tails!
> The Tigers couch upon the prey & suck the ruddy tide:
> And Enitharmon groans & cries in anguish and dismay.
>
> Then Los arose; his head he reard in snaky thunders
>   clad:
> And with a cry that shook all nature to the utmost
>   pole,
> Call'd all his sons to the strife of blood.[34]

These two poems are forceful, mythological reflections on recent history, but the struggles are represented in deeply human terms: in particular, sons must rebel against punitive fathers. In *Europe*, women – mothers in particular – are shown to be slightly more devious than men in the pursuit of power. Los, a much milder father than Urizen, is sympathetic to his rebellious son.

Frontispiece to *America*

The Ancient of Days

In some of his illustrations to *America* and *Europe*, Blake searches for an exact correspondence to the events in the text, as in his depiction of Urizen in Plate Eight or Orc in Plate Ten of *America*. His growing sophistication also leads him to expand visually the meaning of the text, as in Plate Eleven of *Europe*, where two women, one with considerable trepidation and the other with cool detachment, await the moment an almost-dead child can be placed in a pot. One woman is caring but helpless, the other unconcerned. Although they have opposing sentiments about the baby, it will nevertheless meet a grim end. Deep-seated passivity and corrupt luxury have led to the same unhappy result: cannibalism. Here Blake demonstrates how political corruption has invaded domestic life. The dominion of Urizen is splendidly shown in the frontispiece to *Europe*, where, in the solitude he craves, he measures out the universe.

The earlier *The Marriage of Heaven and Hell* is even more experimental than the two prophecies. Here, Blake assaults the eye with a wide range of verbal and visual material: proverbs of hell, a short history of poetry, a critique of *Paradise Lost*, a miniature history of the conflict between the just man and unctuous villainy, a severe condemnation of Swedenborg, and five 'Memorable Fancies'.

Blake's denunciation of Swedenborg was a short time brewing. In 1788, he was slightly irked by the assertion in Swedenborg's *Heaven and Hell* that there were 'particular Hells of different extent in length, breadth, and depth': 'under every *Good* is a hell; i.e. hell is the outward or external of heaven & is of the body of the lord . . .'.[35] About a year later, he still saw much with which he could agree in *Divine Love and Wisdom*; a year after that he peppered his copy of *Divine Providence* with snide rejoinders, some of which, incorrectly, accuse Swedenborg of believing in predestination. Initially, Blake might have been attracted to Swedenborg because he claimed that a new dispensation had commenced in 1757, the year of Blake's birth. By 1790, Blake was not so sure, as he makes plain in *The Marriage*:

> As a new heaven is begun, and it is now thirty-three years since its advent: the Eternal Hell revives. And lo! Swedenborg is the Angel sitting at the tomb; his writings are the linen clothes folded up.[36]

Blake might have been shocked by the amount of gossip whirling about in 1789–90 concerning the Swedenborgians. First of all, some members of the New Jerusalem Church, including Hindmarsh, were expelled because they affirmed that male adherents, under certain circumstances, should be permitted to have concubines. Also, in about 1790, the tomb of Swedenborg, who had died in London in 1772, was opened. Although the corpse was well preserved, it quickly turned to dust. The attack on Swedenborg in *Marriage* might be by way of an ironical commentary on that event. Blake would also have known that the New Jerusalem Church, in an attempt to ensure its survival in an edgy society, increasingly distanced itself from Tom Paine and radical politics. The Church had become institutionalized: catechisms, hymn books and ministers' garments were approved in 1790–1. Clearly, Swedenborg was not the bearer of a new gospel but a rather simple-minded, literal messenger of conformity. Blake, a disillusioned convert, later countered Swedenborg's *Memorable Relations* with 'Memorable Fancies'.

However, his rift with Swedenborgianism might have been most strongly influenced by his increased realization that the New Jerusalem Church held that heaven had dominion over hell. In 1788, Blake had become convinced that heaven and hell were connected. By 1790, he had come to believe that the world of hell was the only alternative open to him. In fact, it was superior to the world of heaven and, paradoxically, it was the source of revolutionary fervour. George III's government *and* Swedenborg had got everything backwards.

Blake had become certain that the ills of earthly existence were compounded by the fact that, in an extremely Manichean way, reason had become associated with moral goodness, and, in the process, passion – and all the energy associated with it – was regarded as evil. This startling realization is captured in *Marriage* by Blake's decision to present his text and illustrations in an extremely non-linear manner. The way of reason consisted of the logical exposition of a narrative, with clearly defined beginnings, middles and ends. However, if that vision of the world was essentially incorrect, it was no longer possible to use the rhetoric of reason. Since the errors being dissected are the inherited traditions of Western man, Blake once again employs Menippean satire as the appropriate vehicle in which to cast his counter-vision. Here and elsewhere, the experimental nature of Blake's work derives from his conviction that a new method of vision must have a distinct form of expression. If the verbal and visual language of the past is used to describe an innovative concept, that idea will be immediately corrupted and tarnished by such dependency.

For some time, he had been aware that he did not wish to write employing the conventions of the printed book. In *The Marriage*, he removes himself even further from accepted discourse by assaulting his audience with a series of *seemingly* random pieces of material flung disparately together.

First, there is Rintrah, who 'roars & shakes his fires in the burdened air'.[37] He is an Orc-like figure whose lands have been removed from him by villains. The censure of Swedenborg follows; then a series of claims: 'Without Contraries is no progression. Attraction and Repulsion, Reason and Energy, Love and Hate, are necessary to Human existence.'[38] Then the Voice of the Devil announces that 'Energy is the only life and is from the Body and Reason is the bound or outward circumference of Energy.'[39] A bit later are the proverbs of hell, which attack conventional notions of moral virtue: 'The pride of the peacock is the glory of God. / The lust of the goat is the bounty of God.'[40] The aim of the text is to throw the audience off-centre, to engender an emotional response which will lead to a questioning of accepted values.

Blake's concession to the narrative tradition is found in the five 'Memorable Fancies', which are interspersed throughout *Marriage*. These constitute a spiritual autobiography, a portrait of the artist as a young man in the process of becoming a young devil. First, the narrator

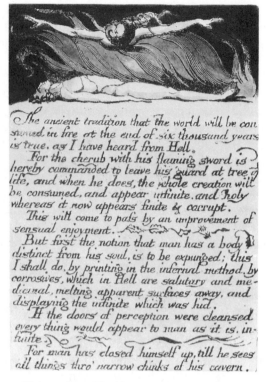

The ancient tradition that the world will be consumed in fire at the end of six thousand years is true. as I have heard from Hell.

For the cherub with his flaming sword is hereby commanded to leave his guard at tree of life, and when he does, the whole creation will be consumed, and appear infinite. and holy whereas it now appears finite & corrupt.

This will come to pass by an improvement of sensual enjoyment.

But first the notion that man has a body distinct from his soul, is to be expunged; this I shall do, by printing in the infernal method, by corrosives, which in Hell are salutary and medicinal, melting apparent surfaces away, and displaying the infinite which was hid.

If the doors of perception were cleansed every thing would appear to man as it is, infinite.

For man has closed himself up, till he sees all things thro' narrow chinks of his cavern.

Plate 14 from *The Marriage of Heaven and Hell*

visits the 'fires of Hell' and dispassionately collects some of its proverbs. He only flirts with that mode of existence until he dines with the prophets Isaiah and Ezekiel, whom he questions about the vocation of prophet. He asks Isaiah: 'does a firm perswasion that a thing is so, make it so?' In a profoundly non-Aristotelian and deliberately illogical reply, the prophet tells him: 'All poets believe that it does, & in ages of imagination this firm perswasion removed mountains; but many are not capable of a firm perswasion of any thing.'[41] But the narrator is capable of such beliefs, and in the next 'Memorable Fancy' he is in 'a Printing house in Hell'. There he sees the dragon-man, a viper, an eagle, lions and unnamed forms; men receive such revelations but tame them by consigning them to libraries.

The longest 'Memorable Fancy' dramatizes the quarrel between the intrepid young narrator and an angel. The two decide to exchange fantasies. The angel goes first and summons up the Leviathan.

his forehead was divided into streaks of green & purple like those on a tyger's forehead: soon we saw his mouth & red gills hang just above the raging foam, tinging the black deep with beams of blood, advancing toward us with all the fury of a spiritual existence.[42]

This apparition has no power over the narrator, but the angel is outraged by what he sees in one of seven brick houses conjured up by his adversary:

in it were a number of monkeys, baboons, & all of that species chain'd by the middle, grinning and snatching at one another, but withheld by the shortness of their chains: however I saw that they sometimes grew numerous, and then the weak were caught by the strong and with a grinning aspect, first coupled with & then devour'd, by plucking off first one limb and then another till the body was left a helpless trunk. This, after grinning & kissing it with seeming fondness, they devour'd too; and here & there I saw one savourily picking the flesh off of his own tail....[43]

The narrator is reminding his opponent that repression leads to the repulsive conduct seen in the house, but the angel can only upbraid him: 'thy phantasy has imposed upon me & thou oughtest to be ashamed.'[44] In the final 'Fancy', the narrator witnesses a quarrel between an angel and a devil. The latter asserts that he is a follower of Christ the revolutionary: 'did he not mock at the sabbath, and so mock the sabbath's God? ... turn away the law from the woman taken in adultery?' This was the Jesus who was 'all virtue, and acted from impulse: not from rules'. In a nice touch, the angel becomes a devil and the narrator's fraternal companion, with whom he now reads the Bible in its 'infernal or diabolical sense, which the world shall have if they behave well'.[45]

In each succeeding 'Memorable Fancy', the consciousness of the narrator is heightened and thus raised. Blake obviously hoped that his unconventional description of his own conversion to devilry would serve as an impetus to the reader, who is being assaulted in an attempt to force him into a parallel regeneration. This illuminated book concludes on a note of genuine triumph: Blake does not reject reason, but he claims that it has held pride of place for far too long. His message is implicit in his title: the worlds of heaven and hell must be united, but this can be done only if the claims of passion and energy are recognized. The dead corpse of rationality must allow itself to be resurrected by the angel of passion.

There are no central mythological figures in this text, which was published earlier than *America* or *Europe*. But Blake did not need a character such as Orc in *Marriage* because he himself – the nameless 'I' – is the hero of this text, which is by way of being his own *Pilgrim's Progress*, a guide to the paths which must be followed for full enlightenment.

7

Fearful Symmetry

1792–1795

DESPITE relative prosperity, the early 1790s were years of lost financial opportunities. In June 1793, Blake confided to his Notebook:

> I say I shan't live five years
> And if I live one it will be a
> Wonder.[1]

Time had certainly taken its toll on Catherine. When he returned from Italy in 1794, John Flaxman was astounded by the change in her appearance: he 'never saw a woman so much altered'.[2]

Blake undertook twelve plates for Stockdale's edition of Gay's *Fables* (1793) and was announced as one of the engravers of the same publisher's 'Splendid Edition of Barlow's Aesop's Fables ... embellished with ONE HUNDRED and FOURTEEN beautiful Copper Plates'. However, eventually he did none of the engravings for that edition. In 1805, he remarked that the publishers of such ambitious books looked upon him as 'Incapable of Employment'.[3] And there must have been many days when, 'between Two & Seven in the Evening', he was filled with 'Despair'.[4]

Although his place in the publishing world was precarious, Blake was willing to take on the sympathetic Joseph Johnson on behalf of a (supposedly) aggrieved client. Blake might have done this because it was second nature for him to support an under-dog, but he might also have been resentful about *The French Revolution*. Another possible source of irritation with Johnson is contained on the title-page of the emblem book *For Children: The Gates of Paradise*, which reads in part: '1793. Published by W Blake ... and J Johnson St Pauls' Church Yard'.[5] There is no other evidence that Johnson was involved in this project. But, as with *The French Revolution*, he may have agreed to publish *For Children* and then have rejected the idea.

Through Joseph Johnson, Blake met the prickly John Gabriel Stedman, thirteen years his senior, the son of an officer in the Scots Brigade, a regiment of mercenary troops stationed in the Netherlands, and an aristocratic Dutchwoman. He was the ninth but first-surviving child of that marriage. At ten, Stedman was sent to Scotland to be educated under the supervision of an uncle, Dr John Stedman, who treated him badly. He had made a speedy return to Holland. Since John Gabriel was unusually precocious at drawing, his parents decided to train their son as an artist, but the young man, in a headstrong manner not dissimilar to that of the hot-headed Blake, rebelled:

> I embraced the proposal of becoming a painter, and masters were chosen at Bergen op Zoom, to instruct me in first beginnings, but which I all peremptory refused from merely a motive of pride, scorning to be instructed by block-heads in their profession which I, though a boy, easily discover'd and proved them to be.
>
> What then, I proposed to be sent to Italy, or Antwerp, where I was convinced I might learn the art in full perfection.
>
> But no! from the danger of my again being made a papist, and some other pecuniary reason, this was refused me, and from which moment I refused to be a painter.[6]

When he first wrote to Blake in 1791, Stedman was a retired soldier of fortune, who had served in the same Scots Brigade as his father. Up to 1773, when he arrived in Surinam as part of an expedition to protect the planters against the rebellion of their black slaves, the twenty-nine-year-old Stedman's life had been a picaresque series of adventures and mishaps: duels, escapades with prostitutes, true love crushed by an irate father, a feigned suicide, drunken brawls, orgies, a stint posing as a doctor. In Surinam, Stedman's emotional life changed when he met Joanna, a fifteen-year-old mulatto girl, the slave daughter of Kruythoff, a planter, and a slave called Cery. Joanna nursed the impetuous young man when he became ill, and the two soon fell in love.

Stedman and Joanna married on 8 May 1773, but a month later he had determined to 'lie [with her] no more for certain good reasons. Give her a gold medal to remember me.'[7] The 'certain good reasons' centred on the infamy that Joanna's behaviour might elicit among her fellow slaves and the possibility of pregnancy, which would make her a more valuable commodity. However, despite his ramshackle existence, Stedman's devotion to Joanna grew, although she was sold in early October 1773 to the firm of Passalage and Son. Despite this, Joanna and he were allowed to meet, and a son, Jack, was born on 27 November 1774.

The relationship between husband and wife was rhapsodic, as appears from this description of a meeting in April 1774: 'Free like the roes in the forest, and disencumbered of every care and ceremony, we breathed the purest ether in our walks, and refreshed our limbs in the limpid stream.'[8] Conjoined to their strong sexual and spiritual attraction was Joanna's desire to bestow gifts upon her lover and her unwillingness to accept any from him. She recognized his 'generous intentions' but wanted to act selflessly to prove her 'disinterested disposition'. Her nobility is enshrined in her declaration:

> I am born a low contemptible slave. Were you to treat me with too much attention, you must degrade yourself with all your friends and relations; while the purchase of my freedom you will find expensive, difficult, and apparently impossible. Yet though a slave, I have a soul, I hope, not inferior to that of an European: and blush not to avow the regard I retain for you, who have distinguished me so much above all others of my unhappy birth. You have, Sir, pitied me; and now, independent of every other thought, I shall have pride in throwing myself at your feet, till fate shall part us, or my conduct become such as to give you cause to banish me from your presence.[9]

Accompanying Stedman's devotion to Joanna was an increased realization on his part of the horrible plight of the slaves, as emerges from his description of the death of Neptune, who had murdered a plantation owner:

> for these offences of course he was sentenced to be *broken alive upon the rack*, without the benefit of the *coup de grâce* or mercy-stroke. Informed of the dreadful sentence, he composedly laid himself down on his back on a strong cross, on which, with arms and legs expanded, he was fastened with ropes: the executioner, also a black man, having now with a hatchet chopped off his left hand, next took up a heavy iron bar, with which, by repeated blows, he broke his bones to shivers, till the marrow,

blood, and splinters flew about the field; but the prisoner never uttered a groan nor a sigh.[10]

Before he left Surinam in 1777, Stedman arranged for the manumission of his son and placed Joanna – whom he could not afford to buy and who therefore refused to leave Surinam – with the wealthy Mrs Godefoy. Five years later, Joanna died, apparently having been poisoned. Eventually, Jack joined his father, enlisted in the Navy and was drowned at the age of seventeen. In poor health, Stedman, who married again in 1782, retired to Tiverton in Devon on full pay with the rank of major, where he wrote his memoirs and *Narrative of a Five Years Expedition against the Revolted Negroes of Surinam*.

Stedman, who was an assiduous correspondent, recorded in his diary on 8 February 1791 that he had sent 'a large parcel with manuscripts &c., and lists of names [subscribers], and proposals to London ...'.[11] Well before this time, he had probably concluded an agreement to publish with Johnson; that February, he may have been dispatching the eighty-six drawings which were to be engraved for this book. By the autumn, arrangements had been made by Johnson for the hiring of engravers for this edition, for on 1 December Stedman had written to Blake twice to thank him for his excellent work. Characteristically, Blake did not bother to answer either letter.

Johnson would have been immediately sympathetic to Stedman's account of Surinam, for which he paid a minimum of £500.[12] Astutely, Johnson parcelled out the drawings to a team of engravers, probably choosing them according to their specialities. Bartolozzi, an expensive but prestigious choice, did the frontispiece of Stedman and a drawing of Joanna. Blake was assigned sixteen, including *The Skinning of the Aboma Snake*, two of monkeys, and most of the engravings which depicted the more dire aspects of slave life.

More than most publishers, Joseph Johnson was very concerned with what he set in type. Although he had responded warmly to Stedman's text, he felt it needed extensive reworking and hired a 'literary dry-nurse', William Thomson, to edit the book.[13] Such interference was a constant source of vexation to Stedman. A *Narrative* was not published until 1796, probably because of the author's continual interference. On 24 June 1795 he found his book 'quite mard' and on 17 January 1796 he claimed: 'My book was printed full of lies and nonsense, without my knowledge. I burnt two thousand vols. and made them print it over again, by which they lost 200 guineas.'[14] Stedman now approached the printer Luke Hansard, refusing to deal

Engraving from Stedman's *Narrative*

directly with Johnson, 'who I would now not Save from the gallows'. Evidently, Johnson altered the dedication to the Prince of Wales, thus proving he was a 'damn'd infernal Jacobin scoundrel'.[15]

Blake and Stedman may not have met until 2 June 1794, but their friendship quickly flowered after the obstacle of unanswered letters was surmounted. By August 1795, cordiality – prompted by gifts of a blue sugar cruse to Catherine and an oil portrait to William – had given way to an affection warm enough for Blake to 'undertake to do busness' for Stedman, who left all his papers at Hercules Buildings when he was not in London.[16] Blake made this offer even though he knew full well just how disturbed and scatterbrained Stedman had become, as this stream of incoherence from a diary entry of 1795 amply shows: 'Met 300 whores in Strand. French prisoners come home. Abershaw &c., hang'd 8. Saw a mermaid.'[17]

Stedman, Dutch-born and stranded in Devon, was clearly an outsider to the London establishment, and Blake would have been sympathetic on these grounds. It is probable that Blake too nursed a wound which he thought Johnson had inflicted on him. What remains peculiar about this alliance is that Blake must have realized just how much he and Stedman differed on slavery. Despite his manifest sympathies, Stedman asserted that black Africans were savages and would be harmed by sudden emancipation. Blake should also have been uncomfortable with the fact that Stedman's beliefs were almost identical with those of the Abolition Society, which in 1792 did not seek the emancipation of slaves: they demanded only that the slave trade be stopped. On one of the plates he engraved, Blake shows a slave with Stedman's initials stamped on his flesh; in *Visions of the Daughters of Albion*, the evil Bromion says: 'Stampt with my signet are the swarthy children of the sun.'[18]

It is a measure of Blake's isolation in the early 1790s that he maintained a friendship with such an obviously cranky person, whose opinions on slavery he would have loathed. Stedman, a former soldier turned writer and artist, would have appealed to Blake as someone who had rejected the norms of society, but, at a deeper level, Blake would have perceived him as a spiritual enemy. This was a pattern he would increasingly follow: outer conformity led to venomous hatred of the supposed friend.

At the time he was engraving the plates for Stedman's *Expedition*, Blake was working on the illuminated book, *Visions of the Daughters of Albion*, which begins, like *Thel*, with Oothoon, the protagonist,

Frontispiece to *Visions of the Daughters of Albion*

questioning a marigold: 'Art thou a flower? Art thou a nymph? ... I dare not pluck thee from thy dewy bed!' Such a fate does not upset the marigold 'because the soul of sweet delight/Can never pass away'.[19] Oothoon follows her advice, places the flower between her breasts and goes to offer herself to Theotormon, her lover. On the way there, Oothoon is assaulted by Bromion. As a result of his rape of her, he views Oothoon as a 'harlot'. Unfortunately, this is an opinion shared by Theotormon, who folds 'his black jealous waters round the adulterate pair',[20] whom he ties up back to back.

Although Oothoon proclaims her transparent purity, Theotormon is both unable and unwilling to accept her innocence. In fact, he deems himself the injured party: 'Tell me where dwell the joys of old! & where the ancient loves?'[21] More directly and honestly than Theotormon, Bromion asserts his belief in the primacy of the real world; however, he has little concern or interest beyond immediate physical sensation.

In a long monologue where her increasingly raised sensibility is vividly dramatized, Oothoon rhapsodizes 'happy happy Love! free as the mountain wind!' In her mind this is contrasted to jealous love, which 'drinks another as a sponge drinks water'.[22] Like Thel, Oothoon has found the world of experience a cruel one, but she does not reject the existence into which she has hurled herself, although she sits bound to Theotormon at the end of the poem. Indeed, she is certain that 'every thing that lives is holy!'[23]

In the tragic history of Oothoon, Blake comments on some of the major injustices of his day: slavery, the oppressive marriage laws which gave women no rights to their own property, the exploitation of 'children bought with money'.[24] The daughters of Albion, in a manner reminiscent of some members of British society, are made unhappy by the plight of Oothoon, but all they do, as in the conclusion of the poem, is 'hear her woes, & echo back her sighs'.[25] These choral figures have no visions.

At a superficial level, Stedman's delineation of the cruelty of slavery influenced Blake's text, but the moral centre of the poem resides in the depiction of female consciousness and Blake might have had in mind Joanna's stirring speech to Stedman when she declares her independence. Another piece of Blakean irony comes to the fore when Oothoon, still hoping to be reconciled to Theotormon, tells him that she will catch for him 'girls of mild silver, or of furious gold':

> I'll lie beside thee on a bank & view their wanton play
> In lovely copulation bliss on bliss with Theotormon:
> Red as the rosy morning, lustful as the first born beam,
> Oothoon shall view his dear delight. . .[26]

This is a masculine fantasy of free love and goes against the tenor of the remainder of the poem. Here Blake is demonstrating how even the liberated perceptions of his heroine have been corrupted by the prevailing pettifogging norms of 'Lawful Bread Bought with Lawful Money & a Lawful Heaven seen thro a Lawful Telescope by means of Lawful Window Light'.[27]* According to Blake, his society was precariously held together by a patriarchal concern with property which extended itself to women, blacks and children – even the pleasures of sex were held in thrall.

Many of the issues raised in *Visions* are re-examined in *Experience*.

---

*However, it must be kept in mind that the sentiments expressed by Oothoon are quite similar to those of Mary Green in the 'William Bond' poem.

'The Chimney Sweeper'

These lyrics do not appear to have as specific a social focus, although the work of the charity schools, praised in the corresponding poem in *Innocence*, seems to have become ineffectual in the new 'Holy Thursday'.

> Is this a holy thing to see,
> In a rich and fruitful land,
> Babes reduced to misery,
> Fed with cold and usurous hand?[28]

The voice of the chimney sweeper now contains no ambiguity:

> And because I am happy, & dance & sing,
> They think they have done me no injury:
> And are gone to praise God & his Priest & King
> Who make up a heaven of our misery.[29]

The streets of London offer no charters of freedom; they are chartered in the sense of being places of confinement which are under the control of an oppressive regime. The nurse considers her charges' playtime a 'waste'. The sunflower whose colour betokens its immortality is 'weary of time'; the gates of the Garden of Love are shut with 'Thou shalt not' written over the entrance. Birth in such a desolate wasteland is perilous, Blake reaffirming his doubts about coming into being:

> My mother groand! my father wept.
> Into the dangerous world I leapt:
> Helpless, naked, piping loud;
> Like a fiend hid in a cloud.
>
> Struggling in my father's hands:
> Striving against my swadling bands:
> Bound and weary I thought best
> To sulk upon my mother's breast.[30]

In the frontispiece to *Innocence*, the piper had looked to the child for inspiration; in the corresponding plate to *Experience*, he rigidly supports the baby and stares soberly ahead. To maintain any kind of contact with the child within himself, he has to hold desperately on, and the grimace on his face shows how difficult a balancing act this can be.

In the chilling 'Nobodaddy', a poem written about this time, Blake links Urizen and fatherhood. The evil male figure is a 'daddy' whom the speaker wants to reduce to a 'nobody', but that task is arduous, if not impossible.

> Why art thou silent & invisible
> Father of Jealousy?
> Why dost thou hide thyself in clouds
> From every searching Eye?
>
> Why darkness & obscurity
> In all thy words & laws
> That none dare eat the fruit but from
> The wily serpent's jaws?
> Or is it because Secresy
> Gains females' loud applause?[31]

In this macabre Oedipal lyric, political, religious and personal concerns are uneasily blended.

The same disquietude about motherhood and fatherhood is apparent in two of the plates in the emblem book, *For Children*. In Plate One, a mother with two infants in her lap uproots a third mandrake child from under a willow, a tree of paradise. She goes about her task of removing the child from the garden in a businesslike manner. Since

Blake was the third offspring of his parents, there may be, as we have seen, an autobiographical touch here. In Plate Eight, a proud son exhibits his youthful potency before a Urizen-like father. The son's spear has a sharp, threatening barb whereas the flaccid parent seems to lack the energy for combat.

Experience and *For the Children* betray the loneliness which now enveloped Blake. Although he eked out a living from his engraving, his own publications were not finding an audience, as he sadly but defiantly announced 'To the Public' in an engraved broadside of 10 October 1793.

> The Labours of the Artist, the Poet, the Musician, have been proverbially attended by poverty and obscurity; this was never the fault of the Public, but was owing to a neglect of means to propagate such works as have wholly absorbed the Man of Genius.

In having discovered a method of publishing his own work which 'combines the Painter and the Poet', the author claims he 'is sure of his reward'. However, pervasive insecurity reigns here, as when Blake boasts that he has 'very early engaged the attention of many persons of eminence and fortune'. He also concludes this advertisement with a slight sneer: 'No Subscriptions for the numerous great works now in hand are asked, for none are wanted; but the Author will produce his works, and offer them to sale at a fair price.'[32] Blake, obviously seeking purchasers for his illuminated books and historical engravings, perversely insults those very individuals.*

Blake continually undermined his stated hopes. As his isolation increased, he also became aware of a contradiction with which he had not previously grappled: is not the artist – by the very fact that he places order on experience in the act of creating – a Urizenic figure? Earlier, he had relegated Urizen, angels, kings and fathers to a rubbish heap. What if such tyrannic impulses were within himself? One of his

---

* There were some early purchasers of the illuminated books: Baron Dimsdale probably bought his copy of *Urizen* before 1800, and Francis Douce, the antiquary who served as keeper of the manuscripts at the British Museum, owned copies of *Thel* and *The Marriage of Heaven and Hell*.

Several of the illuminated books (especially *America* and *Europe*) contained passages which might be considered seditious. So Blake would have had to exercise caution in selling them.

Until recently, it was considered likely that copies of the illuminated books were prepared when Blake received orders for them. According to Joseph Viscomi ('The Myth of Commissioned Illuminated Books: George Romney, Isaac D'Israeli, and "ONE HUNDRED AND SIXTY designs ... of Blake's",' *Blake/An illustrated Quarterly* 23 (1989) 65: 'Yet, the shared stylistic features and materials among copies of the same title prove just the opposite, that the books were produced in limited editions and, hence, that production could not have been motivated by commission.'

first examinations of this question is in 'The Tyger' from *Experience*. The plate depicts an innocuous animal which looks like a stuffed toy, but the text asks who framed that animal's 'fearful symmetry'.

> And when thy heart began to beat,
> What dread hand? & what dread feet?
>
> What the hammer? what the chain,
> In what furnace was thy brain?
> What the anvil? What dread grasp,
> Dare its deadly terrors clasp! . . .
> Did he smile his work to see?
> Did he who made the Lamb make thee?[33]

The 'dread grasp' might be an essential part of any creative act, thus making any attempt at symmetry 'fearful'.

Blake had previously attacked the enemies of passion and the promoters of inhuman political and social systems. From the vantage point of the outsider, he had catalogued and analysed the monumental history of ancient and modern failures to take full advantage of man's potential, capacities which can be seen in Jesus the radical, the prophets and the early history of England. Suddenly, it was no longer possible for him to proceed in this single-minded way. He had to examine that part of himself which was Urizenic, that portion of the self which sought control.*

The divisions within Blake are explored in the illuminated books which are concerned with creation: *The Song of Los*, *The Book of Los*, *The Book of Ahania* and, especially, *The First Book of Urizen*. (There is only one book of *Urizen*, the title being a play on 'The First Book of Moses' of *Genesis*.) Here Blake presents the creation itself as a destructive act. Following the lead of the German mystic Jacob Boehme, he maintains that it was caused by a weak moment of introspection on the part of an eternal being, which took place in two stages, the latter involving the division of Adam into two beings, male and female. Of course, as we have seen, Blake was suspicious of the mere act of giving birth. He emphasizes this discomfort anew in *Urizen*.

Urizen, an immortal, separates himself from his fellow Eternals and seeks to dominate them with laws. When his confrères rebel, he flees from them, and Los, also an immortal, is set to guard him. Although

---

*Blake was also flirting with the notion that the assumption of power is not necessarily an evil act. God the Father is often portrayed by Blake as a figure who manifests the benign aspects of control, organization and authority.

he imposes order, Urizen really lives in chaos, and Los attempts to place some restraints on him. Urizen's enclosure becomes the universe, his own form eventually hardening into that of man. Urizen's offspring, most of whom settle in cities, propagate his crimes. The exception to the rule is the fiery Fuzon, who in a manner reminiscent of Moses leads his followers away from the corrupt 'pendulous' earth.

Despite its title, *Urizen* is centred on the plight of Los, who valiantly attempts to hold himself together, and the self-destructive pity he feels for Urizen.

> Los wept, obscur'd with mourning:
> His bosom earthquak'd with sighs;
> He saw Urizen, deadly black,
> In his chains bound, & Pity began,
>
> In anguish dividing & dividing –
> For pity divides the soul;
> In pangs, eternity on eternity,
> Life in cataracts pourd down his cliffs.[34]

After Los splits into male (Los) and female (Enitharmon), the child Orc is born from their union, and the cycle of conflict – at the centre of an illuminated book such as *America* – begins anew.

Earlier, Blake had identified with Orc, but now he could not do this: Los, the immortal who is cleaved in two, embodies his new psychic state. Unlike Urizen, who is a caricature of the beneficent God of Michelangelo's Sistine Chapel, Los cannot impose uniformity in a simple-minded way. He is uncomfortably aware that the enjoining of order sometimes comes through weakness and leads to suffering and further oppression. Blake also came to the painful conclusion that art originates just as much in the artist's inner conflicts as it does from an exterior examination by the artist of conflicts in the world. He could no longer place blame outside himself. Now he had to do battle with the monster lodged within himself.

Blake had to look inwardly to move beyond the grimness he had pictured so poignantly in *Experience*. Was a higher innocence leading to redemption possible? Or was he forever stuck in a universe into which he had been rudely cast? Would he be cowardly like Thel or would he, despite the constricting bonds which held him down, have the resolute valour of Oothoon?

Blake was courageous, but the realization of his own Urizenic tend-

Los howld in a dismal stupor

'He Cast him into the Bottomless Pit, and Shut him up'

encies was accompanied by tremendous guilt. Increasingly, he tried to purge himself of such loathsome feelings by vesting them in others. If his male friends were Urizenic monsters masquerading as friends, he did not have to deal with his own inner demons. (As we shall see, a similar, devastating pattern can be seen in his characterizations of women.) In many ways, the tendency to blame others for his own failings was the most damaged portion of Blake's personality. He habitually consigned his own most unpleasant qualities to a host of friends and acquaintances who desperately wanted to aid him. And since these persons were perceived as power-hungry fiends, Blake ultimately had to spurn their offers of assistance.

8

To Fame Unknown

1795-1798

THE further decline in Blake's popularity as an engraver is reflected in a letter of Richard Cosway – 'Mr Jacko' in *Island in the Moon* – of December 1795 to George Cumberland, who had called at Schomberg House and left behind a drawing of his own after Leonardo. Cosway admired Cumberland's work, but he was especially anxious to 'get Blake to make an engraving' of it.

> I shou'd think he wou'd be delighted to undertake such a Work & it wou'd certainly *pay him very well* for whatever time & pains he may bestow upon such a Plate, as we have so *very few* of Leonardo's Works well engrav'd & the composition of this Picture is so very graceful & pleasing I am convinc'd he might put allmost any Price on the Print & assure himself of a very extensive Sale.[1]

There is no evidence that Cumberland extended such an invitation, although in 1794-5 Blake engraved eight plates for his *Thoughts on Outline* (1796). Cosway was probably responding to accurate information on Blake's precarious finances, which are difficult to reconstruct.* What is certain is that, more and more, Blake could not find work.

---

* If, for example, Blake received an *average* of £10 for each plate he engraved and designed or simply engraved, his basic income would have been £130 in 1790, £260 in each of 1791 and 1793, and £90 in 1792. And he would have been reduced to £60 in 1794 and 1795 and £30

The publishers might well have found Blake uncompliant, thus shying away from him when many competent, presumably milder-mannered, engravers were readily available. Hostile reviews of his work did him no good, as is demonstrated by this comment (in Joseph Johnson's *Analytical Review*) on his three designs for Burger's *Leonora* (1796), engraved by one Perry and published by W. Miller: 'This edition is embellished with a frontispiece, in which the painter has endeavoured to exhibit to the eye the wild conceptions of the poet, but with so little success, as to produce an effect perfectly ludicrous, instead of terrific.'[2] A similarly harsh notice appeared in the *British Critic*: 'Nor can we pass by this opportunity of execrating that detestable taste, founded on the depraved fancy of one man of genius, which substitutes deformity and extravagance for force and expression, and draws men and women without skins, with their joints all dislocated; or imaginary beings, which neither can nor ought to exist.'[3] Earlier, in January 1792 William Bowyer announced an edition of Hume's *History of England* in sixty parts ('FIVE magnificent volumes'). Barry, Cosway, Fuseli and Stothard were some of the painters, whose canvases were to be exhibited at the publisher's. William Sharp, Francesco Bartolozzi and William Blake were among the 'Gentlemen ... actually' engaged as engravers. Ultimately, Blake signed none of the 195 plates issued between 1793 and 1806.

Not surprisingly, Blake's reputation at the Royal Academy was in shambles. Joseph Farington, landscape painter, topographical draughtsman and diarist, listened in disdainful silence in February 1796 as Benjamin West, Ozias Humphry and Cosway 'spoke warmly in favour of the designs of Blake the Engraver, as works of extraordinary genius and imagination'.[4] The ever-fashionable Farington's hostility was subtly abetted by Fuseli, who told him that Blake had 'a great deal of invention, but that "fancy is the end, and not a means in his designs." He does not employ it to give novelty and decoration to regular conceptions; but the whole of his aim is to produce singular shapes & odd combinations.'[5] Fuseli also confided to Farington that Catherine had 'imbibed something of [her husband's] singularity'.[6]

Almost a year later, in January 1797, Farington was a member of a committee of Academicians, including Thomas Stothard and John Hoppner, who were studying the recent, supposed discovery of Titian's secret of colouring. At a meeting at Wright's Coffee House, the group

---

in 1796. However, average fees for engraving are dependent upon (a) size of the engraving, (b) degree of finish and (c) the friendliness of the commissioner.

had a 'laughable conversation' in which Blake's 'eccentric designs' were mentioned. Stothard defended Blake, but acknowledged that he had been seduced into 'extravagance'. Stothard 'knew by whom' but was careful not to mention Fuseli by name: 'Hoppner ridiculed the absurdity of [Blake's] designs, and said nothing could be more easy than to produce such. – They were like the conceits of a drunken fellow or a madman: "Represent a man sitting on the moon, and pissing the Sun out – that would be a whim of as much merit."'[7] When the assemblage burst into laughter, Stothard became offended, although Farington, rather improbably, thought that the company had responded only to the humour in Hoppner's metaphor.

In the mid-1790s William was reminded of how much he missed Robert when he noticed a young man walking daily by his house. This person, who looked 'interesting & eager, but sickly', carried a portfolio under his arm. Blake instructed Catherine to invite the young man to visit with them. He was indeed a would-be artist and Blake offered to give him lessons. Sadly, the young man's illness soon overtook him. When he was confined to bed, William and Catherine 'never omitted visiting him daily & administering medicine, money, or Wine & every other requisite until death relieved their adopted of all earthly care & pain. Every attention, every parental tenderness, was exhibited' by husband and wife.[8] Blake's profound sense of loneliness since Robert's death was rekindled.

Increasingly, Blake felt alienated from his environment. Now he became Hercules, subjected to the whims of Omphale: Lambeth was 'ruin'd and given / To the detestable Gods of Priam, to Apollo: and at the Asylum / Given to Hercules, who labour in Tirzah's Looms for bread'.[9] And this happened in the midst of his spiralling sense of professional estrangement. Just before and after *Urizen*, he produced three smaller illuminated books: *The Song of Los*, *The Book of Los* and *The Book of Ahania*. Most of his efforts in 1795 and 1797 centred on his illustrations and engravings for Edward Young's *Night Thoughts*.

Blake had probably met James Edwards in about 1784 through Joseph Johnson. Later, James, one of the publishers co-operating in the Hume project, was also the co-publisher of Stedman. At the very least, he would have been kept up to date by Johnson on all the agitation generated by that book. Blake was included in the list of 'eminent engravers' chosen to make engravings of Fuseli's Milton paintings in the never-realized edition to be issued by Johnson and Edwards. In September 1791, Richard, James's twenty-three-year-old younger brother, opened his own shop at 142 New Bond Street. Like his elder brother, he was fascinated with illustrated books. Although the list of publications which can be traced to him is small, it includes the splendid *A Select Collection of Views and Ruins in Rome and Its Vicinity*, the first part of which was published in 1797.

Fully aware that Blake needed book commissions to survive. Richard Edwards asked him to prepare a four-volume engraved edition of Edward Young's *Night Thoughts*. The young publisher had in his possession the poet's own autographed copy of that celebrated text, and the choice of Young was probably his. He felt – or hoped – that an illustrated edition of one of the century's most popular poems would find its financial feet in a marketplace which still seemed eager for such books, even though the war with France had, from 1793 onwards, exhausted that lucrative export market. However, knowing that such ventures were precarious if teams had to be hired, Richard Edwards proffered the work to Blake as sole illustrator and engraver.

Defiantly, Blake haggled with the publisher about terms. He wanted 100 guineas for the illustrations, but Edwards 'said He could not afford to give more than 20 guineas for which Blake agreed'.[10] In the desperate hope that the engravings of the illustrations selected for the book would net him a comfortable income over the next few years, he succumbed, receiving the miserly sum of approximately $9\frac{1}{2}$d for each of his 537 watercolours. It is not known what Blake obtained for the forty-three engravings which appeared in 1797, at a time when the market in such books was going into decline. However, if he was paid £5 5s 0d each (the amount he received for some smaller outlines he did in the 1800s) he would have collected £225 15s 0d.[11]

Edwards withdrew from the project after publishing only one volume (four of the nine *Nights*), but his motivation in doing so may have been a strange one: he and other members of his family became markedly wealthier in the late 1790s, at which time he began to lose any interest he previously had had in running a business. In any event, publishing may have been only a hobby; in 1799 he relinquished commerce entirely when, through the assistance of the Earl Spencer, he was appointed Head Registrar of the Island of Minorca.

The two-page sheet *Explanation of the Engravings*, probably written by the publisher, shows an extremely limited grasp of Blake's response to Young. Indeed, the *Explanation* is an attempt to homogenize what others might consider eccentric or erratic in Blake's designs. By 1797, the publisher's lack of interest can plainly be discerned in the advertisement, his subdued manner in puffing the book being all too obvious:

If this edition, therefore, of the *Night Thoughts* be found deficient in any essential requisite to its perfection, the circumstance must be imputed to some other cause, than to the oeconomy or the negligence of the editor.

Of the merit of Mr. Blake in those designs which form not only the ornament of the page, but, in many instances, the illustration of the poem, the editor conceives it to be unnecessary to speak. To the eyes of the discerning it need not be pointed out; and while a taste for the arts of design shall continue to exist, the original conception, and the bold and masterly execution of this artist cannot be unnoticed or unadmired.[12]

Edwards had clearly become indifferent to the idea of 'offering to the publick an embellished edition of an english classick',[13] although he was correct in a later advertisement to claim that the engravings were in 'a perfectly new style of decoration, surrounding the text which they are designed to elucidate'.[14]

This new method probably arose through a collaboration between illustrator and editor. Joseph Johnson might have arranged for Edwards to view some of Blake's illuminated books. Or, conversely, Blake, having been approached by Edwards, might have suggested to the publisher that the look of his illuminated books could be approximated if the printed text of the poem was centred on large pieces of paper, the margins of which could then be given over to a pictorial commentary on the text.

The Complaint, or Night Thoughts on Life, Death, and Immortality, published in parts from 1742 to 1745, made Edward Young famous. As a young man, he had written a series of well-received plays, including *Busiris* (1719) and *The Revenge* (1721), both staged at Drury Lane. When *The Universal Passion,* his satires, met with only lukewarm success, he took orders and was eventually instituted Rector of Welwyn in 1730. *The Night Thoughts* brought him the worldly renown which had previously eluded him, but notoriety was purchased at the price of personal privacy. In 1731, Young had married Elizabeth Lee, the daughter of the second Earl of Litchfield. She died in 1740, and the poem was widely interpreted as an elegy to her, her daughter by a previous marriage, Elizabeth Lee Temple, and her husband, Henry Temple.

Those deaths obviously played a large part in creating the ambience which allowed Young to seize upon the late eighteenth century's overwhelming obsession with 'graveyard' poetry. Imbued, like Blake, with a strong sense of personal loss, Young attempted to reassure himself and his audience about the immortality of the soul.

Young's 10,000-line poem would have appealed to Blake because of its insistence on an underlying meaning to the seeming transitoriness of human existence. Blake would also have responded to the fierce admonitions that the poet bestows upon one of his central characters, the corrupt Lorenzo – variously portrayed as a libertine and atheist – whom he is trying to convince of the validity of religious experience. In his remonstrances with Lorenzo, the poet is consoling himself, defining his own reaction to death.

Before 1795, Blake's own verse displays a wide-ranging indebtedness to Young. In *An Island in the Moon*, Steelyard the Lawgiver makes extracts from *Night Thoughts*, and Blake's 'The Sick Rose' –

> O Rose, thou art sick!
> The invisible worm,
> That flies in the night
> In the howling storm:
>
> Has found out thy bed
> Of crimson joy:
> And his dark secret love
> Does thy life destroy.[15]

– may have been derived in part from Young: 'Death's subtle seed within ... working in the Dark ... beckon'd / The Worm to riot on that Rose so red, / Unfaded e'er it fell; one moment's Prey.'[16]

What Blake disliked about *Night Thoughts* was Young's dependency upon the rational Christianity of latitudinarian divines such as John Tillotson and his advocacy of a Newtonian universe: 'What Order, Beauty, Motion, Distance, Size! / Concertion of Design! how exquisite!'[17] Such mathematical exactitude would have been repulsive to Blake. Pope had been accused (incorrectly) of harbouring deistic sentiments in *An Essay on Man*, and Young was following – despite his stated intention of not falling into such a trap – in his footsteps.

Perhaps surprisingly, Blake was even-tempered in his ripostes to Young, probably because he knew that a full-scale repudiation of the theology of *Night Thoughts* would have immediately alienated Edwards. What Blake did was to Christianize the rational elements in Young: through this amplification he offered a remarkable reinterpretation of the text in which he juxtaposed a severe Urizenic God with a warm, caring Christ. Blake also appropriated characters from his illuminated books – Los, Enitharmon, Orc – and gave them a place in his visual commentary, but the principal focus of his reading of the poem is centred on the soothing presence of Christ. In *Night Four*, Young celebrates the:

> Long golden Chain of Miracles, which hangs
> From Heaven thro' all Duration, and supports
> In one illustrious, and amazing plan,
> Thy Welfare, *Nature!* and thy God's Renown;
> *That Touch*, with charm celestial, heals the Soul
> Diseas'd, drives Pain from Guilt, Lights Life
>   in Death,
> Turns Earth to Heaven, to heavenly Thrones
>   transforms
> The ghastly Ruins of the mould'ring Tomb.[18]

Blake personalizes such ruminations by emphasizing the 'touch' of Christ, who in one illustration reaches out to bestow his redeeming hand on a prone nude figure very much in need of his assistance.

Although the Young project may have fallen well below financial expectations, it led to a commission from the indefatigable John Flaxman, who found yet another way to help his old friend. For years, Flaxman had been in the habit of presenting his wife with a special birthday present, usually a picture book. In about 1804, John gave Nancy a volume containing portraits of their friends and in 1812 he himself made for her an illustrated manuscript, *The Casket*. Nancy's rhapsodic response in March 1796 to a glimpse of the Young water-colours gave her devoted husband the notion to commission Blake for the 1797 gift.

According to Nancy, Blake was a 'genius [who] soars above all rule. [The illustrations to Young] will be a very lilly of the Valley or the meadow's queen. Twill be in short the choicest wild flower in Linneas' system.' So moved was Nancy that she intended to read Young, whose work she was not acquainted with: 'from what little I have seen his writings seem like the orient Pearls at random strung.'[19]

A year and a half later, Nancy mentioned to a friend that her husband had employed Blake 'to Illuminate the works of Grey for my library'.[20] It is not known who chose Gray as the subject for embellishment. As a young man, Blake had in 1785 submitted a now lost watercolour of *The Bard* to the Royal Academy. Having restored true Christianity to the text of Young, with whom he was in substantial agreement, Blake might have wanted to turn to a secular poet whose

(39)

Than that, which touch'd Confusion into Form,
And Darkness into Glory ; Partial *Touch* !
Ineffably pre-eminent Regard !
Sacred to Man, and Sovereign thro' the whole
Long golden Chain of Miracles, which hangs
From Heaven thro' all Duration, and supports
In one illustrious, and amazing Plan,
Thy Welfare, *Nature* ! and thy God's Renown ;
That Touch, with charm celestial, heals the Soul
Diseas'd, drives Pain from Guilt, Lights Life in Death,
Turns Earth to Heaven, to heavenly Thrones transforms
The ghastly Ruins of the mould'ring Tomb.

Do'st ask me when ? when *He* who dy'd returns ;
Returns, how chang'd ? where then the man of Woe ?
In Glory's terrors all the Godhead burns ;
And all his Courts exhausted by the Tide
Of Deities triumphant in his Train,
Leave a stupendous Solitude in Heaven ;
Replenisht soon ; replenisht with encrease

Of

Night Thoughts watercolour

work was decidedly in need of a full-scale revision. Also, Blake's work on Young had been for the marketplace: he had had to temper himself. In private work for friends, he was more free to vent a reforming spirit. Another important consideration was that Young's large poem was rambling, necessitating over 500 watercolours, whereas the chronological arrangement of Gray's spare oeuvre – which required 116 watercolours – allowed Blake to impose a cyclical structure, almost as if his illustrations are a critique of Gray's life. In so doing, Blake constructed yet another spiritual autobiography in contradistinction to Gray's severely constrained existence, which, he felt, had been passed without any real intuitive understanding or true inner enlightenment: Blake's world of innocence has a counterpart in Gray's *Ode on the Spring*, his concept of experience to *Ode on a Distant Prospect of Eton College*, his search for a suitable means of expression to *The Progress of Poesy*, his misogynistic fantasies to *Ode on the Death of a Favourite Cat*, and his fascination with the world beyond death to *Elegy Written in a Country Churchyard*.

It is possible that Fuseli, who labelled the *Night Thoughts* 'Pyramids of Dough',[21] suggested Gray to the Flaxmans or Blake. Although Gray had written little, Fuseli claimed, 'that little is well done'.[22] By any reckoning, this was a splendid opportunity for Blake. In a short space of time, he would be able to measure himself against two of the most distinguished versifiers of the century and, in each case, he would show them the errors of their corrupt poetical ways.

Much more than *Poetical Sketches* and *An Island in the Moon*, these two commissions gave Blake the chance to reveal how deeply he understood the literary traditions of his century. In any event, he had amplified Young – now he would correct Gray. The spirit of reformation is slyly hinted at in the dedicatory poem 'To Mrs Ann Flaxman' where Blake uses, in a droll way, her metaphor of the wild flower.

> A little Flower grew in a lonely Vale;
> Its form was lovely but its colours, pale.
> One standing in the Porches of the Sun,
> When his Meridian Glories were begun,
> Leapd from the steps of fire & on the grass
> Alighted where this little flower was.
> With hands divine he movd the gentle Sod
> And took the Flower up in its native Clod;
> Then planting it upon a Mountain's brow –
> ''Tis your own fault if you don't flourish now.'[23]

There is no room for false modesty in this lyric. Blake's 'divine' hand has transplanted the weak flower, assisting it to grow in a much more dramatic landscape than that in which it previously existed. Through his illustrations, he has done all he can for Gray, who must now sink or swim on his own. Blake is willing to lend a fraternal hand, but he can only go so far in making a silk purse out of a sow's ear.

The overwhelming passivity of Gray exasperated Blake. For him, this is the crucial distinction between Young and Gray. The parson from Welwyn may have paid too much heed to Newton and Tillotson, but there is a soaring grandeur in his use of blank verse. By contrast, Gray is far more timid and correct, although he had been intimately aware of the landscape of the graveyard and the power of the Gothic. Much more than Young's, Gray's poetry reflects strong doubts about his ability to versify and to be truly inspired. Through parody, Blake had commented on such issues in *Poetical Sketches*. Now, he presented his alternative interpretation alongside Gray's text. As in his illustrations to Young, Blake is, in an extremely sober way, defining himself in opposition to another poet's vision. In those portions of Gray's text which are comical, Blake even allows his own sense of playfulness to infiltrate his watercolours.

Gray's middle-class origins (his father was a scrivener; his mother and aunt kept a milliner's shop) were not very different from Blake's. What separated the two men was Gray's education at Eton and Cambridge, his friendships with the likes of Horace Walpole, and his Grand Tour to France and Italy. Despite severely limited finances, Gray led a comfortable life as a recluse at Cambridge and disdained honours, such as the Poet Laureateship. He could devote himself to antiquarian and botanical pursuits, never having to worry about foraging for a living. Gray's pervasive melancholia, readily apparent in the small number of poems he allowed to survive his rigorous prunings, repulsed Blake.

What Blake could admire about Gray was his absorption with the powers of the imagination. In the *Elegy Written in a Country Churchyard*, he reflected on the nature of death, using many of the trappings employed by Young. But Gray was not absolutely sure of his own place in the world beyond death, and his poem is concerned with the unused potential of those buried at Stoke Poges and with the reputation of a poet – such as himself – who takes the time and trouble to write of such unheralded lives. In fact, the poem ends with Gray's staging of his own death and his own brief elegy for himself when some 'kindred spirit' enquires his fate and a 'hoary-headed swain' points to the epitaph over his grave:

Here rests his head upon the lap of Earth
A Youth, to Fortune and to Fame unknown:
Fair Science frown'd not on his humble birth,
And Melancholy mark'd him for her own.

Large was his bounty, and his head sincere,
Heav'n did a recompense as largely find:
He gave to Mis'ry all he had, a tear,
He gain'd from Heav'n, 'twas all he wish'd, a Friend.

No farther seek his merits to disclose,
Or draw his frailties from their dread abode,
(There they alike in trembling hope repose)
The bosom of his Father and his God.

Samuel Johnson's contempt for Gray was overcome by the *Elegy*; for Blake, this text was filled with pernicious error. Self-abnegation was a repugnant idea, and, moreover, Gray accepted all too easily the dominion of God the Father.

In his eighth illustration to the *Elegy* Blake introduces a whimsical, self-reflexive touch: the tombstone of William Blake with the legend, 'Dust Thou Art'. In the next, the 'hoary-headed swain' points to a wrapped body with thorny vines binding it. That corpse disappears from the next two, but in the concluding watercolour 'William Blake' soars in the air, guiding another male – Gray – upwards. Blake is not concerned with the physical fact of death – that is commonplace and can be dealt with as such. He is more interested in the world beyond the apparent one, and, he is broadly hinting, Gray never cultivated that plane of existence. Literally, Blake has to show him the way.

Gray's viewpoint in these illustrations is, like himself, bleak and pale but, hovering in the background and often pushing itself to the foreground, is the vividly coloured world of the imagination, a world from which he has perversely excluded himself. Blake shows Gray in a variety of prone positions, often consulting books: the poet fails to use his inner eye and thus never comes into contact with the inspiration he could summon up if only he would allow himself to get in touch with it. Far too much time has been spent reading about life rather than living it. In the final illustration to *The Progress of Poesy* Blake condemns Gray's self-imposed subservience to Shakespeare, Milton and Dryden –

Yet oft before his infant eyes would run
Such forms as glitter in the Muse's ray,
With orient hues, unborrow'd of the sun:

A PINDARIC ODE. 91

Nor the pride, nor ample pinion,
That the Theban Eagle bear,
Sailing with supreme dominion
Thro' the azure deep of air:
Yet oft before his infant eyes would run
Such forms as glitter in the Muse's ray,
With orient hues, unborrow'd of the sun:
Yet shall he mount, and keep his distant way
Beyond the limits of a vulgar fate,
Beneath the Good how far—but far above the
    Great.

G   THE

Illustration to Gray's 'Progress or Poesy'

> Yet shall he mount, and keep his distant way
> Beyond the limits of a vulgar fate,
> Beneath the Good how far – but far above the Great

– by showing a young man, his back to the viewer. His 'Muse's ray' is transparent and apprehensive; on the ground, a dead child lies stretched upon a bed of cut wheat. For Blake, Gray is too concerned with avoiding a 'vulgar fate' and being numbered among the 'good'. In so doing, he condemns himself to spiritual and artistic death.

In addition to the enormous amount of energy consumed by the 663 watercolours and 43 engravings to the poems of Young and Gray, Blake increasingly concentrated from 1795 on the purely pictorial aspects of his imagination. Unlike the other prophetic books, *The Book of Ahania* and *The Book of Los* were etched in intaglio and colour-printed and show far less ambition in the extension of Blake's verbal imagination – indeed, like *All Religions are One* and *There is No Natural Religion*, they have a perfunctory, primitive quality, betokening their status as experiments.*

Urizen, completed in 1795, was to be Blake's last major illuminated book for years to come. As we shall see, he increasingly found writing cumbersome and forbidding. A good indication of this preference can be discerned in his decision to market 'a selection from the different Books of such [of the Illuminated Books] as could be Printed without the Writing'.[24] *The Small Book of Designs* is derived principally from *Urizen, The Marriage* and *Thel*, but some of the plates in *The Large Book of Designs* contain material, including *Dance of Albion* and *The Accusers*, not in any illuminated book.

Having flirted briefly with a new form of illuminated book and having tried to find a new way of selling his work, Blake made twelve large colour prints in 1795, which have no accompanying text and which are not arranged in any fixed order. Although these prints are technically monotypes (single imprints in heavy opaque pigment from a plate, probably of millboard), approximately three copies of each survive. The thick colours were applied to the plate once, successive pulls being taken while the pigment was still wet. Each succeeding print would receive less pigment than the one beforehand and require more finishing in pen and watercolour. All of the principal themes of the illuminated books are repeated in these prints. In addition, at

---

* Some of the other, earlier illuminated books *printed* at this time were done in this new process as opposed to the earlier watercolouring by hand.

Elohim Creating Adam

approximately the same time as he was 're-writing' Gray and Young, Blake shows a masterful knowledge of Milton and Shakespeare.

In *Elohim Creating Adam* and *God Judging Adam*, the compelling majesty of a corrupt Urizenic God is plainly visible, although Elohim seems to have some doubts about the power he wields. A guilt-ridden devil holds Eve in thrall in *Satan Exulting over Eve*. This repressive world is one of 'one law for the lion and ox' wherein the only knowledge valued is that which can be quantified (*Newton*). Such tyranny leads to a breakdown on the part of the repressed ruler who seeks to repress others (*Nebuchadnezzar*). *The House of Death* is the true outpost of a fallen world, and divisions within that world are underscored in *Lamech and his Two Wives* and *Naomi Entreating Ruth and Orpah to Return to the Land of Moab*. The possibility of redemption is raised in *Christ Appearing to the Apostles after the Resurrection*.

The conflict between reason and passion – the central theme of *The Marriage of Heaven and Hell* – is dramatically recreated in *The Good and*

Hecate

Evil Angels Struggling for Possession of a Child, where the contest is between the excessively zealous blind youth and the well-intentioned good angel. For Blake, an overabundance of energy can lead to evil, but he usually shows such turnings taking place at the instigation of an evil woman.

Two of the most powerful images in the series, *Pity* and *Hecate*, are devoted to the demonic powers of women, both illustrations inspired by Shakespeare. *Pity* is taken from a metaphor spoken by Macbeth:

> And pity, like a naked new-born babe,
> Striding the blast, or heaven's cherubim, hors'd
> Upon the sightless couriers of the air,
> Shall blow the horrid deed in every eye,
> That tears shall drown the wind. . . .

The infant leaves behind a dying mother, the division of mother and child being symbolic of 'man begetting his likeness, / On his own divided image'. In Shakespeare's play, Macbeth's own 'horrid deed', the murder of Duncan, is symptomatic of the chaos unleashed by an act which breaks familial and societal ties. The fact of birth deeply troubled Blake, and, here again, he dramatizes his discomfiture.

Pity is anti-feminist in the sense that women's ability to conceive and give birth is seen as metaphoric of disharmony. *Hecate* is even more startling in its condemnation of female evil and error. The witch, Hecate, who appears in *Macbeth* and *A Midsummer Night's Dream*, is immediately likened to Urizen by her crouching position over an open book whose pages are undecipherable. And the evil of women would be a major theme in *Vala, or the Four Zoas*, where Blake would attempt once again to unravel the mysterious forces at the heart of human darkness.

9

The Female Will

1798–1800

Aᴸᴛᴇʀ the heavy work-load from the Edwards and Flaxman commissions eased in 1797, Blake had little in hand during the next
three years: an engraving for Joseph Johnson for *Elements of Algebra*
(1797), eight plates for the same publisher's *History of England* and
Roman History (1798; the designs for both were probably by Fuseli),
three plates for Flaxman's *A Letter to The Committee for Raising the
Naval Pillar* (1799) and one plate for Boydell's *Dramatic Works of
Shakespeare* (not published until 1803). In 1800, Blake engraved eleven
plates for two further items published by Johnson: *Gymnastics for Youth*
and a portrait of Lavater.

The few jobs that he was able to obtain were channelled to him
through the triumvirate of Johnson, Fuseli and Flaxman. Blake had
become even more suspect to the publishing trade: he could obtain
commissions only through the loyalty of old friends.*

Despite the shadow of public disapproval, he still clung to the idea
of popular success, as his submission to the Royal Academy in May
1800 of his pen-and-tempera drawing on copper, *The Miracle of the
Loaves and Fishes*, testifies. Any hopes that Blake had for recognition,
however, were fast disappearing. In increasingly straitened circum-

---

*In 1794–5 – before beginning work for Edwards – Blake had engraved eight plates for another
comrade, George Cumberland (*Thoughts on Outline*).

stances, he looked at both the fraught political climate and his own, often terrifying, inner landscape in *Vala, or the Four Zoas*.

For Blake, any possibility of genuine political transformation in England was dimmed by the continuing war with France and the emergence of Napoleon. In March 1796 Bonaparte was named commander-in-chief of the French army in Italy. The Directory further increased his power in 1797 and 1798, and in November 1799 Bonaparte, Sieyès and Ducos were appointed consuls; a month later Napoleon became First Consul, eventually – through a deft series of manoeuvres – proclaiming himself Emperor on 18 May 1803. In the ascension of that Urizenic figure, Blake saw how completely the revolution in France had failed in its attempt to promote even a semblance of democratic reform. If France was infertile, England – which had not experienced a social upheaval since the seventeenth century – was inflexibly rocky ground. The English establishment – which viewed Napoleon's ambitions with an understandably terrified eye – became even more repressive in the late 1790s.

Blake's most persistent metaphor for the ensuing political and social distress is the absence of bread. In 'Gwin, King of Norway' 'our wives / And children cry for bread',[1] and this theme finds its most vehement expression in *Vala* when Urizen proclaims:

> Compell the poor to live upon a Crust of bread by soft
>   mild arts;
> Smile when they frown, frown when they smile & when a
>   man looks pale
> With labour & abstinence say he looks healthy
>   & happy
> And when his children sicken, let them die.[2]

The economic reality in London in the late 1790s was that the price of bread had risen so steeply that it was beyond the reach of many of the poor. By September 1800, it cost 1s 9d a quartern loaf, whereas 9d had been a high price a short time before. This led to the storming of the Corn Market, and the immediate lowering of the price.

Rather than simply looking at urban squalor as he had done in *Experience*, Blake now examined the very machinery of such devastation by investigating the thriving factories, a by-product of war. In such places, the poor worked for paltry sums. They were also the ones slain in battle. Their hopeless situation is evoked in this lamentation by Vala, which describes the smoking brick kilns, which employed women, on the outskirts of London:

> O Lord, wilt thou not look upon our sore afflictions
> Among these flames incessant labouring? Our hard masters
>   laugh
> At all our sorrow. We are made to turn the wheel for water,
> To carry the heavy basket on our scorched shoulders, to sift
> The sand & ashes, & to mix the clay with tears & repentance.[3]

The horrors of the factory are linked to another part of the corrupt economic chain:

> First, Trades & Commerce, ships & armed vessels [Urizen] builded
>   laborious
> To swim the deep; & on the Land children are sold to trades
> Of dire necessity, still laboring day & night;
>   till all
> Their life extinct, they took the spectre form in
>   dark despair:
> And slaves in myriads in ship loads burden the
>   hoarse sounding deep,
> Rattling with clanking chains. The Universal
>   Empire groans.[4]

England and its overseas empire are tainted with the blood of the working poor – white and black – who must bear the high cost of economic expansion and the ensuing militarism, England's quarrels with France being largely concerned with the ownership of overseas colonies.

In his analysis of the ways in which various iniquities interlock with each other, *Vala* is Blake's most acute examination of the English political system, but that dissection is really the backdrop to an investigation of the evil lurking in the hearts of individual men, William Blake in particular. In *Urizen*, Blake had empathized with Los, who becomes contaminated because he feels pity for Urizen. Los becomes a jailor trapped in the prison of the self. In *Vala* Blake tried to find a way out of such a snare, and, here, he identified with Orc.

Vala exists as a manuscript largely written on the proof sheets of the *Night Thoughts* engravings. Like Young, Blake divided his poem into nine nights, envisaging it as a much more intricate response to Young than his earlier illustrations. The title-page is dated 1797, but this is only the year in which Blake began the poem; most of the text was probably completed by 1800 with significant changes being made by 1803, although some additions were entered as late as 1810.

Much more psychological than any other of Blake's poems, *Vala* tells the story of Albion, the Eternal or Universal Man, who is the subject and the landscape of the poem. Albion is severed into four Zoas: Urizen (reason), Luvah (passion – previously called Orc), Urthona (imagination and repressed anger – previously called Los) and Tharmas (compassion). Each of these males has, as a result of a split within himself, an emanation (respectively, Ahania, Vala, Enitharmon, Enion). Also, each of the Zoas has a spectre: the rational portion of the self which – like the Angel in *Marriage* – often acts in an extremely irrational manner.

The conflicts within Albion are indicative of the divisions within society as well as the self: his constituent parts are fragmented and battle for dominance. Near the beginning of the poem, when Albion falls asleep, Urizen and Luvah fight over him. Later, when he becomes ill, Albion hands authority over to Urizen. This preference for one of the Zoas over the others is symptomatic of something deeply wrong with him, and, as long as he remains ill, there is no possibility of any kind of salvation for either nations or individuals. This is the dilemma with which the poem opens. Consciously, Blake wants to unify the warring parts of Albion, but, as *Urizen* demonstrates, he is aware of the irreconcilable splits within himself which are indicative of the discords tearing England apart. Blake desperately *wants* to find unity, but his own psyche and civilization go against any kind of resolution.

Blake named the poem after Luvah's emanation. Of the four Zoas, he was the one with whom Blake most clearly sympathized. Luvah is passionate, imaginative and irascible. His female counterpart shows an excess of energy: she is inordinately pleasure-loving, unrestrained and power-hungry. If Vala can somehow re-enter Luvah, that fusion will be symbolic of personal and societal rejuvenation.

The action of *Vala* is extremely Homeric in that a series of altercations among a number of pampered, self-centred gods is at the heart of the text. Among those characters, it is Vala who personifies the danger of having too much wilful energy. In her struggle for control, she becomes Urizenic. Blake may be suggesting that women have a strong desire to impose themselves on hapless male wills, but he is also revealing how an excess of any one character trait simply leads to the emergence of its corresponding vice.

Many of the most startling moments in *Vala* are in the confrontations of the Zoas with their emanations, as in Urizen's brutal response to well-meant advice from Ahania.

> Shall the feminine indolent bliss, the indulgent self of weariness,
> The passive idle sleep, the enormous night & darkness of Death,
> Set herself up to give her laws to the active
>   masculine virtue?
> Thou little diminutive portion that darst be a counterpart![5]

Urizen's harsh words are uttered as 'he seizd her by the hair / And threw her from the steps of ice that froze around his throne'.[6] The domestic arrangements are very much those of *Tiriel*, Blake's early evocation of male–female discord.

Much of *Vala* is taken up with the struggles between Urizen and Vala, until these two potent characters join forces to destroy Luvah/Orc. Blake's own inner strifes as poet–creator surface when he presents two conflicting narrative strands in Night Eight: (1) the final victory of Vala and (2) the appearance of a manifestation of Luvah, whom Urizen and Vala cannot destroy: Christ, the Lamb of God. The second plot introduces a female character even more sinister than Vala: Rahab the harlot, who *apparently* triumphs over Christ when he is crucified. Los reminds Rahab that by killing Christ she has allowed his redemptive love to enter into her world of death. Thus she will be the author of her own eventual destruction.

The glimmer of hope embedded in Night Eight serves as a prelude to the 'Last Judgment' of the final Night, which has a landscape taken from the Book of Revelation. Albion, having finally awakened, summons Urizen to his side. At that moment, the former tyrant is restored, becoming a young man 'glorious bright Exulting in his joy'.[7] Orc, the inferior form of Luvah, is burnt away. Then Luvah and Orc are briefly dismissed from Eternity. An idyllic description of Vala's childhood follows. Finally, Vala, in her redemptive state, bestows loving tenderness on Tharmas and Enion:

> Where is the voice of God that calld me from the silent dew?
> Where is the Lord of Vala? Dost thou hide in clefts of the rock?
> Why shouldst thou hide thyself from Vala, from the soul that wanders
>   desolate?
> She ceas'd, & light beamd round her like the glory of the morning.[8]

If the ending to the poem has a *deus ex machina* quality, that is probably as far as Blake could go in settling the problem of human destiny.

There is no real resolution of the dispute between the Zoas and their emanations, Urizen and Vala, male and female.

More convincing is the sacramental imagery of the Final Harvest, which brings the poem to a triumphant conclusion. Urizen gathers in and thrashes the corn. Then Luvah carries out his task, the vintage. Those chores completed, they partake of bread and wine.

> The Sun has left his blackness & has found a fresher morning
> And the mild moon rejoices in the clear & cloudless night
> And Man walks forth from midst of the fires. The evil is all
>   consumd.[9]

Blake's unwillingness or inability to achieve closure, and his introduction of narrative lines which are sometimes completely opposed to each other betray pervasive uneasiness but also a realization that life itself is indeterminate. However, human and divine are conjoined in Christ, and the poem ends in a luminous moment of calm expectation of the arrival of the millennium. On a political level, the poem celebrates the one bright spot Blake could discern in foreign affairs: the peace of Amiens of October 1801. That month Blake wrote to Flaxman: 'Peace opens the way. ... The Kingdoms of this World are now become the Kingdoms of God & his Christ, & we shall reign with him for ever & ever.'[10] The commingling of Christian bread and wine and the hoped-for restitution of bread to the poor are neatly dovetailed. But the discord between men and women is not satisfactorily resolved.

In *Visions*, Oothoon's cry for reform is boldly uttered, Blake obviously agreeing with his heroine's sentiments. Much earlier, he had contrasted the heroic efforts of women such as Jane Shore and Queen Emma to instances of masculine brutality, and there is a deeply compassionate pen-and-watercolour drawing of 1805 of *The Woman Taken in Adultery*. Intellectually, Blake did not view woman as the second sex. And yet there is a strong undercurrent of anger directed against women and erotic love in his writings and art. Blake believed that human beings had first existed in an androgynous state, from which they had been expelled – just as Los was divided into Los and Enitharmon in *Urizen*. Such a doctrine implies that unity can be achieved only by a joining together of male and female. On the surface, this is the paradigm which has to be followed in order for harmony to exist. Continually, Blake *wants* to move *Vala* in that direction. And yet he is never really comfortable with such a notion. From childhood, he abhorred the very idea of dependency. As an adult, his bitterness

towards parental figures was displaced by a deep rage against the fact
that he relied upon another person for the gratification of his sexual
appetites, his autonomy being undermined in a newer and more subtle
way.

Some of his fury can be found in the explosive 'The Chapel of Gold':

> I saw a chapel all of gold
> That none did dare to enter in;
> And many weeping stood without,
> Weeping, mourning, worshipping.
>
> I saw a serpent rise between
> The white pillars of the door;
> And he forcd & forcd & forcd
> Down the golden hinges tore;
>
> And along the pavement sweet,
> Set with pearls & rubies bright,
> All his slimy length he drew,
> Till upon the altar white
>
> Vomiting his poison out,
> On the bread & on the wine.
> So I turnd into a sty
> And laid me down among the swine.[11]

Literally, this poem is concerned with the chapel as an oppressive
institution which is invaded by the Orc-like serpent, a revolutionary.
More primitively, 'The Chapel' is about sexual intercourse, which is
described as necessary but repulsive. The snake-like penis is inserted
into the vagina – the chapel of gold – and achieves orgasm. But coitus
here is described in a deeply negative manner: the serpent has to force
his way into the chapel, tearing its hinges down. The violence of this
act is accompanied by a description of the semen as poison, which is
spilled on to the sacramental bread and wine. The world of religion
and the world of human sexuality are divorced from each other. The
speaker, a repulsed but fascinated voyeur, realizing that sex is a
debasing activity, transforms himself into a sty, and lies 'down among
the swine'.

Blake's identification of a chapel of repressive religion with the
vagina is clearly made in one of the *Vala* drawings. The manuscript is
also embroidered with an illustration showing a woman with a penis;
some pages show random acts of brutal and perverted sexual activity.
Blake's fear that sex is evil can be seen in other poems:

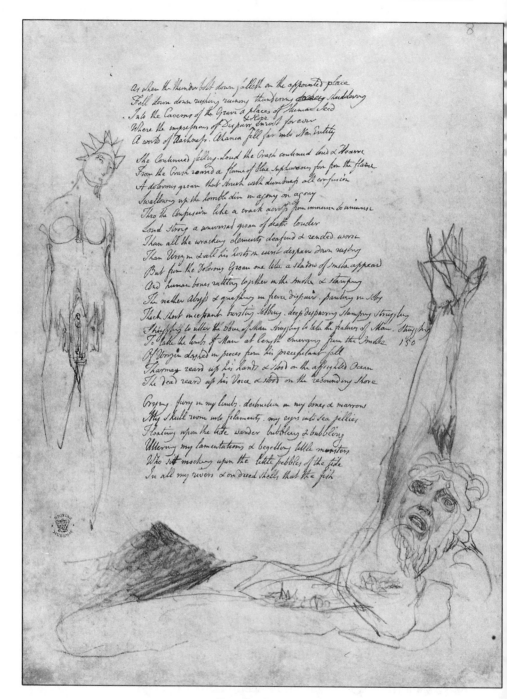

Page from *Vala*

> When a Man has Married a Wife,
>   he finds out whether
> Her knees & elbows are only
>   glued together.[12]

> In a wife I would desire
> What in whores is always found –
> The lineaments of Gratified desire.[13]

In both these verses there is the suggestion that copulation is shameful, something which can be indulged only in guilty secrecy. There is a hint of violence in the first lyric and in the second the hope is expressed that a wife will perform like a whore so that lust can be appeased.

As in 'William Bond' Blake is tempted to view himself as trapped by female wiles. In 'The Crystal Cabinet' a maiden catches the speaker while he is 'dancing merrily' and locks him up. From within his prison, the speaker sees another maiden with a smile that 'filld me, that like a flame I burnd'.

> I strove to seize the inmost Form
> With ardor fierce and hands of flame
> But burst the Crystal Cabinet
> And like a Weeping Babe became.

> A weeping Babe upon the wild
> And Weeping Woman pale reclind
> And in the outward air again
> I filld with woes the passing Wind.[14]

By imprisoning the speaker, the first maiden provides him with a comfortable home but when he strays beyond her approved confines, in pursuit of another partner who can gratify him, he is reduced to a 'Weeping Babe'.

A similar view of the destructive power of women is at the centre of 'The Mental Traveller' where Orc, the male infant, is given to an old woman 'who nails him down upon a rock / Catches his Shrieks in Cups of gold'.

> She binds iron thorns around his head;
> She pierces both his hands & feet;
> She cuts his heart out at his side
> To make it feel both cold & heat.

The Christ-like Orc survives to become a 'bleeding youth' and the old lady is transformed into a 'Virgin bright' to whom he is attracted:

He plants himself in all her Nerves
Just as a Husbandman his mould,
And She becomes his dwelling place
And Garden fruitful seventy fold.

Despite a life of travail, Orc survives into old age, at which time a 'little Female Babe does spring'. Later, she conspires with the man she loves to drive the old man from his own home. Eventually, Orc 'becomes a wayward Babe / And she a weeping Woman Old'. The frown on the face of the infant makes him so repulsive that no one dare touch him except the old woman: 'She nails him down upon the Rock / And all is done as I have told.'[15] This is a profoundly sad piece of poetry, its circularity suggesting that woman in all her guises is to be distrusted.

In *Vala*, all of the female emanations – especially Enitharmon and Vala – are rigidly controlling. Her joy 'is in the Death of her best beloved / Who dies for Love of her / In torments of fierce jealousy & pangs of adoration'.[16] Women, exultant in the quest for power, delight in causing pain and lust. The reintegration of the Zoas with their emanations is not psychologically realized in the conclusion of *Vala*, betraying the fact that Blake was not sure how the gulfs separating the sexes could be bridged.

The need for gratification embodies one of the central paradoxes of existence for Blake: man is a creature divided between the corporeal and the spiritual. However, his sexual organ ties him to the demands of the body, and thus men dislike women because they inhibit their search for a higher existence. Although Blake can envisage orgasms – as does Oothoon – as moments of intense, transcendent self-realization, women remain very much feared: he resents the fact that he is dependent upon them for satisfaction and that sex removes him from full contact with the divinity within himself. Not surprisingly, he once claimed that true regeneration through Christ can be inhibited by 'Sexual Generation'.[17]

The separation into male and female remains for Blake *the* metaphor for the fragmented nature of life. In another piece of pure male resentment, Blake envies the ability of women to reproduce the species: this is a form of creativity to which men cannot aspire. His own attempts at art are but second-best next to such fecundity. In *Vala*, so much blame is squarely placed on the shoulders of women that the issues raised in *Urizen* can be temporarily shelved: he does not have to be overly concerned with the male artist as a repressive, domineering figure. (That theme will be dealt with later in *Milton*.)

The Whore of Babylon

In Blake's poems and illustrations, women are often mothers or whores, and he does not approve of either. (However, his blowzy Whore of Babylon seems embarrassed by the threat she poses.) Or sometimes, women are over-idealized. All of these are, however, works of the imagination, in which Blake allows his fantasy to wander freely. Nevertheless, Blake's own conflicts about his own wedded state are reflected here. He was probably a faithful husband, but he envisaged marriage as a clever societal trap. He shares Oothoon's revolutionary sentiments in *The Daughters of Albion*, but it is not likely that they are feelings he was able to bring into everyday reality.

The scant surviving evidence of the Blake marriage in the 1790s and early 1800s suggests that Catherine was of inestimable assistance to her husband in his various engraving tasks. William certainly taught Catherine 'to take off his proof impressions and print his works'.[18] Also, she had an 'excellent Idea of Colouring' and 'was no small use in the completion of his laborious designs'.[19] In July 1802, William Hayley was convinced that Catherine 'suited [William] *exactly*. They have been married more than 17 years & are as fond of each other, as if their Honey Moon were still shining':

> the good woman not only does all the work of the House, but she even makes the greatest part of her Husband's dress, & assists him in *his art* – she draws, she engraves, & sings delightfully & is so truly the Half of her good Man, that they seem animated by one Soul. . . .[20]

The image of the faithful wife doing her husband's bidding is on the surface probably accurate. And Blake was a dutiful spouse: 'he made a constant practice of lighting the fire, and putting on the kettle for breakfast before his Kate awoke.'[21] But underneath this complacent portrait of domestic calm lingers a world of mutual distrust.

The Blakes certainly endured an isolated, claustrophobic existence. Commissions for the book engravings were becoming few and far between. In any event, husband and wife worked incessantly on their 'real' tasks – William's illuminated books, watercolours, separate engravings. When these did not gain recognition, bitterness was commingled with loneliness. Although husband and wife gave room to the occasional pet cat (Blake 'used to say how much he preferred a cat to a dog as a companion because she was so much more quiet in her expression of attachment'[22]), theirs was not a marriage which would likely have welcomed children, although the reason for their childlessness is not known. These two people often had only each other for company and, in increasingly fraught circumstances, they must have vented their rage upon each other.*

---

* Also, these mysterious words of Gilchrist (*Life of William Blake* (London: J.M. Dent, 1945), pp. 314–15; henceforth, **Gilchrist**) must be borne in mind: 'There *had* been stormy times in years long past, when both were young; discord by no means trifling while it lasted. But with the cause (jealousy on her side, not wholly unprovoked), the strife had ceased also.'

10

The Perils and Pleasures of Patronage

1799–1803

INCREASINGLY, Blake relied on Cumberland or Flaxman to rein in work for him. It was Cumberland who told the Revd John Trusler of the middle-aged engraver desperately in need of commissions. Trusler, sixty-four in 1799, had been educated at Westminster and Emmanuel College, Cambridge. A cleric who at one time served as chaplain to the Poultry-Computer (the ancient sheriff's prison situated east of Grocer's Hall Court, London), Trusler's energies were resolutely focused on a number of ingenious projects: he invented a method of teaching oratory 'mechanically'; in 1765, he took charge of a literary group formed for the purpose of abolishing publishers. A bit later, in 1769, Trusler circularized every parish in England and Ireland with a scheme to reproduce sermons in script type. The idea was that the resulting talks would look as if they had been handwritten by the parson who was stepping into the pulpit.

This prolific virtuoso was the author of more than twenty-five books, many of the do-it-yourself variety: *Practical Husbandry, or the Art of Farming, with Certainty of Gain* (1780), *Poetic Endings, or a Dictionary of Rhymes* (1783), *The Way to be Rich and Respectable* (1796) and *A Sure Way to Lengthen Life* (first edition in 1770; *With Vigour* was appropriately added to the title in 1819). Unlike Blake, Trusler's tremendous energy eventually brought him great wealth. He commissioned paintings of *Malevolence* and *Benevolence*, with, if these were a success, *Pride* and *Humility* to follow. If Trusler found the designs acceptable, he intended to have Blake engrave them and thus act as the publisher of four large prints.

Not surprisingly, Trusler told Blake exactly what the first picture, *Benevolence*, was to look like. Blake could not obey what he saw as simple-minded instructions, as he diplomatically informed Trusler on 16 August 1799:

> I attempted every morning for a fortnight together to follow your Dictate, but when I found my attempts were in vain, resolvd to shew an independence which I know will please an Author better than slavishly following the track of another, however admirable that track may be. At any rate, my Excuse must be: I could not do otherwise, it was out of my power![1]

These are brave words for a struggling artist. As he confided to Trusler, he held firm opinions as to how *Malevolence* was to be done: 'A Father taking leave of his Wife & Child is watchd by Two Fiends incarnate, with intention that when his back is turned, they will murder the mother & her infant'.[2]

Trusler was not about to take any insolence. Flatly, he informed Blake that he knew nothing of motivation: '*Your Fancy* ... seems to be in the other world or the World of Spirits, which accords not with my Intentions, which, whilst living in This World, Wish to follow *the Nature of it.*'[3] Trusler also implied that Cumberland, although he was a friend of Blake, lived in the real world. Stung by this rebuke, Blake did not try to conceal his hatred of Trusler's standards.

> I really am sorry that you are falln out with the Spiritual World, Especially if I should have to answer for it. I feel very sorry that your Ideas & Mine on Moral Painting differ so much as to have made you angry with my method of Study. If I am wrong, I am wrong in good company.... That which can be made Explicit to the Idiot is not worth my care.[4]

Blake also defended himself against the charge that he had not shown any causality in the depiction of *Malevolence*: 'Is not Merit in one a Cause of Envy in another, & Serenity & Happiness & Beauty a Cause of Malevolence?'[5]

Rubbing salt into the wounds he was inflicting, Blake claimed that Trusler's arguments were 'Ill proportiond' and his eye 'perverted by Caricature Prints'. He even included some gratuitous observations:

> Fun I love, but too much Fun is of all things the most loathsom. Mirth is better than Fun & Happiness is better than Mirth – I feel that a Man

Malevolence

may be happy in This World. And I know that This World Is a World of Imagination & Vision. I see Every thing I paint In This World, but Every body does not see alike.[6]

Blake's point is that he is going to paint the imaginative life visible to him and damn the consequences. Then, suddenly, he becomes boastful and a trifle grandiose. He reminds Trusler that he is an engraver who has obtained thirty guineas for engravings of the same size.

Engraving is the profession I was apprenticed to, & should never have attempted to live by any thing else, If orders had not come in for my Designs & Paintings, which I have the pleasure to tell you are Increasing Every Day. Thus if I am a Painter, it is not to be attributed to Seeking after.[7]

Blake was not quite so cavalier when he told Cumberland of the débâcle with Trusler, who, he claimed, wanted him to 'Reject all Fancy' from his work: 'But I cannot paint Dirty rags & old Shoes where I ought to place Naked Beauty or simple ornament.'[8]

People like Trusler, Blake warily realized, could never be pleased. Although he stuck to his own strongly held convictions, he was despondent when both Joseph Johnson and Henry Fuseli had not used him as an engraver after the failure of the *Night Thoughts* edition. Nevertheless, he tried to be optimistic:

as I know that He who Works & has his health cannot starve, I laugh at Fortune & Go on & on.... It is now Exactly Twenty years since I was upon the ocean of business, & Tho I laugh at Fortune, I am perswaded that She Alone is the Governor of Worldly Riches, & When it is Fit She will call on me; till then I wait with Patience in hopes that She is busied among my Friends.[9]

Blake's faltering spirits could be so raised in August 1799 only because of the generosity of his most devoted, persistent and unquestioning patron: Thomas Butts.

Of the same age as Blake, Butts in 1783 became an assistant clerk in the office of the Commissary General of Musters, which acted as an adjunct to the Paymaster's office. The Commissary General was responsible for ascertaining that those receiving money were actually alive and in uniform, that equipment was in order and that various kinds of records were accurate. On 2 June 1788, Butts became Chief Clerk at an annual salary of £91 5s. As was the case with many other government posts of the time, a number of perquisites brought Butts's income to over £750. However, he had to share his work with another clerk, thus reducing his portion to the still hefty £375. Although he held a position which was lucrative, the job was unduly tedious: 'The Employment is irksome, admits of little variety, and affords no mental improvement; – exacting patience, unwearied application, and undivided attention.'[10]

In Blake's miniature, the curly-haired Butts looks the epitome of fashion in a bright blue coat with gold epaulettes and buttons. Butts's dandyism is confirmed by the 'smart embroidered coats, waistcoats, and lace ruffles preserved by his descendants'.[11] Butts's sensitive nature is also enshrined in the portrait: the face is refined – almost too delicate – and the eyes are alert and searching.

Blake's patron was certainly anxious to extend his own financial success to other members of his family and on 8 June 1799 his son, Joseph Edward, was appointed a clerk in his father's office at an annual income of £80. Another son, Thomas junior, joined at Christmas 1806. In a nice, additional bit of nepotism, Butts augmented his sons' salaries from 1808 through 1810 with large doses of overtime. After 1814, Butts even helped Blake's brother James to find employment.

Butts, not satisfied with the revenues he was able to generate from the Commissary General of Musters, served as an extra clerk at the General Post Office from 1793 to 1795; clerk of the two-penny Post Office from 1795 to 1796; principal clerk in the same office at £150 a year, and Clerk of the Letter Bills at £50, from 1797 to 1806. Of course, as was frequently done, Butts no doubt had deputies acting for him at these various posts. However, he would probably have been receiving most of the proceeds from such appointments. Some of these activities were being carried on at the same time as he was draining filial overtime from the budget of the Musters office.

Although Butts's position in the bureaucracy suffered severe setbacks by the mid-1810s, he had invested considerable money in real estate (including properties in Grafton Street and Fitzroy Square in central London) and in canals, water works, mines, banks and insurance. Earlier, he had inherited £700 from an uncle. When he retired in 1817 at the age of sixty, he was a comparatively rich man.

It is not known how Blake and Butts met, but it was probably in the mid-1790s. The Blakes and the Buttses even saw each other socially, as a diary entry by twelve-year-old Tommy Butts of 13 May 1800 testifies: 'Mr. and Mrs. Blake ... drank tea with mama.' And there were elegant tea parties: the Butts family kept a 'George III Tea Pot and Stand' and a 'George III silver Mug' used by Blake.[12] Mr and

Mrs Butts probably entertained William and Catherine by themselves, without introducing them to many of their other friends.*

Butts was a man who used the system to advantage, but he was the one person who, for a long time, bestowed wholehearted approval on Blake. As his surviving letter to him shows, Butts, who obviously had a sense of humour, was entranced with the ethereal world Blake inhabited:

> you cannot but recollect the difficulties that have unceasingly arisen to prevent my discerning clearly whether your Angels are black, white, or grey, and that of the three on the whole I have rather inclined to the former opinion and considered you more immediately under the protection of the black-guard; however, at any rate I should thank you for an introduction to his Highness's Court, that, when refused admittance into other Mansions, I may not be received as a Stranger in this.[13]

Despite his steady, relentless climb to financial prosperity, Butts was aware of a transcendental dimension from which he did not wish to be excluded. He saw in Blake a man who clung to truths beyond mere material success, and Butts held out a generous hand, gradually filling his house with paintings and engravings by Blake, almost as if he were literally storing up treasures from heaven. In this way, he bought himself into daily contact with a vision of the world from which he had, at his spiritual peril, closed himself. Like many collectors, Butts was obsessive: he had to be constantly fed by the artist he revered.

Butts's surviving letter to Blake amply shows his comprehension of Blake's mission, but it also betrays uneasiness with the artist's self-indulgence and 'confined Conversation'. He hopes that Blake's opinions will eventually 'harmonize' with society. Then Blake can become:

> a more valorous Champion of Revelation & Humiliation than any of those who now wield the Sword of the Spirit; with your natural & acquired Powers nothing is wanting but a proper direction of them, & altho' the way is both straight & narrow I know you too well to fear your want of resolution to persevere & to pursue it – you have the Plough & the Harrow in full view & the Gate you have been prophetically told is Open, can you then hesitate joyfully to enter into it?[14]

The reprimand in this letter is couched in gentle, persuasive terms –

---

* An exception was John Birch, a surgeon of St Thomas's Hospital, London, and a proponent of the use of electricity in medicine. His 'Electrical Magic' was of great help to Catherine in December 1804.

in contrast to Trusler – and there is also the sense that Butts's veneration is unconditional: it will survive even if Blake perversely goes against the grain of commercial success.

Unlike Flaxman, Fuseli and Stothard, Butts was not an artist and posed no threat to the frequently insecure – and thus envious – Blake. Unlike Johnson and Trusler, Butts did not have the power to place Blake's name before a large public. In one sense, Blake could simply accept Butts's sincere love, hoping that it would not be withdrawn even if he acted badly. At another level, Blake must have marvelled at the way in which Butts could remain so much within the world and yet disdain its values. Despite temptation, the poet–artist could not do this. And he castigated his artist friends who did succumb. In Blake's life, his friendship with Butts was for many years a calm oasis where he could be constantly refreshed.

Butts's patronage is puffed beyond reasonable dimensions in Blake's letter to Trusler. For Blake, this was a 'Miracle' which kept him spiritually and physically alive and which helped him 'Emerge from a Deep pit of Melancholy':[15] 'My work pleases my employer & I have an order for Fifty small Pictures at One Guinea each, which is Something better than mere copying after another artist.'[16] Such understanding generosity allowed Blake to explore the possibility of merging his vision with that of artists he professed to despise – Rembrandt, Titian, Correggio and Rubens – at the very same time as he was praising the precision of 'Greek workmanship' which he felt received its most sublime expression by Raphael, Durer and, especially, Michelangelo. Trusler had tried to shackle Blake whereas the freedom Butts gave Blake allowed him, ironically, to experiment with the traditional modes of interpretation favoured by Trusler.

Blake's first series of biblical subjects was done in 'fresco', a form of tempera, although, strangely, he mentioned to Trusler that he was experimenting with oil painting, which he despised because he considered it too stolid. However, Blake's colour printing in the 1790s, although it has excellent colour density, is sometimes extremely dark. His investigation of fresco was a bid to gain the clarity of watercolour without the heaviness of oil painting.

In his frescoes, Blake placed a ground of whiting and carpenter's glue on copper, panel or canvas; he then mixed his watercolours with glue which had been thinned; he would then periodically affix a transparent wash of glue-water over parts of his work; finally, he would apply a finish to the complete painting. The resulting pictures are often extremely Rembrandtesque, particularly in the ways 'in which light picks up contours and cool colours emerge imperceptibly from the warm and dense'[17] backgrounds and the manner in which warm glows are positioned against dark backgrounds. The fifty subjects may have been planned, like a conventional collector's cabinet, to hang in a single room, although religious subjects were not usually grouped in such an arrangement, which in the eighteenth century was reserved for Dutch and decorative pictures.

The Butts tempera cycle was devoted to the life of Christ – thirty-five paintings – with typological antecedents from the Old Testament accounting for the remaining spaces. Blake would have been aware of Benjamin West's similar, abortive scheme for St George's Chapel, Windsor, and his cycle stays well within the custom of choosing Old Testament subjects customarily interpreted as anticipating the Christian dispensation. He also emphasized the Fall of Man, the event which led Christ to take on human form.

Despite his adherence to a multitude of traditions, Blake, in his most specifically Christian body of work up to this time, does not disdain idiosyncracy, as in *The Temptation of Eve*, where he follows Milton rather than Genesis. A triumphant Eve, her legs placed within the coils

The Temptation of Eve

28 Broad Street, where Blake was born

(*Left*) This is either a self-portrait by Blake or a depiction of his brother, Robert

(*Inset left*) Catherine Blake

BLAKE
23 HERCULES ROAD
F A

13 Hercules Buildings, where Blake lived from 1790 to 1800

Blake's cottage at Felpham, where he lived from 1800 to 1803

Robert Cromek

William Hayley

Thomas Phillips' oil portrait of Blake

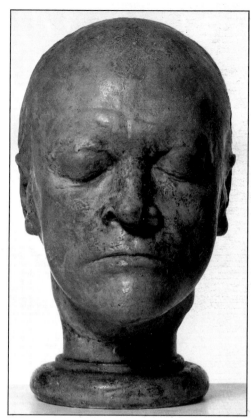
Deville's life mask of Blake

17 South Molton Street, where Blake lived from 1803 to 1821

3 Fountain Court, Strand, where Blake lived from 1821 to 1827

Samuel Palmer

John Linnell

of the serpent, stands in the middle of the picture area, Adam asleep at her side. Here, Eve, who clearly relishes her perverse behaviour, is very much like Vala. She is a troublemaker who welcomes the sexual embrace of the serpent.

What Butts gave Blake was what he most needed: the opportunity to experiment with a new method of painting, the occasion to discover how closely he could align his religious convictions to the traditions of representing Christ's life, and, most significantly, unqualified financial support. Butts probably had a limited intellectual understanding of Blake's work in that he intuitively felt the poet–artist's greatness without being able to challenge him in any serious manner. In that sense, Blake could be said to have admired Butts because the Musters Clerk venerated him. However, Butts, in his sole extant letter to Blake, did take issue with him. No doubt he did the same when they met. The lack of tension in their relationship may have been due to the plain fact that Butts's life, with the exception of his dealings with Blake, did not touch upon any of the petty jealousies and intrigues of the circles in which his artist friend precariously moved. Because of that, Butts could bestow upon Blake the fraternal love he desperately craved. The same would not be true of Blake's strained friendship with the well-known poet, dramatist and man-of-letters William Hayley.

Hayley, twelve years older than Blake, was the second son of Thomas Hayley and his wife, Mary, of Chichester. He went to Eton in 1757 and in 1763 entered Trinity College, Cambridge, which he left in 1767 without taking a degree. He was admitted to the Middle Temple in 1766. Three years later he married Eliza Ball, the daughter of the Very Revd Thomas Ball, Dean of Chichester. Eliza, who was five years older than her husband, was mentally unstable, and her father opposed the match. The couple finally parted in 1789, but before that the alliance between the two had been precarious, and there had been long intervals of separation. Thomas Alphonso, Hayley's only child, was the son of a Miss Betts, a housemaid, although any relationship between her and Hayley seems to have been over by the time of Tom's birth in 1780. There was a polite fiction that Eliza was the mother of Tom; the boy himself may not have known the identity of his real mother. In 1774, Hayley settled at Eartham, Sussex, and it was to this place that many of his literary and artistic friends were summoned for long visits.

Hayley began his publishing career with *Ode on the Birth of the Prince of Wales*, which appeared in 1762, and which was reprinted in the *Gentleman's Magazine* the next year. Shortly after his marriage, he wrote a play, *The Afflicted Father*, and composed a number of cele-bratory epistles (including the *Epistle on Painting* in 1777 to Romney and *Essay on History* in 1780 to Gibbon), but his first success came with *The Triumphs of Temper* (1781). *A Philosophical, Historical, and Moral Essay on Old Maids* (1785) brought him notoriety.

By the mid-1780s, Hayley was a celebrity. A kindly man, who was also excitable and flamboyant, he surrounded himslf with people who were, like himself, devoted to literature and art. It has become fashion-able to see Hayley as a cultivated hanger-on, a man of no talent who wanted to be involved with the genuinely gifted. Horace Walpole's view of him has been taken as the correct measure: 'if you love incense, he has fumigated you like a flitch of bacon.... For Mr. Hayley himelf, though he chants in good tune, and has now and then pretty lines amongst several both prosaic and obscure, he has, I think, no genius, no fire and not a grain of *originality*.'[18] Blake would have vehemently agreed with Walpole.

In the 1790s and early 1800s, Hayley was not simply a lionizer or a person whose sense of importance was established only by being in the company of the great. He was a famous writer who sought out the best-known artistic people of his generation. A deeply insecure man, he recognized the limits of his own talents when he opined in 1792 that if his beams were 'shorn like a sheep's coat ... they would not have made a golden fleece large enough to have loaded a mouse'.[19] In his play, *The Mausoleum*, he parodies himself: 'Poor Facile wants force; yet may frequently please / By a light airy mixture of mirth and ease.'[20] Politically, Hayley believed that royal authority should be diminished and parliamentary power increased, which is to say that he was a Whig reformer. Above all else, Hayley was the Man of Sentiment par excellence.

Hayley's closest friendship had been with William Cowper, the most celebrated poet of the last fifteen years of the eighteenth century, to whom he introduced himself in a letter of 7 February 1792. Hayley did this because he had been told, incorrectly, that Cowper was writing a biography of Milton which would be in direct competition with the life of the poet which Boydell and Nicol had asked him to do for them. Cowper, immediately touched by Hayley's warmth, reassured him that this was not the case: he was simply translating the Italian and Latin poems of Milton into English and preparing a commentary on *Paradise Lost*. Quite soon, the men became fast friends, as Cowper told his cousin, Lady Hesketh: 'He glows with benevolence to all men, but burns for my service with a zeal for which you will adore him.'[21] By

June 1792, the two men wrote to each other with an alacrity which Cowper said 'all but youthful lovers must despair to imitate'.[22] Hayley was also the Robin 'Red-breast' who, in a dream, crept into Cowper's bosom: 'I never in my waking hours felt a tenderer love for any thing than I felt for the little animal in my sleep.'[23]

Constantly, Hayley tried to relieve Cowper's deep-seated melancholia: he invited him to Eartham – an invitation which, to Cowper's own surprise, he accepted; he obtained a royal pension for the reclusive poet. Hayley suggested that he and Cowper collaborate on the Milton, the poet responding enthusiastically to this suggestion. Without doubt, Hayley intruded himself into Cowper's affairs, but the simple truth is that Cowper welcomed such advances. Hayley – who immediately obtained an 'electrical machine' when the poets' companion Mary Unwin suffered a stroke – acted as a physician to his friends. He was also the amiable father, who yearned to supply all of Cowper's needs. The friendship cooled only when Cowper moved to Norfolk in 1795 and retreated into a severe depression.

Hayley probably learned of Blake in 1794* when Flaxman sent him a copy of *Poetical Sketches*, together with this measured praise:

> they are the writings of a Mr. BLAKE you have heard me mention, his education will plead sufficient excuse to your Liberal mind for the defects of his work & there are few so able to distinguish & set a right value on the beauties as yourself, I have beforementioned that Mr. Romney thinks his historical drawings rank with those of Mi[chel] Angelo; he is at present employed as an engraver, in which his encouragement is not extraordinary.[24]

By 1796, Blake and Hayley must have met, since Thomas Alphonso, who was then in London as an apprentice to Flaxman, told his father he was planning to visit Hercules Buildings: 'I have not been able to call on Blake yesterday as I intended but I will lay hold on the first opportunity.'[25]

The next reference to Blake is three years later on 21 December 1799, when Thomas Alphonso was dying of a congenital spinal disease. The distraught father wanted his *Essay on Sculpture*, which included a reproduction of Flaxman's portrait medallion of Thomas, to be ready as soon as possible. Henry Howard's drawing of the

---

*From 1769 until 1774, Hayley lived at 5 Great Queen Street; Blake lived at Basire's, 31 Great Queen Street, from 1771 to 1778. It is possible that the two met during that time.

medallion was delayed because the artist had inflammation of the eyes, and in February 1800 Hayley desperately hoped that 'the dear departing angel will see his own engraved portrait arrive before his own departure'.[26] Part of the subsequent delay was due to Blake, who was engraving the drawing and who sent it to Hayley in April: 'With all possible Expedition, I send you a proof of my attempt to Express your and our Much Beloved's Countenance.'[27] Blake's words suggest that he was on friendly terms with both father and son.

Upon receiving the engraving, Hayley realized that he was going to have to be even more heroic. As far as he was concerned, the portrait, instead of 'representing the dear juvenile pleasant face', displayed 'a heavy sullen sulky Head which I can never present to the public Eye as the Image of a Being so tenderly & so justly beloved'.[28] Tom evidently agreed with his father, and Hayley then asked Blake to improve the plate. Judiciously, Hayley placed most of the blame on Flaxman, whose original Hayley had never considered 'a *very very strong* similitude of the *Individual*'.[29]

When Thomas died on 2 May, Blake wrote a moving letter of consolation in which he compared Hayley's loss to his own of Robert in 1787: 'I am very sorry for your immense loss, which is a repetition of what all feel in this valley of misery & happiness mixed.'[30] Cowper's death a week earlier on 25 April compounded Hayley's grief.

Hayley, who was as persistent as he was generous, prodded Blake to produce another version of the engraving – and a drawing of Tom. Characteristically, Hayley invited Blake down to Sussex, at which time he presented him with Tom's own copy of *The Triumphs of Temper*, in which he inscribed a dedicatory peom:

> Accept, my gentle visionary, Blake,
> Whose thoughts are fanciful and kindly mild;
> Accept and fondly keep for friendship's sake,
> This favour'd vision, my poetic child!
>
> Rich in more grace than fancy ever won,
> To thy most tender mind this book will be,
> For it belong'd to my departed son;
> So from an angel it descends to thee.[31]

Despite such exuberant emotions, Hayley never saw the obscure Blake as being in the same class as the famous Cowper, Blake being someone to whom Hayley mistakenly thought he could condescend. He characterized Blake to Lady Hesketh as 'a most worthy, enthusiastic, affectionate engraver';[32] for him, Blake remained a talented, would-be artist whom he could assist. There is certainly an air of shared superiority in Flaxman's letter to Hayley of 19 August 1800, after William and Catherine had moved to Felpham, near Bognor, on the Sussex coast. According to Flaxman, Blake had to trim the sails of overweening ambition:

> I see no reason why he should not make as good a livelihood there as in London, if he engraves & teaches drawing, by which he may gain considerably as also by making neat drawings of different kinds but if he places any dependence on painting large pictures, for which he is not qualified, either by habit or study, he will be miserably decieved.[33]

Both Fuseli and Johnson had warned Blake that he had to concentrate on 'the mere drudgery of business'[34] to survive, and Hayley was obviously fully aware of the artist's falling fortunes.

In 1800 Hayley was deeply affected by the deaths of his son and Cowper, although Anna Seward shrewdly commented: 'He who can bewail his sorrows to the world, will not become their victim. There is a mournful luxury in such pains, which has nothing to do with the severity of despair. Mr. Hayley will always love to deplore....'[35]

Earlier, in 1797, Hayley had begun construction of a 'Marine Turret' in the middle of Felpham so that Thomas could come into the Eartham estate. In an attempt to escape painful memories of his son, Hayley moved to the Turret in 1800 and sold Eartham. Hayley's new residence was surrounded by a high wall made of large pebbles set in red-brick quoits. The house, nestled inside the jail-like walls, was two-storeyed with delicate windows and elaborate roof parapets. The Turret itself, which allowed a view of the ocean, was made of wood and glass, with an iron handrail. In this secluded spot, Hayley intended to get on with his literary career.

He did not thrive in isolation, and, when Blake responded enthusiastically to the balmy air and ocean views of Felpham in July 1800, Hayley suggested that he and Catherine rent a vacant cottage about 130 yards from the Turret. By 22 July, as Hayley told Lady Hesketh, Blake had agreed to this scheme. Blake had done this, Hayley claimed, because 'he has attached himself so much to me'.

> He has taken a cottage in this little marine village to pursue his art in its various Branches under my auspices, & as He has infinite Genius with

a most engaging simplicity of character. I hope He will execute many admirable things in this sequestered scene.[36]

Hayley had a shrewd sense of how to market himself and, he obviously felt, Blake's halting career could be advanced under his 'auspices'. He could also provide Blake with some work falling directly from his multitudinous enterprises. And, like Flaxman, he was sure that Blake did not have sufficient acumen in business matters: he would show him the way. The excessively self-centred Hayley may possibly have conceived of Blake as a collaborator. However, his prime motivations were an amalgam of forlornness and condescension.

Not unexpectedly, Blake's initial reaction to the scheme was one of unalloyed delight. His tendency to idealize blinded him from reality, to which, when it finally confronted him, he would respond with overwhelming rage. Unbounded gratitude was bestowed in the form of poetry upon Flaxman just before the move: 'Flaxman hath given me Hayley, his friend, to be mine, such my lot upon Earth.'[37] And when Catherine Blake wrote to Nancy Flaxman on 14 September, Blake inserted an exuberant lyric:

> Away to Sweet Felpham, for Heaven is there;
> The Ladder of Angels descends thro the air;
> On the Turret its spiral does softly descend,
> Thro' the village then winds, at my Cot it does end.
>
> You stand in the village & look up to heaven;
> The precious stones glitter on flights seventy seven;
> And My Brother is there, & My Friend & Thine
> Descend & Ascend with the Bread & the Wine.
>
> The Bread of sweet Thought & the Wine of Delight
> Feeds the Village of Felpham by day & by night;
> And at his own door the blessd Hermit does stand,
> Dispensing Unceasing to all the whole Land.[38]

Even for Blake, this is strong language. Hayley had become a brother who dispensed 'unceasingly'; the image of the bread and wine – a symbol of the merging of the rational and spiritual worlds – indicates just how high Blake's hopes had soared. He had found a patron who was literally a saviour, a writer who could unlock the success which had so far eluded him. Sussex had become his 'first temple & altar'. Catherine was 'like a flame of many colours of precious jewels whenever'[39] she heard the place named.

Blake must have had mixed feelings on leaving London. Eighteen-hundred was a famine year, bread being in especially short supply – Blake's submission to the Royal Academy was *The Loaves and Fishes*. That autumn, the shopkeepers of London were denied their ancient right to petition the King on the throne. In November, the Privy Council ordered the police to put down a meeting of tradesmen, artisans, journeymen and labourers that threatened to become a riot. However, George III and his ministers were discussing the possibility of forming a National Gallery. Perhaps, after all, there was some hope that art might be fostered in a nation which had previously devalued artists.

At this time, Blake did not consider the likelihood that financial well-being would continue to elude him, that Hayley might be a difficult person to live with on a daily basis, that he might become deeply envious of Hayley's enormous success, that Hayley might pester him, that Hayley might be jealous of him, that Hayley – acting under instructions from Flaxman – might try to curb and manipulate his imagination.

Such obvious possibilities evaded Blake as he, Catherine and his sister packed 'Sixteen heavy boxes & portfolios full of prints' and changed chaises six times after they left Lambeth between six and seven on the morning of Thursday, 18 September. They did not reach their cottage in Felpham until half-past eleven that evening. Despite a trying day, there had been 'No Grumbling, All was Chearfulness & Good Humour'. The cottage was a 'perfect Model' of such dwellings, Hayley displayed his 'usual brotherly affection' and a 'New Life' in which 'another covering of earth [was] shaken off' had begun. At that moment, Blake could, in a detached way, accept the limits of the new existence which confronted him.

> I am more famed in Heaven for my works than I could well concieve. In my Brain are studies & Chambers filld with books & pictures of old, which I wrote & painted in ages of Eternity before my mortal life; & whose works are the delight & Study of Archangels. Why, then, should I be anxious about the riches or fame of mortality? The Lord our Father will do for us & with us according to his Divine will for our Good.[40]

But Blake was deeply anxious about 'mortal life'. Soon those trepidations would work their way to the surface. For the time being, the residents of Felpham were not 'mere Rustics' but 'polite and modest'. Meat was cheaper than in London and the 'sweet air & the voices of winds, trees & birds, & the odours of the happy ground' made it 'a dwelling for immortals'. 'A roller & two harrows' lay by his window, and there was a plough by the gate.[41] Some evenings, when Catherine and William were sitting by their cottage fire they would be pleasantly surprised to hear Hayley's 'voice calling over at the gate'.[42]

However, they did not have much time to settle 'the sticks & feathers of'[43] their nest of a cottage, which they were renting for £20 a year from Mr Grinder, who owned the nearby Fox Inn. Hayley, upon hearing of the sad plight of a certain Widow Spicer and her children, wrote a ballad, *Little Tom the Sailor*. This poem tells the story of a mother who leaves Tom at home at Folkestone in order to visit her husband, who is dying in a distant hospital. Tom cares for the two younger children, one an infant and one feebleminded, until he must attempt a dangerous sea voyage in search of his mother. Hayley asked Blake to illustrate and print the ballad as a broadsheet, the proceeds of the sale of which were to assist Mrs Spicer. The mawkish poem was still popular enough at the end of November for Catherine to be printing copies in dark-brown ink, touched up with sepia wash; some copies were even hand-coloured by William or Catherine. Presumably, Hayley paid them for the various 'rough sailors'.[44]

There were other tasks. Hayley, after some laborious negotiations with Lady Hesketh, had decided to write the life of Cowper. Engravings for that book would be essential. Also, Hayley had for some time determined to decorate the library, built in a garret at the top of the Turret, with portraits of eminent poets: this was a long, narrow room with a fireplace at one end; eight portraits were placed on each long wall with two on the wall facing the hearth.

By 26 November Blake was 'absorbed by the poets ... whose physiognomies have been my delightful study',[45] although the portraits were not completed by September 1801 when he mentioned that work on Hayley's library was 'still unfinishd but is in a finishing way & looks well'.[46] Eventually, Blake executed these eighteen portraits in pen and tempera. Originally, in 1797, Hayley had envisaged the portraits, all of which consist of wreathed heads set in oblong panels, as a memorial to his favourite poets, culminating in the great poet of his own time, William Cowper. This arrangement was disrupted by Thomas's death, the focus shifting from pantheon to memorial: Tom's portrait was now to be the centrepiece over the fireplace. Hayley probably decided to abandon some of the poets he had planned to include in favour of those admired by his son. In any event, Blake, who had strong opinions on literary history, might have disagreed with his patron's choices (especially the inclusion of Pope), such reservations causing him to have the first of his many qualms about Hayley's judgement.

Hayley was so enraptured with Blake's work on the heads that he urged him to try his hand at miniature portrait painting, a potentially lucrative enterprise. On 13 May 1801, Hayley told a friend that he had 'formed a new artist for this purpose'.[47] Hayley's choice of verb shows just how much he misunderstood the essential nature of Blake. Then, a year later, his fertile imagination came up with yet another scheme to assist his artist friend. He would compose some animal ballads, get Blake to illustrate them à la *Little Tom* and request the genial, often drunk Chichester printer Joseph Seagrave to typeset the texts of the poems on sheets on which the Blakes had already printed William's illustrations. These would be sold as broadsheets, the resulting profits being Blake's.

On 6 August Hayley told John Johnson, Cowper's cousin: 'our good Blake is actually *in Labour with a young Lion.* – The new born Cub will probably kiss your Hands in a week or two.'[48] The principal method of marketing the four broadsheets was to ask members of the Hayley–Cowper circle and some London and provincial booksellers to act as ballad-mongers. This ploy was a flop, although Hayley paid twelve guineas towards Seagrave's printing bill of £30.

Blake was gratuitously insulted by the acerbic Lady Hesketh, who sold some of the 'Sussex Elephants'[49] and the other three beasts. She believed in a no-nonsense approach: 'if Mr. B. is but New in the world, may it be not *in reality kinder* to point out his failings, than to suffer him to think his performances faultless?'[50] She answered her own question a week later when commenting on 'The Eagle'. According to her, Blake had insufficient respect for the 'Human Face Divine': 'the *figure* of the woman hovering over her child is fine, but her *Countenance* is to me rather unpleasant, and that of the child extremely so, without any of those Infantine Graces which few babies are without.... in short the faces of his babies are *not young*, and this I cannot pardon!'[51]

Whether Hayley passed this criticism on is not known, but what is certain is that Blake was getting more and more involved in the sad life history of William Cowper, who had become famous almost by accident when *The Task* was a surprise bestseller in 1785. Cowper perceived his constant melancholia as arising from the persecutory anger of a savage God, whom he had in some way offended. Blake, well aware of the power of the Urizen fixed in his own heart, admired the bravery with which Cowper had faced such horrible feelings, although he believed that Cowper had incorrectly attempted to deal

Engraving of 'The Eagle'

rationally with suicidal impulses which were emotional in origin. For Blake, such sensations had to be embraced in order to be experienced fully – and then expunged. Years later, Cowper spoke to Blake in a dream:

> O, that I were insane, always. I will never rest. Can you not make me truly insane? I will never rest till I am so. O! that in the bosom of God I was hid. You retain health & yet are as mad as any of us all – over us all – mad as a refuge from unbelief – from Bacon, Newton & Locke.[52]

Blake is 'mad' in the sense that he does not accept the bleak rationality of Bacon, Newton and Locke; he retains his 'health' (mental stability) because, unlike Cowper, he does not try to reason himself out of intense mental anguish. In 1800, Hayley, who had deftly manoeuvred Lady Hesketh into allowing him to write Cowper's life, was with this book on the verge of his greatest triumph, so intense was the interest in Cowper's life – particularly his madness.

Although Hayley's invitation for Blake to live at Felpham came in the midst of his fraught negotiations with Lady Hesketh, he probably intended, at the time he issued the summons to Sussex, for Blake to engrave the illustrations to the planned book. When Lady Hesketh did agree, Blake was drawn into the baroque, cumbersome dealings between the difficult cousin and the wily biographer. Lady Hesketh wanted to conceal the truth; Hayley knew that the success of his book depended on being able to tease Cowper's overprotective cousin into allowing him to tell as much of the truth as possible. Blake became increasingly sure that Hayley was manipulating events so that he, in the reclusive retreat of the Turret, could tell the sensational life history of an even more famous recluse and, in the process, advance his fame and fortune. Hayley was feeding on the corpse of Cowper and, Blake became convinced, Hayley was doing exactly the same thing to himself.

Such a view may not have been true to Hayley's conscious intentions, but Blake saw into what he considered to be the inner reality of the situation. In February 1801, Hayley told Lady Hesketh that Blake's 'excellent versatile Talents' had been markedly improved by the lessons he had given him in miniature painting, lessons which had been abetted by the works on hand by George Romney and Thomas Alphonso. Hayley now announced that Blake was to engrave the plates for the biography: 'I am persuaded He will produce a Head of Cowper, that will surprise & delight you; & assuredly it will be executed *con amore*, as he idolizes the Poet.'[53]

As usual, Hayley had spoken much too soon. Lady Hesketh had never liked the faint hint of madness which she felt could be seen in George Romney's portrait drawing of 1792. Not surprisingly, she was outraged when she saw Blake's miniature taken from Romney: 'the Sight of it has in *real truth* inspired me with a degree of horror.... I cannot restrain my Pen from declaring that I think it *dreadful! Shocking!*'[54] Dexterously, Hayley contrived to be silent on this matter, although he was determined to print an engraving after the Romney.

Meanwhile, in May 1801, Blake remained serenely contented at Felpham. 'Mr. Hayley acts like a Prince. I am at complete Ease.' Miniature portrait painting had become a 'Goddess' in his eyes; he had received 'a great many orders'. He told Butts: 'Sussex is certainly a happy place & Felpham in particular is the sweetest spot on Earth.'[55] He was even giving lessons in drawing to a Mr Chetwynd, 'a Giant in body, mild & polite in soul, as I have in general found great bodies to be'.[56] In June 1802, there was the distinct possibility that Blake would engrave a drawing of a local prize bull.[57]

Blake's happiness was probably not broken by the condescending tone of Flaxman's letter to him of 7 October, wherein the sculptor compares the rustic tranquillity of Sussex to the tribulations of the 'great City' of London, where his many commissions continually demanded 'an attention neither to be remitted or delayed'.[58] Blake did not take offence at this saccharine, patronizing reminder: 'the All besto[wing] Hand deals out happiness to his creatures when they are sensible of His Goodness.'[59] In fact, from October 1801 – when peace with France was announced – to the signing of the Peace of Amiens on 27 March 1802, Blake glowed with optimism at the symbolic import of this event. Many years earlier, he had longed to visit Italy. Now, he thought of visiting France: 'I hope to see the Great Works of Art, as they are so near to Felpham, Paris being scarce further off than London. But I hope that France & England will henceforth be as One Country and their Arts One.'[60] Flaxman had even sent a new patron, the Revd Joseph Thomas of Epsom, to call upon him at Felpham. From 1801 to 1809, this parson bought watercolour sets of Blake's illustrations to *Comus*, *Paradise Lost* and *On the Morning of Christ's Nativity*, and six extra-illustrations to a second folio edition of Shakespeare.

Blake's discontent with rural Sussex reached breaking point just as the Peace collapsed on 10 May 1803. Earlier, during the winter of 1802, Hayley had quarrelled incessantly with Lady Hesketh concerning the form of a monument to Cowper, designed by Flaxman, which was to be engraved by Blake. The first glimmering of trouble between the Blakes and Hayley can be discerned in a passing reference by Hayley in a letter to John Johnson of 16 May 1802: 'both my good Blakes have been confin'd to their Bed a week by a severe Fever.'[61] Increasingly, one or other of the Blakes fell ill, their bad health being a psychosomatic barometer of depression and discouragement.

Even by the middle of July 1802, the genially undiscerning Hayley knew things were going badly. He began to see more and more evidence of Blake's misery when, in an intemperate letter to the excitable Harriot Hesketh, he compared Blake's 'perilous powers of an Imagination utterly unfit to take due Care of Himself' to Cowper's similar deficiencies:

his sensibility is so *dangerously acute*, that the common rough Treatment which true genius often receives from *ordinary Minds* in the commerce of the World, might not only wound Him *more than it should do*, but really reduce Him to the Incapacity of an Ideot without the consolatory support of a considerate Friend.[62]

Blake was ill again at the end of July, and the often obtuse John Johnson felt something was wrong when he asked Hayley in December: 'By the bye is our dear Blake *dead*? You are as silent about him as the *grave*!'[63] That month, Hayley, who was just about to send Lady Hesketh a copy of the Cowper biography, in which Blake's engraving of the Romney portrait appeared, remarked that Blake had told him 'that all the Demons, who tormented our dear Cowper when living, are now labouring to impede the publication of his Life'.[64] In her reply, the perverse Lady Hesketh remarked that Blake had 'Softened' the Romney portrait.

But by this time, Blake's dislike of Hayley had hardened. He no longer wanted any scraps from his table, being dissatisfied, for example, with the sixty guineas he received from Cadell & Davies for engraving the appalling designs of Maria Flaxman – the sister of the sculptor – to Hayley's *Triumphs of Temper*. In January 1803, Blake was frank with Butts about the sheer drudgery in which he had become engulfed and he was frightened of the 'intimations that if I do not confine myself to this, I shall not live'.[65] Finally he realized that he had been far too 'sanguine'. He had been 'ignorant' of many things, chiefly the unhealthiness of living in a damp cottage near the ocean. But he did not 'repent' of the move, holding out hopes that Hayley would 'lift' him out of difficulty. Still, he sadly reflected, 'this is no easy matter to a man who, having Spiritual Enemies of such formidable magnitude, cannot expect to want natural hidden ones'.[66]

Gradually, Hayley's status changed from that of 'natural hidden' enemy to spiritual foe. There were, however, some droll, even relaxing moments on the Sussex coast in 1801 and 1802. Hayley, who was collating John Johnson's edition of Cowper's translation of Homer, taught Blake to read Greek. Tryphena, the widow of Lord Bathurst, tried to get Blake to paint a set of handscreens for her, but there were certain tasks to which Blake, even in a reduced condition, would not stoop. He did, however, give lessons in drawing to some members of her family.[67] And then there were visits to Harriet (her real name was Henrietta and she was sometimes called Paulina) Poole at Lavant, three miles north of Chichester. From the mid-1790s, Hayley would ride the ten miles to see her on Tuesdays and Fridays and usually breakfasted with her. Blake – riding Tom's pony Bruno – often accompanied Hayley on his horse Hidalgo to these meetings, where the conversation was often of literature and art. And Blake and Hayley called on William Metcalfe, Hayley's old servant: they were present when he died at the Eartham estate in October 1801.

What Blake became increasingly aware of was that his time was being frittered away in inconsequential work, which offered him no financial advancement. Also, the spectacle of Cowper's unhappy life drew him closer and closer to death, perhaps to Robert's passing:

> I labour incessantly & accomplish not one half of what I intend because my Abstract folly hurries me often away while I am at work, carrying me over Mountains & Valleys, which are not Real, in a Land of Abstraction where Spectres of the Dead wander.[68]

Only sixteen months later did Blake fully realize that he had been wandering off course as an artist: 'I have recollected all my scatterd thoughts on Art & resumed my primitive & original ways of Execution in both painting & Engraving, which in the confusion of London I had very much lost & obliterated from my mind.'[69] Specifically, Blake might be referring to the temperas for Butts but, in a general way, he knew he had to recapture the strong feelings which had overwhelmed and transformed his art in 1787.

Felpham quickly became for him a vast wasteland rather than a fertile watering spot. But, Blake felt, he had proved his mettle: 'I have traveld thro Perils & Darkness not unlike a Champion. I have Conquerd, and shall Still Go on Conquering.'[70] His 'Enlarged' sense of his artistic destiny had to be achieved away from Felpham and by the end of January 1803 he had resolved to leave.

Although he and his brother James were not close, Blake respected his elder sibling's business acumen – and James had been a wary but sympathetic observer of his brother's commercial aspirations. James and his sister Catherine had visited their brother at Felpham and thus knew the situation there at first hand. In a guarded letter to James of 30 January, Blake shows little self-knowledge: 'You know that it is my way to make the best of every thing. I never make myself nor my friends uneasy if I can help it.' He also continues to show a sorry lack of acquired wisdom about the publishing world, when he claims, somewhat improbably, that he was:

> getting before hand in money matters. The Profits arising from Publications are immense, & I now have it in my power to commence publication with many very formidable works, which I have finishd &

ready. A Book price half a guinea may be got out at the Expense of Ten Pounds & its almost certain profits are 500G.[71]

Blake's letter is full of boasting and self-aggrandizement, designed to show his brother that the Felpham years had been a commercial success. Possibly, 'immense' profits could be gained through having, like Hayley, an extensive network of friends. But the *Ballads* scheme, which utilized such an approach, had not worked.

The tremendous acclaim visited upon Hayley's *Life of Cowper* – published earlier that month – obviously wounded Blake, especially when he knew at first hand Hayley's limited capacities in comparison to his own. Perhaps sibling rivalry did not allow him to divulge to James the erosion of his financial aspirations, but the hurt which was eating away at him nevertheless rises to the surface in this piece of fraternal confidence:

> H. is jealous as Stothard was & will be no further My friend than he is compelld by circumstances. The truth is, As a Poet he is frightend at me & as a Painter his views & mine are opposite; he thinks to turn me into a Portrait Painter as he did Poor Romney, but this he nor all the devils in hell will never do. I must own that seeing H. like S Envious (& that he is I am now certain), made me very uneasy, but it is over & I now defy the worst & fear not while I am true to myself, which I will be.[72]

Initially, Blake considered moving to 'some village further from the Sea, Perhaps Lavant. & in or near the road to London for the sake of convenience'.[73] Increasingly, he saw the Felpham years as his 'three years' Slumber on the banks of the Ocean'.[74] London, in place of Sussex, was suddenly idealized: 'Every one who hears of my going to London again Applauds it as the only course for the interest of all concernd in My Works, Observing that I ought not to be away from the opportunities London affords of seeing fine Pictures and the various improvements in Works of Art going on in London.'[75] Although he had not been able to do so before, he was of the firm opinion that he could carry on in London 'unannoy'd'. He would 'See Visions, Dream Dreams & prophecy & speak Parables unobserv'd & at liberty from the Doubts of other Mortals', his devastating experience of Hayley having convinced him of the 'decided' truth of Christ's assertion: 'He who is Not With Me is Against Me.'[76]

Hayley's claim that Blake was 'not very fit to manage pecuniary Concerns to his own advantage'[77] is crisply accurate. That winter,

Blake evidently did not tell Hayley of his plan to leave Felpham. Meanwhile, Hayley secretly tried to help Blake by arranging for him to paint Lady Hesketh's portrait. She did not wish to exhibit her 'Wrinkles to the Publick',[78] but was quite willing to give Blake a gift of five guineas. Hayley thought this a good idea but warned her that Blake had to be treated gingerly: when he made her generosity known to Blake he would have to 'contrive to do it with the utmost caution as I know his honest pride would be otherwise hurt by the Idea'.[79] At about the same time, Hayley attempted to interest the Countess of Portarlington in providing assistance to the poet, whose finances were in the 'narrowest state'.[80] He also spoke warmly of Blake's visionary art, although the artist remained convinced that Hayley disliked such work.

By May, Hayley knew of Blake's imminent departure. At that time he told Flaxman that the bad climate of Felpham and the execrable state of the cottage were the chief reasons that the Blakes were removing themselves. A reasonable semblance of friendship was maintained, with plans for Blake, back in London, to engrave further work for Hayley. 'Thus,' Blake told Butts, 'I hope that all our three years' trouble Ends in Good Luck at last & shall be forgot by my affections & only rememberd by my Understanding.' In fact, out of this disastrous experience, he would construct a 'Grand Poem' (*Milton*) full of 'Sublime Allegory'.[81] In this way, good would come out of evil.

In addition, Hayley, although he could not really come to grips with Blake's imagination, had been impressed by the poet's recent 'Firmness', which had made the older man less grandiose and lofty. As far as Blake himself was concerned, he had been a model of 'Patience & Forebearance of Injuries upon Injuries'. He had 'labourd hard indeed, & [had] been borne on angels' wings'.[82]

This idealized self-portrait is contradicted by a close examination of the relationship between Blake and Hayley. Hayley's understanding had certainly been stretched beyond its limits. Ultimately, he responded to Blake with 'Genteel Ignorance & Polite Disapprobation'.[83] Also, he had been irritated when Blake had demanded a total of seventy guineas for two plates for his *Life of Romney*. Hayley told him that Romney's life would not be as popular as Cowper's and that he would have to print it 'entirely at [his] own risk'.[84] Such was Hayley's response to Blake's 'Firmness'.

The lavish extent to which Blake could distort reality and the excessive limits of Hayley's generosity can be seen in the fracas with John Scolfield. In the midst of his preparations to leave Felpham, Blake had a calamitous encounter on Friday, 12 August with Scolfield, a private soldier in the Dragoons, who, upon the invitation of the caretaker, called William, had entered the cottage garden. Blake 'politely' asked the soldier to leave whereupon Scolfield, in a fierce manner, refused. Blake, maintaining his poise, repeated his request. At that point, Scolfield 'affronted [Blake's] foolish pride. I therefore took him', he claimed, 'by the Elbows & pushed him before me till I had got him out.'[85] Scolfield, now off the property, continued to threaten and swear at Blake, who ventured off the cottage grounds and pushed him fifty paces down the road. Meanwhile, Scolfield tried to turn around and strike Blake. The soldier's curses were so loud that some neighbours came to see what had happened. Eventually, Blake and Scolfield reached the Fox Inn where the soldier was quartered. Grinder, the owner of the cottage and the Fox, forced Scolfield and another soldier, Cock, who had joined the mêlée, to go indoors after a series of abusive threats against Blake and his wife were uttered by the soldiers.

Such was Blake's account, which differs sharply from Scolfield's deposition against him sworn on 15 August. According to Scolfield, Blake had had a lot to say to him. First, he had exclaimed:

[The people of England] were like a parcel of Children, that they would play with themselves 'till they would get scalded and burnt, that the French knew our strength very well, and if Buonapart should come he would be master of Europe in an hour's time, that England might depend upon it that when [Napoleon] sat his Foot on English Ground that every Englishman would be put to his choice whether to have his throat cut or to join the French & that he was a strong Man and would certainly begin to cut throats and the strongest Man must conquer – that he Damned the King of England – his Country and his Subjects – that his soldiers were all bound for Slaves & all the poor people in general.

Then Catherine rushed up to them, interrupting her husband's disquisition: 'This is nothing to you at present but that the King of England would run himself so far into the Fire that he might [not] get himself out again.' She maintained that, although only a woman, she would fight 'as long as she had a Drop of Blood in her'. Blake rejoined: 'My Dear, you would not fight against France?' 'No,' she said, 'I would fight for Buonaparte as long as I am able.' Then Blake turned to Scolfield: 'Though you are one of the King's Subjects I have told what I have said before greater people than you.' Blake then invited Scolfield to have his commanding officer call on Hayley to verify this, whereupon Catherine ordered her husband to turn Scolfield out of the garden.

The hapless soldier turned round to do so peacefully whereupon Blake manhandled him, twice taking him by the collar 'without any resistance' on his part. At the same time, Blake '*damned the King & said the* _____ *Soldiers were all Slaves –*'.[86]

Clearly, both men lied, the truth of this acerbic confrontation lying somewhere in the middle of the two narratives. First, it is unlikely that Scolfield was so entirely the polite gentleman he pictures himself in response to being physically abused by Blake. Second, before the altercation, Scolfield was unlikely to have known of Blake's radical sentiments. A Manchester man trained as a fustian cutter, he had enlisted in the Dragoons on 19 March 1793 at Sarum. Eventually promoted to corporal, then to sergeant in September 1797, he was reduced to the ranks on 30 December 1798, evidently because of habitual drunkenness. Possibly, he hoped that his exposure of a traitor would enable him to regain his corporalship. Scolfield's comrade, Private John Cock, claimed that he heard Blake utter seditious words near the stable door, once an audience had gathered. This is probably mendacious, since none of the townspeople heard any such statements: obviously, Cock and Scolfield were well aware that Scolfield's unsupported testimony could not convict Blake.

In August 1793, Blake was tortured by fears about what the future held for him in London. Paranoid suspicions were aroused when he saw a soldier in his garden. Obviously, he acted without considering the consequences. Although Scolfield no doubt garbled what Blake had screamed, his recollection of the abuse hurled at him by William and Catherine was probably substantially accurate. In April 1815, Blake observed to George Cumberland that he was 'fearful they [the French] will make too great a Man of Napoleon and enable him to come to this Country'. Catherine rejoined that 'if this Country does go to War, our K—g ought to loose his head'.[87] The language and sentiments of 1815 are reminiscent of what Scolfield professed to have heard in 1803.

In the midst of this imbroglio, Blake became convinced that Scolfield had, at Hayley's instigation, been sent to prod him to say things which would land him in trouble with the authorities. Blake was fortunate that he had his say before an audience gathered: he was canny enough to keep his mouth closed in a public forum. In fact, he seized upon this very detail in his memorandum of refutation:

> Mrs. Haynes says very sensibly, that she never heard People quarrel, but they always charged each other with the Offence, and repeated it to

those around, therefore as the Soldier charged not me with Seditious Words at that Time, neither did his Comrade, the whole Charge must have been fabricated in the Stable afterwards. —[88]

As his letter eight months earlier to his brother James shows, Blake was quite capable of distorting the truth. Very much on the edge in the summer of 1803, he had acted very imprudently and then had to lie his way out of a predicament. A man who had little awareness of the practicalities of life, he had again chosen precisely the wrong moment to entangle himself in a charge of sedition: the war with France had resumed in May, and fear of invasion was rife on the Sussex coast. That August, women were ordered away from the coast, when rumours spread that French transports had sailed in that direction. In a sense, the oafish Scolfield chose precisely the right instant to ingratiate himself with his superiors: an alert soldier would be one who could sniff out a French sympathizer.

The ever resourceful Hayley, who shared Blake's political opinions regarding the tyrannical and inefficient Government of England, quickly came to his aid and stood bail for £50 when the magistrate, John Quantock, bound Blake over for the Quarter Sessions (Seagrave provided an additional £50). And so, just as Blake was escaping from dependency on Hayley's Urizenic-inspired kindness, he had to accept his help in ridding himself of a serious criminal charge. Blake's retreat from Sussex was accomplished with more flair than even he could have wished.

11

Further Hazards of Patronage

1803–1805

A FTER a brief stay with James on Broad Street, William and Catherine, reduced to a hand-to-mouth existence, took rooms in the autumn of 1803 at 17 South Molton Street, about a mile north-west of Golden Square. Not only were the couple robbed of the open fields of Felpham, but they were confined to the first floor of a house, where their landlord was one Mark Martin. There were other lodgers there, including the 'young & very amiable Mrs Enoch'. More than ever before, William and Catherine were poised precariously between bare subsistence and complete destitution.

Nevertheless, Blake, at first, was delighted to be back in London, which he unrestrainedly praised: 'The shops in London improve; everything is elegant, clean, and neat: the streets are widened where they were narrow.'[1] A year and a half later, the faddishness of London became irritating, as can be measured in his response to the meteoric rise to fame of William Henry West Betty, the actor:

> The Town is Mad. Young Roscius like all Prodigies is the talk of Every Body. I have not seen him & perhaps never may. I have no Curiosity to see him, as I well know what is within the compass of a boy of 14. & as to Real Acting it is Like Historical Painting, No Boy's Work.[2]

Back in London, William and Catherine remained worried about the charge of sedition laid by Scolfield. Their anxieties increased when, on 4 October, Blake being present, a jury at the Michaelmas Quarter Sessions at Petworth found true bills of sedition and assault against him, which meant the case could now go for trial. The sureties which Blake had to provide were raised to £1000, those funds probably being supplied, again, by Hayley and Seagrave. Blake arrived back from the 'contagion of the Court of Justice' to find Catherine in 'very poor health',[3] no doubt as a result of frayed nerves.

At about this time, Hayley also arranged for Samuel Rose, the frail lawyer whom he had met through Cowper, to defend Blake. Meanwhile, Lady Hesketh was very upset about these proceedings – she was especially disturbed about 'some reports' that 'Mr. B: was more *Seriously* to blame than you were at all aware of ...'.[4] Lady Hesketh, who was on good terms with Rose, had perhaps heard from him that the charges against Blake were substantially accurate.

When Blake returned to Sussex for the trial at the Guildhall at Chichester on 11 January, he probably stayed with Hayley at the Turret. Rose's opening speech to the Duke of Richmond, the six other magistrates and the jury rightly stressed the inconsistencies in Scolfield's assertions and impugned his character. He pointed out that Scolfield claimed that the seditious words were uttered in the garden whereas Cock swore that they were made in the vicinity of the Fox. The testimony of the townspeople, 'you will then agree with me', he proclaimed, 'totally overthrows the testimony of these Soldiers'.[5] At this juncture, the highly strung Rose broke down, unable to continue. Despite this setback, 'the verdict of the Jury was in favour of his calumniated client'.[6] When the acquittal was announced, the court was 'in defiance of all decency', the *Sussex Weekly Advertiser* announced, 'thrown into an uproar by [the] noisy exultations'[7] of the audience.

Hayley was ecstatic, especially as he had noticed the Urizenic conduct of the Duke of Richmond, who was 'bitterly prejudiced against Blake; & had made some unwarrantable observations in the course of the trial, that might have excited prejudice in the Jury'. As soon as the verdict was rendered, Hayley approached the Duke – who had sat in place from ten in the morning until eight at night – with a flamboyant declaration: 'I congratulate your Grace, that after having been wearied with the condemnation of sorry Vagrants, you have at last had the gratification of seeing an honest man honorably delivered from an infamous persecution. Mr Blake is a pacific, industrious, & deserving artist.' The Duke, who had no trouble recognizing heavy-handed, self-righteous sarcasm, bluntly replied: 'I Know nothing of Him.' Triumphantly, Hayley sneered back: 'True, my Lord, your Grace can Know nothing of Him; & I have therefore given you this Information: I wish your Grace a good Night.'[8]

Blake also had his moment during the middle of the trial, when, during Scolfield's testimony, he called out ' *"False"* ... in a tone which electrified the whole court and carried conviction with it'.[9] Many years afterwards, a man who as a boy had been in the courtroom remembered being transfixed by Blake's 'flashing eye'.[10] When the triumphant Blake reached home, Mrs Enoch assured him that Catherine had been 'near the Gate of Death';[11] the news of her husband's vindication quickly 'resumed' her.

Hayley behaved as a loyal friend during the Scolfield imbroglio – his kindness extended to paying Rose's fee – and this meant that Blake's reliance upon him increased. So Blake came to loathe him even more. Yet Blake knew that any chance he had of establishing himself on a secure financial footing was linked to his association with Hayley. At Felpham, Blake had seen how effectively Hayley was able to utilize a large network of friends to promote himself. Now came the painful realization that he would have to imitate Hayley's entrepreneurial style of self-publicity.

When he had settled back in London, Blake became more poignantly aware than ever that every 'Engraver turns away work that he cannot Execute from his superabundant Employment. Yet no one brings work to me.'[12] Why, when art in London was flourishing, was he so isolated?

> How is it possible that a Man almost 50 Years of Age, who has not lost any of his life since he was five years old without incessant labour & study, how is it possible that such a one with ordinary common sense can be inferior to a boy of twenty? ... O that I could live as others do in a regular succession of Employment, this wish I fear is not to be accomplishd to me.[13]

Blake's answer to these nagging questions was that there was a Devil side of himself which constantly led him 'very much to my hurt & sometimes to the annoyance of my friends'. When he managed to vanquish this creature, he promised himself to 'do double the work I do now'.[14] As he knew, he lived very much a 'Divided Existence' where commerce and artistry did not meet.[15] In this passage, Blake shows that he was very well aware of the self-destructive streak in his character.

Blake despised Hayley for his art of compromise, but, briefly – from 1803 to 1805 – in a sometimes ridiculous parody of Hayley, he tried to become a businessman-cum-artist. He forced himself to conform, to be grateful for favours which he hated himself for accepting. Underneath the surface of amiability dwelt rage. Some of these activities were initiated by Hayley, who wished Blake to help him collect information for his new project, the life of George Romney. For example, Hayley wanted to get in touch with Emma Hamilton, who had sat many times for the infatuated artist. Blake could not immediately locate the Hamilton house in Piccadilly: 'She left some time ago. Mr Edwards will procure her address for you & I will send it immediately.'[16]

Blake was also working on the two plates for Volume III of the *Life of Cowper*, which was published in 1804, a year after the first two volumes. He was also assigned three of the forty plates for Flaxman's *Iliad*, which appeared in 1805; Prince Hoare, the painter, asked him to engrave a drawing of Ceres by Flaxman. Also, Blake was involved in April 1804 with the thirty-seven-year-old publisher of the *Monthly Magazine*, Richard Phillips, who, incarcerated in Leicester jail eleven years earlier for selling Paine's *Rights of Man*, had asked Cowper to write a sonnet on his behalf. 'So you see,' Blake assured Hayley, 'he is spiritually adjoined with us.'[17] Acting as Phillips's agent, Blake pleaded with Hayley to assume the editorship of a new periodical, into which Phillips was willing to sink £2000. Blake pushed Hayley to acquiesce: 'Literature is your Child. She calls for your assistance!'[18] Meanwhile, Blake was getting behind in the plates he was supposed to be preparing for the Romney biography. He reminded Hayley that 'Endless Work is the true title of engraving,' but in case Hayley was becoming agitated, he rather untruthfully told him that this observation was borne out by 'the things I have in hand day & night'.[19]

Moreover, there was a serious discrepancy between Blake's blithe assertion to Hayley of 27 January 1804 –

> I write now to satisfy you that all is in a good train. I am going on briskly with the Plates, find every thing promising. Work in Abundance; & if God blesses me with health doubt not yet to make a Figure in the Great Dance of Life[20]

– and the fact that Hayley was justifiably irritated that he was seeing little promised work. In May 1804, he sent Blake a copy of William Falconer's *The Shipwreck* in hopes that his dilatory friend would look at the engravings and be inspired to engrave Romney's painting of the same name.

A month later, Blake was again trying to get more money out of Hayley. He suggested that the true genius of Romney could be realized only by a combination of engravings which were 'highly finishd' and 'less finishd'. In fact, Blake had checked with his old partner, James Parker, who assured him that thirty guineas was the proper price for the former, half that for the latter. Not very subtly, Blake notified Hayley that most engravers had their hands full – he would never be able to hire eight men to do the eight plates he wanted by November. He also implied that he was quoting bargain prices. That very day, Parker had informed him that he had 'turned away a Plate of 400 Guineas because [he was] too full of work'. When Blake consulted Flaxman, the sculptor had extended almost identical advice. Blake is conveying this news 'immediately ... because no time should be lost in this truly interesting business'.[21]

Blake then observes that the head of Romney, which he has been working on for six months, is 'in very great forwardness'.[22] Three months later, he tells Hayley 'the favor of ten Pounds more will carry me thro the [Shipwreck] plate & the Head of Romney'.[23] A month later, he was still working on the portrait of Romney and, in December, the 'Dreamer', as he dubbed himself, wanted another £10: 'I am very far from shewing the Portrait of Romney as a finishd Proof.'[24] Such dilatoriness in part explains the reluctance of publishers to employ Blake.

Meanwhile, after Hayley had rebuffed Phillips's earlier offer of an editorship, Blake tried to persuade the Sussex recluse to allow Phillips to become his publisher, even though this would displease Seagrave, who usually co-published Hayley's books with London firms. Phillips's 'connexions are Universal', he informed Hayley: 'his present House is on the most noble scale & will be in some measure a Worthy Town Vehicle for your Beautiful Muse.' Also, Blake entreated Hayley, perhaps Phillips could publish an edition of the Ballads with his engravings?: 'whatever you command I will zealously perform, & Depend upon it, I will neither Do nor say but as you Direct'.[25] For Blake, Phillips was a potential Maecenas, whose treasure house could be unlocked if only Hayley would co-operate.

In order to entice Hayley into his net, Phillips was indeed willing to publish the Ballads. Of this offer, Blake told the Hermit: 'I consider myself as only put in trust with this work, and that the copyright is for ever yours.'[26] By 22 March, Phillips had offered Blake twenty guineas each for five plates to be completed by 28 May. In the suppressed Advertisement to these animal pictures, Blake said that he was confident that the public would 'approve of my rather giving few highly labourd Plates than a greater number & less finishd'. He wistfully concluded: 'If I have succeeded in these more may be added at Pleasure.'[27] On 4 June 1805, Blake pleaded with Hayley to include the ballad of *The Horse*: 'I write to entreat that you would contrive so as that my plate may come into the work, as its omission would be to me a loss that I could not now sustain, as it would cut off ten guineas from my next demand on Phillips, which sum I am in absolute want of.'[28]

So distanced was Blake from many of the sentiments he vigorously held that he could congratulate Hayley on 4 May 1804 on his poem concerned with George III's recovery from (supposed) mental illness: 'it is one of the prettiest things I ever read, and I hope the King will live to fulfil the prophecy and die in peace; but, at present, poor man, I understand he is poorly indeed.'[29] Blake also ingratiated himself when he told Hayley that John Boydell's eyes had lit up at the mention of his name.[30]

Only occasionally did Blake risk offending Hayley, as when he told him that Joseph Johnson did not like acting as co-publisher with Seagrave. The Unitarian might be honest and generous, but he was self-serving. At times, he had written 'such letters to [Blake] as would have called for the sceptre of Agamemnon rather than the tongue of Ulysses'.[31] Blake then offered Hayley his 'settled opinion':

> if you suffer yourself to be persuaded to print in London, you will be cheated every way; but, however, as some little excuse, I must say that in London every calumny and falsehood utter'd against another of the same trade is thought fair play. Engravers, Painters, Statuaries, Printers, Poets. We are not in a field of battle, but in a City of Assassinations.[32]

Blake's portrait of London as a cesspool of depravity is a reflection of his inability to obtain recognition. Now Blake idealizes Sussex, where Hayley's lot is 'truly enviable': 'the country is not only more beautiful on account of its expanded meadows, but also on account of its benevolent minds.'[33]

In the midst of his deeply conflicted pursuit of reputation, Blake witnessed Fuseli's advancement to the rank of Master at the Royal Academy; he knew that Thomas Banks's death would clear the way for Flaxman to become Professor of Sculpture there. What Blake clung to in the midst of activities which he would ultimately see as degrading was the figure of George Romney, 'whose spiritual aid has not a little conducted to my restoration to the light of Art'.[34]* As Blake was well

---

*Evidence has recently been discovered which demonstrates that by 1799 Romney had purchased at least four illuminated books. Romney probably bought these directly from Blake.

aware, Romney had achieved worldly acclaim as a portraitist, a calling he despised. Romney's real interests were in the irrational forces of the mind and the Gothic. In February 1787, weary of a daily schedule which sometimes included five sitters told Hayley: 'This cursed portrait-painting! How I am shackled with it! I am determined to live frugally, that I may enable myself to cut it short, as soon as I am tolerably independent, and give my mind up to those delightful regions of imagination.'[35] From 1803 to 1805, Blake desperately wanted to make a similar adaptation which would allow his visionary ambitions to become compatible with financial success.

In October 1804, in part inspired by Romney, Blake was 'enlightened with the light I enjoyed in my youth, and which has for exactly twenty years been closed from me as by a door and by window-shutters'.[36] This crystalline moment – 'on the day after visiting the Truchsessian Gallery' – occurred when Blake viewed examples of the kinds of painting which he would have been exposed to in 1784 had Hawkins sent him to Italy. (As Blake knew, Romney had undertaken such a pilgrimage from 1773 to 1775.)

In August 1803 the vast collection of Joseph, Count Truchsess was shown in a gallery that had been built in the New Road, Marylebone, opposite Portland Place. Lighted from the top, the building comprised eight rooms filled to bursting with over 900 canvases. Truchsess, who claimed to have lost a fortune as a result of the revolution in France, wanted to sell his collection and used the exhibition as a marketing ploy. Many great painters were said to be represented in the collection, but a substantial portion of these were merely copies. Thomas Lawrence said 'there was scarcely an original picture of a *great master* among them'.[37] Despite this, Blake was able to view samples of the work of artists such as Michelangelo, Raphael and Durer, artists whom he had hoped to emulate as a young man. In close proximity to them he glanced at pieces of 'Venetian and Flemish Ooze'[38] by Correggio, Veronese and Rubens.

The time Blake spent in the Truchsessian Gallery transformed him – he saw clearly that he had to return to his original aspirations. He experienced an 'altered state' and became 'drunk with intellectual vision'. 'I thank God', he proclaimed, 'that I courageously pursued my course through darkness.'[39] But, during his first three years back in

---

See Joseph Viscomi, 'The Myth of Commissioned Illuminated Books: George Romney, Isaac D'Israeli, and "ONE HUNDRED AND SIXTY designs ... of Blake's" ', *Blake/An Illustrated Quarterly*, 23 (1989) 48–66.

London, Blake was very much in danger of abandoning that sacred vision.

Hayley clung tenaciously to his belief in Blake's merit as an artist, even though Lady Hesketh's hair stood on end to think that he persevered in this friendship. 'I don't doubt', she told John Johnson, that Blake 'will poison him in his Turret or set fire to all his papers, & poor Hayley will consume in his own Fires.'[40] To that stern lady, Hayley maintained that he supported Blake because 'he is *very apt to fail in his art*: – a species of failing peculiarly entitled to pity *in Him*, since it arises from nervous Irritation, & a *too vehement desire to excell*'. Cowper, he assured her, would have understood that this gifted man 'has *often appeared to me on the verge of Insanity*'.[41] This was Hayley's hapless response to Blake's rage, which he did not realize was largely directed against himself.

Hayley wanted to assist Blake in overcoming his streak of perversity. However, Blake's procrastinations and price hikes rankled. Also, he did not want Phillips to serve as his publisher. Without telling his difficult friend, Hayley made enquiries through Flaxman about hiring an engraver or engravers to supplant Blake. In June 1804, Flaxman recommended his friend Robert Cromek as a 'man of independent Spirit [who] is very handsomely employed as he well deserves'.[42] Hayley thought this man would be particularly well suited to do *The Shipwreck*, but 'since Blake has just got in his own apartments the three designs of Romney', he did not wish to wound his feelings. Eventually, Caroline Watson – even though Flaxman was appalled by her work – was given seven of the twelve Romney plates: Blake's rendition of *The Shipwreck* was his sole contribution to that volume. Watson also did the engraving of Romney's portrait of Cowper for the second edition of the Cowper biography. This move was initiated by Lady Hesketh, Blake being excessively polite when informed:

> The Idea of Seeing an Engraving of Cowper by the hand of Caroline Watson is, I assure you, a pleasing one to me; it will be highly gratifying to see another Copy by another hand & not only gratifying, but Improving, which is better.[43]

At this time, chivalry was Blake's outward way of coping with an increasingly trying financial existence. The other side of his feelings was confided to the privacy of his Notebook, where Hayley is a consummate villain:

> When H—y finds out what you cannot do
> That is the Very thing he'll set you to.
> If you break not your Neck tis not his fault
> But pecks of poison are not pecks of salt.
> And when he could not act upon my wife,
> Hired a Villain to bereave my life.[44]

The last couplet suggests that Hayley made sexual overtures to Catherine. When these were rebuffed, he employed Scolfield to accuse Blake of sedition. Blake's self-contempt for deferring to Hayley is captured in these lines:

> I write the Rascal Thanks, till he & I
> With Thanks & Compliments are quite drawn dry.[45]

Samuel Rose is perfunctorily denigrated in the Notebook, but Blake did express genuine sorrow at his premature death: 'Farewell, Sweet Rose! thou hast got before me into the Celestial City.'[46] Blake was able to hold conflicting ideas about friends and aquaintances but such understandable ambivalences disturbed him. He did not really respect divisions within himself – or others.

The juvenile side of Blake can be plainly discerned in the jottings he entered in his Notebook. Blake tried to transcend such feelings and to find, once again, a semblance of balance in his 'Grand Poem', *Milton*. For him, the 'Divine countenance' was more readily seen in the faces of Cowper and Milton 'than in any prince or hero'.[47] However, if he looked too closely at Cowper, he might be drawn into his madness. In Milton, he saw a man who, like himself, had become tainted – despite true imaginative vision. If Blake could redeem Milton, he could perhaps save himself.

In *Vala*, Blake had revived the 'Universal Man' from his coma. He had been able to sort out the disparate, warring Zoas and had imposed a pacific, millennial ending. However, that poem was left unfinished and unengraved, the text being full of unresolved conflicts upon which a conclusion is forced. Blake worked on *Vala* at Felpham, but at some point during his stay there he abandoned it in favour of *Milton*, where he was able to discuss many of the same issues in a more precise way. Rather than concentrating on the unhealthy 'Universal Man' he turned to John Milton, who exists in eternity in a similar infirm state. The result is much more successful because the poem is also a deeply felt autobiographical meditation on the fate of William Blake, who is sick unto death in the fallen world. Although dated 1804, *Milton* was not engraved until about 1809.

Blake had previously identified – to a limited extent – with Young and Gray when he had reinterpreted and corrected their works. Milton, a dissenter who attempted to define political, religious and personal freedom on an epic scale, was the great national poet of England. Despite good intentions, his poetry was seriously flawed by an undue reliance on perverted beliefs centred on a Urizenic God. The task in *Milton* was twofold: to save the seventeenth-century poet and to recover the past glory of an England utterly debauched in the early 1800s.

> And did those feet in ancient time,
> Walk upon England's mountains green? . . .
> I will not cease from Mental Fight,
> Nor shall my Sword sleep in my hand:
> Till we have built Jerusalem,
> In England's green and pleasant Land.[48]

There is also a touch of sibling rivalry at work: Hayley, also a would-be son of Milton, had written a biography of the poet which emphasized his radical sympathies. In his new poem, Blake would perform the supreme act of rehabilitation by helping Milton to purge himself of his weaknesses and inconsistencies. And Blake posed some interesting questions: how could the great poet of political freedom have been corrupted by his sexuality? how could he have placed so much dependence on a rational God?

In part stimulated by the poet's stay in rural Sussex, *Milton* is a poem of varied, evocative landscapes. The site of unhappy human experience is Generation; beyond that is the world of Beulah, a dream place into which one can venture only momentarily; Golgonooza is Los's beautiful city of 'Art and Manufacture' – a reminder of the culture to which man can aspire – located at the edge of Ulro, the place of formlessness; Eden, which partakes of both the world of eternity and mortality, is surrounded by Beulah. The Mundane Shell protects the Mundane Egg, which is the universe as inhabited by man and which he must pass through on his way to Eden and eternity.

These various landscapes share some similarities with the 'fourfold vision' Blake told Thomas Butts of in November 1802: single vision ('Newton's sleep') is an endorsement of the philistinism rampant in Generation; twofold vision, which condemns political and religious repression, sees beyond the confines of Generation; the artist, who is a visionary dreamer, briefly enters Beulah in order to be refreshed and to communicate its essence to fellow mortals; in rare moments, mortals see into the world of Eden – closely allied to Jerusalem – and thus have a glimpse of eternity. The artist creates form from formlessness and is thus intimately aware of the dangers of Ulro.

One of the problems which Blake encountered in *Vala* was his inability to produce a focused narrative. In *Milton*, he avoids this obstacle by relying on a series of analogous tales: the central stories are contained in the Bard's Song and in the description of Milton's voyage to self-renewal. These accounts show two different sides of Blake's own interior landscape. In the Bard's Song, which recounts the domestic squabbles of three brothers, Blake attempts to come to grips with his envious hatred of Hayley. When he turns to the story of Milton – an immortal soul lost in chaos – Blake's attention is directed in a more positive vein to redemption and gratitude.

The Bard's Song tells of rivalry among three sons of Los: Satan the Elect, Palamabron the Redeemed and Rintrah the Reprobate. Satan is a charming individual with a smooth veneer:

> with most endearing love
> He soft entreated Los to give to him Palamabron's station;
> For Palamabron returnd with labour wearied every evening.
> Palamabron oft refus'd; and as often Satan offer'd
> His service, till by repeated offers and repeated intreaties
> Los gave to him the Harrow of the Almighty.[49]

In a manner similar to that of Los, Palamabron succumbs to the deceitful machinations of Satan, who abuses the authority given to him. This leads Palamabron to condemn him:

> You know Satan's mildness and his self-imposition.
> Seeming a brother, being a tyrant, even thinking himself a
> brother
> While he is murdering the just; prophetic I behold
> His future course thro' darkness and despair to
> eternal death.
> But we must not be tyrants also! he hath assum'd my place
> For one whole day, under pretence of pity and
> love to me:
> My horses hath he maddend! and my fellow servants injur'd:
> How should he, he, know the duties of another?[50]

Satan, a player who believes in the script he is acting, counterattacks, asserting that Palamabron is the one who has behaved unjustly. At an assembly of Eternals convened at Palamabron's request, Rintrah – the wrathful one – is condemned. Meanwhile, Satan proclaims that he is God. Then, Leutha – Satan's emanation – accepts culpability: having fallen in love with Palamabron, she 'stupefied' Satan's masculine perceptions. The jealous Satan thus sought to supplant his brother. Later, Leutha, who like Milton's Sin springs from Satan's head, seduces Palamabron and gives birth to Death.

In this creation myth, brotherly enmity comes into being as a result of sexual jealousy. Yet again, men are the pawns of women in the battle of the sexes, since the blame for Satan's atrocious behaviour is attributed to his feminine side. Covertly, Blake may be suggesting that his relationship with Hayley was unbalanced because of sexual jealousy aroused by the older man's interest in Catherine.

Overtly, Blake is showing two sides of himself in Palamabron and Rintrah. Palamabron represents the part of Blake which is conciliatory and which seeks to make its way in the world. Then there is the uncompromising Rintrah, that portion of Blake which writes of unbridled hatred in the Notebook. These are very limited concepts of the self, which do not take Blake beyond the confines of *Vala*.

Then the poem changes direction. Disturbed by what the Bard proclaims, a member of the audience asserts: 'Pity and Love are too venerable for the imputation / Of guilt.' The Bard counters: 'I am Inspired! I know it is Truth! for I sing / According to the inspiration of the Poetic Genius.'[51] However, when Milton, who has been in eternity since 1674 but is dejected because he is separated from his Sixfold Emanation (three wives and three daughters), overhears this song, he is not as blithely self-assured as the Bard. Despite intentions to the contrary, he realizes that unawares he had been in his mortal life a follower of Satan:

> He took off the robe of the promise, & ungirded himself from the
>   oath of God.
> And Milton said, 'I go to Eternal Death! . . .
> When will the Resurrection come to deliver the
>   sleeping body
> From corruptibility? O when, Lord Jesus, wilt thou come?
> Tarry no longer: for my soul lies at the gates of death.
> I will arise and look forth for the morning of the grave.
> I will go down to the sepulcher to see if morning breaks!
> I will go down to self annihilation and eternal death,

> Lest the Last Judgment come & find me unannihilate
> And I be siez'd & giv'n into the hands of my own Selfhood...
> What do I here before the Judgment? without my Emanation?
> With the daughters of memory, & not with the daughters of
>   inspiration?
> I in my Selfhood am that Satan; I am that Evil One!
> He is my Spectre! In my obedience to loose him from my Hells
> To claim the Hells, my Furnaces, I go to Eternal Death.[52]

Milton's moving acceptance of his limitations and his steadfast determination to change himself reflect Blake's awareness that he could no longer be exclusively Palamabron or Rintrah. Like Milton, Blake has to integrate the various parts of his personality – at least, he has to try to do so, even though this might involve killing off portions of himself.

Milton's descent into mortality is in imitation of Christ, who took on human flesh to save mankind. Like another hero, Christian in *Pilgrim's Progress*, Milton finds his way beset with obstacles. In a manner reminiscent of Los, the poet struggles with and nearly succumbs to Urizen – the God the Father to whom he gave form in *Paradise Lost*. In their second confrontation, Milton bests him. He is able to do this because he has become attentive to the missing female part of himself (Ololon), with whom he is finally united in Blake's garden at Felpham. Only then can Milton cast out the spectre of Satan from within himself and tell him: 'I know my power thee to annihilate.' This leads to even greater insights:

> I come in Self-annihilation & the grandeur of Inspiration
> To cast off Rational Demonstration by Faith in the Saviour;
> To cast off the rotten rags of Memory by Inspiration;
> To cast off Bacon, Locke & Newton from Albion's covering;
> To take off his filthy garments, & clothe him with Imagination;
> To cast aside from Poetry all that is not Inspiration,
> That it no longer shall dare to mock with the aspersion of
>   Madness....[53]

Such perceptions are easy to utter, but they are difficult to live. This is the sad realization of William Blake, the other central character in *Milton*. In his attempt to impose order on the full panoply of existence, the artist has to describe both good and evil. And to depict evil, one must know first-hand its chaos and desolation. If an artist does this, he can be badly burned and, eventually, destroyed.

As Blake increasingly perceived, greatness as an artist can be pur-

Plate 18 from *Milton*   Plate 37 from *Milton*

chased at too high a price: misunderstanding, isolation, poverty, condemnation. Did he really want to subject himself to further misery? A
resounding yes is Blake's answer, at that moment in *Milton*, where
the dead poet enters the living poet's left foot 'As a bright sandal formd
immortal of precious stones & gold: / I stooped down & bound it on to
walk forward thro' Eternity.'[54] Immediately, the poet hurls himself
backwards in a gesture of rapt submission. This handing down of the
poetic mantle can be done only because Blake has saved Milton. Now,
perhaps, strengthened by the poet's presence within himself, Blake can
carry on, even though with considerable trepidation, his own poetical
priesthood. The way before him may be arduous, but it no longer
crosses insurmountable terrain.

The success of *Milton* – and the reason why Blake was able to
complete it – lies in his ability to deal directly with the seemingly
impossible difficulties which threatened to overwhelm him during
and just after the Felpham years. Here, he comes to grips with the
horrendous divisions which drive human beings apart in the world

of Generation. And, he sees that reconciliation and restoration are possible.

In the midst of his stay at Felpham, Blake told Butts of this nightmare:

> With my Father hovering upon the wind
> And my Brother Robert just behind
> And my Brother John, the evil one,
> In a black cloud making his mone;
> Tho dead, they appear upon my path
> Notwithstanding my terrible wrath.
> They beg, they intreat, they drop their tears,
> Filld full of hopes, filld full of fears.[55]

Despite his anger, Blake is helpless to banish these spirits. In his new illuminated book, there is a twin plate to the one where the star of Milton enters Blake. There he depicts a star penetrating the right foot of Robert. This illumination is darker than the one showing William, but there are four – not three – steps behind his younger brother. Robert has entered the world of fourfold vision, whereas his brother lives in the fallen world of Generation which permits him only momentary glimpses of Beulah.

Milton is a poem filled with disastrous parental and, especially, fraternal relationships. At Felpham and after his return to London, Blake had to deal with a false brother, Hayley. As he brooded upon his own career, Blake turned his attention to Milton, whom, in a fraternal way, he tried to rid of error. In so doing, he allowed the redeemed poet's inspiration to enter and transform him, making him aware that the divisions – especially sexual – he feared could be overcome. Despite setbacks, he could persevere. He could regain his youthful enthusiasm for a pristine, primitive art. And these thoughts brought him back to his brother and the agonizing realization of just how much he missed him.

Blake's central dilemma – how was he going to survive as an artist? – is clearly reflected in *Milton*. The unworldly poet–painter could never have succumbed to earthly success, but that does not mean the temptation did not exist. That was the painful lesson of 1803–5. But Blake had a rejuvenated sense of his destiny. Unfortunately, this soon brought him into conflict with the man he would see as his greatest enemy: Robert Cromek.

Jerusalem: the Emanation of the Giant Albion, also begun at Felpham and substantially finished by 1807, is a companion piece to *Milton* in that many of the personal conflicts dealt with in the earlier text are

The Union of Contraries (plate 99 from *Jerusalem*)

given, in the later one, more universal scope. As such, *Jerusalem* is concerned with the redemption of Albion, the English nation. As in *Vala* and *Milton*, the central figure is in a slumber and is isolated from his female emanation. England has long been divorced from its destiny as the inheritor of ancient wisdom, which can lead to divine redemption. As we have seen, from his youth Blake was convinced that early English history contained various individuals who were capable of embodying as well as pursuing such goals. For him, the sad history of his own time showed how far England had strayed from the ideals of those dead heroes.

If *Milton* is a deeply personal poem which can be compared to Milton's *Paradise Regained*, *Jerusalem* is Blake's *Paradise Lost*, his attempt to write sacred, epic history. In *Jerusalem*, Los, the true artist, witnesses the disagreements between Albion and his emanation but, ultimately, beholds their reconciliation, which is symbolic of 'Awaking into' the 'Bosom in the Life of Immortality'.[56]

By this time, Blake had serious reservations about allegory, which he saw as Greek and secular. Instead, he preferred 'vision' and that is precisely the note upon which the poem concludes. The final judgement and resurrection, described in the language of Revelation, occur in the London of the early 1800s. When Blake showed *Jerusalem* to Robert Southey in July 1811, the future Laureate dismissively – and rather densely – claimed that Blake's extensive use of urban geography meant that he had written a 'perfectly mad poem' in which 'Oxford Street is in Jerusalem'.[57]

More than any other of the illuminated books, *Jerusalem* shows Blake's sympathy with antinomianism, as he juxtaposes corrupt Albion with the concept of the potentially redemptive city of Jerusalem. The antinomians looked forward to the time when social justice and providential love would be fused together on earth. *Jerusalem* concludes precisely in this fashion, testifying to Blake's return to the religious doctrine he had imbibed during his childhood and adolescence. Blake had nowhere else to turn. Trapped in a mercenary society which did not allow him to earn a decent living, he imagined his sordid world being transformed by the physical intervention of divine love.

12

'Bob Screwmuch' and the Infamy of Patronage

1805–1808

ALTHOUGH Richard Edwards's edition of the *Night Thoughts* had not been a commercial success, Blake's forty-three copper intaglio engravings were of high quality. The designer–engraver could not be held responsible for either the declining market in 1797 for such books or the publisher's half-hearted promotion of the edition. Despite this setback, Blake was clearly seen as a specialist in graveyard material. Such must have been the opinion of Robert Cromek, the engraver turned publisher who approached Blake – possibly at Flaxman's behest – in September 1805 'desiring', as Blake told Hayley, 'to have some of my Designs; he namd his Price & wishd me to Produce him Illustrations of the Grave, A Poem by Robert Blair'.[1]

The first linking of Cromek's name with Blake's occurs in an advertisement of 2 February 1793 mentioning that the two men would be among the engravers of the 'Splendid Edition of Barlow's Aesop's Fables'.[2] In 1805, Cromek engraved the frontispiece after Blake to Malkin's *A Father's Memoirs of His Child*, which was not published until 1806. Born in Hull in 1770, Cromek had been trained by the eminent Francesco Bartolozzi. From 1795 to 1805, he had made a series of bookplates after designs by Stothard. His other work included some of the plates to an edition of the *Spectator* (1803), to Du Roveray's edition of Pope (1804), and to an early edition of Rogers's *Pleasures of Memory*.[3] When his health became poor in about 1804, Cromek, who had never liked the dirty, messy conditions in which engravers had to work, became a print-jobber and publisher. According to Alexander Gilchrist, he had 'a nervous temperament and an indifferent constitution'.[4] A friend of Cromek's told his son that Robert and his wife Elizabeth, whom he married in 1806, 'were handsome – your father, in particular, had a small Classical head, with most gentlemanly manners, and took much in society'.[5] From the time of his marriage, Cromek lived at 64 Newman Street, popularly called 'Artists' Street'. Benjamin West, Thomas Stothard and Ozias Humphry were among those with whom Cromek maintained 'very Friendly terms'.[6] George Cumberland Jr, who was living with the Cromeks in 1808, reached very different conclusions, as he told his father on 20 December: 'It is very unpleasant at Mrs. Cromek's ... they take great liberties with me, my home & abroad amusements & Studies are frustrated by their selfish dispositions.'[7]

Cromek may have determined that there was a market for an illustrated edition of Robert Blair's popular blank-verse poem of 1743, *The Grave*. Or, possibly, he chose the poem because he felt that Blake's expertise in this area would lend itself to this particular text. As a result of Cromek's overture, Blake had, by 27 November, made, as he told Hayley, 'about twenty Designs which pleasd so well that he, with the same liberality with which he set me about the [forty] Drawings, has now set me to Engrave them. He means to Publish them by Subscription.'[8] There is only one more extant letter from Blake to Hayley, that of 11 December. Others might not have survived – or there might be a specific, unknown occasion for dissension which caused Blake to drop Hayley, who had long been a thorn in his side. Another possibility is that Blake, having acquired a new patron, no longer felt bound to continue a painful relationship. If that was so, he had merely exchanged one enemy for another who would cause him even more hurt.

Robert Blair, a minister educated at Edinburgh and in Holland, published *The Grave* in 1743, three years before his death at the age of forty-seven. Although Blair's poem was completed before 1740, it was not published until after the first instalment of *Night Thoughts*. Young's triumph paved the way for the appearance of a poem which received scanty, indifferent notices but which, despite this, became enormously popular. Samuel Johnson did not admire it, but James Boswell did. 'He told me,' said the biographer, 'so long ago as 1748 he had read "The Grave, a Poem", but did not like it much. I differed from him, for though it is not equal through and is seldom elegantly correct, it abounds in solemn thought, and poetical imagery beyond the common reach. The world has differed from him, for the poem has passed through many editions, and is still much read by people of a serious kind.'[9]

The 800 lines of *The Grave* are written in hortatory blank verse which reminded many of its first readers of Shakespearean monologue. The strong-willed voice cajoles its audience, prompting them to recall how vain are attempts to escape or forget the dominion of death. Also, the poet asserts that contemplation of the grave should be the preparation by the virtuous for eternal life with God. The full trappings of the graveyard tradition – tombs, deserted churchyards, death-bed repentances – are evoked in a much more concise fashion than in the *Night Thoughts*.

> Quite round the pile, a row of rev'rend elms,
> Coeval near with that, all ragged shew,
> Long lash'd by the rude winds; some rift half down
> Their branchless trunks, others so thin a-top
> That scarce two crows could lodge in the same tree.
> Strange things, the neighbours say, have happen'd here.
> Wild shrieks have issu'd from the hollow tombs;
> Dead men have come again, and walk'd about;
> And the great bell has toll'd, unrung, untouch'd!
> Such tales their cheer, at wake or gossiping,
> When it draws near the witching-time of night.[10]

As in his illustrations of Young, Blake uses this poem as a vehicle for his own meditations on death and resurrection. So universal are Blair's reflections that Blake subtly augments the text with his own Michelangeloesque vocabulary of heroic figures. As in his illustrations to Young, Blake gives the text a more Christological significance. And in three instances he uses his knowledge of sepulchral statuary – gained from the time he was an apprentice to Basire. As a group, the surviving designs are more sweeping and dramatic than those to Young.

Blake's designs were meant to tell a parallel, complementary story to Blair's: 'By the arrangement here made, the regular progression of Man, from his first descent into the Vale of Death, to his last admission into Life eternal, is exhibited. These Designs, detached from the Work they embellish, form of themselves a most interesting Poem.'[11] Initially, Cromek – who may have written these words* – was delighted by the strong images Blake submitted to him.

* The remarks are possibly by B. H. Malkin.

The Soul Hovering over the Body

Cromek probably had little capital – and this may have drawn him to Blake, whose engraving technique did not have the fashionable edge of Cromek's own practice or training. However, Cromek, who may have found the illustrations to the *Night Thoughts* moving, simply wanted Blake to work in that manner. The publisher's extant correspondence reveals him to have been a shrewd businessman. Even more than Hayley, however, he shared with Blake a passionate conviction of the centrality of art to the well-being of a nation and a corresponding worry about the failure of England to develop a national school of painting. Indeed, his language and vehemence of expression are Blakean:

> The value of genius is considerably enhanced by its rarity – it is by no means a common thing.... As there can be but few Men of Genius so, I grant, to be one of them, is to be, as far as relates to this World, unhappy, unfortunate; the Mock & scorn of Men; always in strife & contention against the World & the World against him; but, as far as relates to another World, to be one of these is to be Blessed! He is a Pilgrim & stranger upon Earth, travelling into a far distant Land, led by Hope &

sometimes by Despair but – surrounded by Angels & protected by the immediate Divine presence. He is the light of the World. Therefore Reverence thyself, O Man of Genius! –

There exists in this Country a vast, formidable Party ... who contemn, & to the utmost of their power spread abroad their contempt for *Poets & Poetry*, & of all the Works of Fancy & Imagination, denying & blaspheming every power of the Mind except reasoning & thence demonstrating their Design is to depress true Art & Science & to set up false Art & science in their stead.[12]

This is vivid, demonstrative rhetoric, written by a man imbued with strong views about visionary art and society's denigration of it.

On 27 November 1805, 'my Friend Cromek' had agreed, Blake told Hayley, to have him engrave twenty prints for the Blair edition. However, the first of two prospectuses issued by Cromek in November 1805 stated that there would be 'Fifteen Prints From Designs Invented and to be Engraved by William Blake'.[13] This seems a slight change, especially in the light of the second prospectus dated that same November but probably printed two or three months later: now there were to be 'Twelve Very Spirited Engravings by Louis Schiavonetti, from Designs Invented by William Blake'.[14] Why was Blake replaced by Schiavonetti? The answer lies in the expression 'Very Spirited'.

Cromek's disagreement with Blake did not come about because mercantile success was not compatible with transcendental art. Rather, Cromek was bitterly disappointed with Blake's inability – or unwillingness – to temper his art for the marketplace. Although he was sympathetic to Blake's inner dictates, he was not willing to lose money because of a depraved disregard for market forces. Blake's reluctance to compromise was no doubt dictated by his struggles against Hayley. So burned was he by that experience that he simply would not make the modest adjustments upon which Cromek insisted.

As soon as he had engaged Blake to illustrate *The Grave*, Cromek, in an attempt to gain the commercial success which had eluded the edition of the *Night Thoughts*, successfully solicited the 'Subscriptions and Patronage' of Benjamin West, the President of the Royal Academy, and fourteen other Academicians, including Cosway, Fuseli, Flaxman and Stothard. In addition, Fuseli wrote a puff for the edition.

Although Blake received only £20 for his drawings, he had hoped to obtain substantially more money for the engravings. Trouble began when Cromek wanted to advertise the edition at his premises. For this purpose, Blake provided him with the white-line engraving of *Death's*

Door: this is an accordance with the first issue of the Prospectus, which states: 'a Specimen of the Stile of Engraving may be seen at the Proprietor's.'[15] However, Cromek told Stothard that this etching was done 'so indifferently and so carelessly ... that he employed' Schiavonetti.[16]

Flaxman might have been aware of this single etching when he wrote on 14 November that Blake was 'in a way to do well' as an engraver 'if he will only condescend to give that attention to his worldly concerns which every one does that prefers living to Starving'.[17] A Flaxman letter to Hayley of 1 December might also be reflecting on Cromek's irritation with the etching:

> Blake is going on gallantly with his drawings from the Grave, which are patronized by a formidable list of R.A.'s and other distinguished persons – I mentioned before that he has good employment besides, but still I very much fear his abstracted habits are so much at variance with the usual modes of human life, that he will not derive all the advantage to be wished from the present favourable appearances.[18]

What exactly was wrong with the etching that upset 'favourable appearances'?

The white-line engraving in which the form of the design stands out in white against a black background is deliberately rough looking: Blake had returned to the conception of art which he had rediscovered the year before. Cromek may have been so repulsed by this sample that he immediately engaged Schiavonetti to do the engravings – or, more likely, he may have shown *Death's Door* to some customers, who expressed dissatisfaction. In any event – afraid of losing the market for the Blair edition – Cromek acted quickly. It is not known whether he offered Blake the opportunity to redo the design in a more acceptable fashion.

At one level, Cromek can be seen as the enemy of visionary art, as a crass businessman* who refused to take a chance on an innovative approach to book illustration. On the other hand, he was a person anxious to market prophetic art if it could be done in a way which would not ensure a severe financial loss. Once again, Blake – having found a person who shared a similar view of the centrality of art in human destiny – was uncompromising. Cromek turned to Schiavonetti – who like himself had been trained by Bartolozzi – because he knew that he would be faithful to Blake's designs while, at the same time,

---

*Cromek did represent some modern forgeries as if they were antique border ballads.

Death's Door (White line etching)

Death's Door (Schiavonetti's etching after Blake's design)

transforming them into engravings which had a *reasonable* chance of commercial success. Even J. T. Smith, Blake's friend, remarked that it would be 'unreasonable to expect the booksellers to embark in publications not likely to meet remuneration'.[19] Schiavonetti's engravings were 'Very Spirited' in a manner to win an audience; Blake's notion of 'Very Spirited' was, as far as Cromek was concerned, outrageous.

Cromek, an indefatigable promoter, managed to obtain a subscription of at least 684 copies, most of which sold at two guineas. In addition to the Royal Academicians, the purchasers included Thomas Bewick, Hayley, Butts, Richard Edwards (six copies), Colnaghi the dealer (six) and John Murray the publisher (six). The large sales in Liverpool, Birmingham, Wakefield, Manchester, Newcastle, Bristol and Edinburgh testify to Cromek's extensive travelling in pursuit of sales. Although Blake had forfeited a significant amount of money by having his engraver's stylus removed from his hand, he remained on amicable but uneasy terms with Cromek until May 1807.

The former engraver had every reason to retain the acerbic artist's good will: after all, it was Blake's designs which were being engraved. It was in Cromek's best interests to boost him, and it was undoubtedly Cromek who invited Thomas Phillips, a Royal Academician, to undertake Blake's portrait, which was etched by Schiavonetti as the frontispiece to *The Grave*, an engraving which was praised by the *Antijacobin Review* in a review which condemned Blake's designs!*

Phillips, who was renowned as a story-teller, was amused by his exchanges with Blake during the sittings at his studio at 8 George Street, Hanover Square in April 1807.[20]

'We hear much', the painter said, 'of the grandeur of Michael Angelo; from the engravings, I should say he has been over-rated; he could not paint an angel so well as Raphael.'

If Phillips was baiting Blake, it worked: 'He has not been over-rated, Sir, and he could paint an angel better than Raphael.'

'Well,' the portrait painter rejoined, 'you never saw any of the paintings of Michael Angelo; and perhaps speak from the opinions of others; your friends may have deceived you.'

'I never saw any of the paintings of Michael Angelo, but I speak from the opinion of a friend who could not be mistaken.'

'A valuable friend truly and who may he be I pray?'

'The arch-angel Gabriel, Sir.'

Not to be outdone, Phillips countered: 'A good authority surely, but you know evil spirits love to assume the looks of good ones; and this may have been done to mislead you.'

'Well now, Sir, this is really singular; such were my own suspicions; but they were soon removed – I will tell you how. I was one day reading Young's *Night Thoughts*, and when I came to that passage which asks "who can paint an angel," I closed the book and cried "Aye! who can paint an angel?" A voice in the room answered, "Michel Angelo could." "And how do *you* know?" I said, looking round me, but I saw nothing save a greater light than usual. "I *know*," said the voice, "for I sat to him: I am the arch-angel Gabriel." "Oho!" I answered, "you are, are you: I must have better assurance than that

---

* According to the *Antijacobin Review*, Phillips *gave* the portrait to Cromek: 'The portrait itself, which the artist, with a most praiseworthy liberality, has presented to Mr. Cromek, is a very fine and well painted picture ...' (*BR*, p. 208). This piece of information may be incorrect, or the circumstances of the presentation may have been obscured. It seems unlikely that Phillips asked to paint Blake; certainly, Blake could not have afforded Phillips's fee.

of a wandering voice; you may be an evil spirit – there are such in the land." :"You shall have good assurance," said the voice, "can an evil spirit do this?" I looked whence the voice came, and was then aware of a shining shape, with bright wings, who diffused much light. As I looked, the shape dilated more and more: he waved his hands; the roof of my study opened; he ascended into heaven; he stood in the sun, and beckoning to me, moved the universe. An angel or devil could not have *done that* – it was the arch-angel Gabriel.'[21]

The Academician 'marvelled' at this tall tale, no doubt composed on the spot to vanquish him. Despite Blake's comical attempts at one-upmanship, Phillips in his portrait shows the poet–painter with an elegant coat and waistcoat, frilled shirt and watch fob or seal. Here he is dressed as a middle-class businessman. The portraitist also captured Blake's fiery, burning, protuberant eyes – the facial feature which captured the attention of most people who met him. The contradictions within Blake in 1807 are here perfectly enshrined: he yearned for public recognition but there was a force within him which would not allow him to accede to such impulses. He saw a world curtained off from most of his contemporaries. And to that sphere he had to pay his fullest allegiance.

However, even after Schiavonetti had replaced him as engraver, Blake, in June 1806, in yet another perverse attempt at popularity, asked Ozias Humphry, the fashionable miniaturist, for help in applying for permission to dedicate his *Grave* designs to the Queen.* When the petition was granted, Blake made a vignette sketch to accompany his dedicatory poem. In the illustration and lyric, the Queen is a Thel-like figure who holds in her 'mild Hand' the golden keys to the golden gate of Heaven, the grave: 'And rich and poor around it wait;/O Shepherdess of England's Fold':

> To dedicate to England's Queen
> The Visions that my Soul has seen,
> And, by Her kind permission, bring
> What I have borne on solemn Wing,
> From the vast regions of the Grave,

---

*Humphry, who was fifteen years older then Blake, had left Bath in 1763, upon the encouragement of Reynolds, to settle in London. In 1772 he had to abandon miniatures because of an accident which affected his eyes and, a year later, he went to Italy for four years. Upon his return, Humphry practised in oils; he eventually resumed miniature painting after a three-year stint in India from 1785 to 1788. When miniatures again taxed his weak eyes, he turned to crayons. He became ARA in 1779 and RA in 1791, eventually becoming Portrait Painter in Crayons to the King.

> Before Her Throne my Wings I wave;
> Bowing before my Sov'reign's Feet....[22]

If Blake did not see any inconsistency between rough, experimental engravings which would fail in the marketplace and gratuitous flattery to the monarch, Cromek did – although he was doubtless pleased to place the Queen's name at the head of his list of subscribers. When Blake demanded four guineas for the vignette sketch, the publisher, upon returning the drawing, vented his irritation.

> The Queen allowed *you*, not *me*, to dedicate the work to *her*! The honour would have been yours exclusively, but that you might not be deprived of any advantage likely to contribute to your reputation, I was willing to pay Mr. Schiavonetti *ten* guineas for etching a plate from the drawing in question.[23]

But Cromek was not going to pay Blake four guineas. In fact, he was furious with him: 'You charge me with *imposing upon you*. Upon my honour, I have no recollection of anything of the kind. If the world and I were to settle accounts tomorrow, I do assure you the balance would be considerably in my favour. In this respect *"I am more sinned against than sinning."*'

As far as Cromek was concerned, he was the one imposed upon. He had tried to create a name for Blake: 'I say the labour was Herculean, because I had not only the public to contend with, but I had to battle with a man who had predetermined not to be served.' Blake, Cromek informed him, was his own worst enemy:

> I can honestly and conscientiously assert that if you had laboured thro' life for yourself as zealously and as earnestly as I have done for you, your reputation as an artist would not only have been enviable but it would have placed you on an eminence that would have put it out of the power of an individual, as obscure as myself, either to add to it or take from it. *I also imposed on myself* when I believed what you so often have told me, that your works were equal, nay superiour, to a Raphael or to a Michael Angelo! Unfortunately for me as a publisher, the public awoke me from this state of stupor, this mental delusion. That public is willing to give you credit for what real talent is to be found in your productions, *and for no more*.

Cromek believed that he had acted selflessly, having set out to bestow fame and financial comfort upon Blake:

> I was determined to bring you food as well as reputation, tho' from your

late conduct I have some reason to embrace your wild opinion, that to manage genius, and to cause it to produce good things, it is absolutely necessary to starve it; indeed, this opinion is considerably heightened by the recollection that your best work, the illustrations of 'The Grave', was produced when you and Mrs. Blake were reduced so low as to be obliged to live on half-a-guinea a week.[24]

Since Blake's income from 23 January to 7 September 1805 was at least £37 18s (or 29s per week), Cromek's estimate was very low. In any event, Cromek had felt the twenty guineas he paid for *The Grave* designs more than he could then afford. This galled Blake because Schiavonetti would have received an engraving fee of at least £540, an immense sum for Blake. In addition, he was no doubt aware that Cromek's profit from the edition ran to a substantial sum, somewhere between £300 and £900.[25]

Cromek's May 1807 letter to Blake – written a year before the edition of Blair was published in 1808 – probably brought their relationship to breaking point, as another overlapping incident provided even more hot fat for a raging fire. Towards the end of his letter Cromek exclaimed, somewhat obliquely: 'Why should you so *furiously rage* at the success of the little picture of "The Pilgrimage"? 3,000 people have now *seen it and have approved of it*. Believe me, yours is *"the voice of one crying in the wilderness!"* ' Cromek is referring to the print he was to advertise at the back of the *Grave* volume: *The Procession of Chaucer's Pilgrims to Canterbury*. This engraving – to be sold by subscription – was from 'the well-known cabinet picture' by Thomas Stothard then on exhibition in London. The advertisement concludes with ironies which would have been hateful to Blake: The engraving was to be 'EXECUTED IN THE LINE MANNER OF ENGRAVING, AND IN THE SAME EXCELLENT STYLE AS THE PORTRAIT OF MR. WILLIAM BLAKE, PREFIXED TO THIS WORK by LOUIS SCHIAVONETTI, Esq. V.A. THE GENTLEMAN WHO HAS ETCHED THE PRINTS THAT AT ONCE ILLUSTRATE AND EMBELLISH THE PRESENT VOLUME'.[26]

According to J. T. Smith, Cromek – at about the time the Blair drawings had been completed and before he saw the engraving of *Death's Door* – asked Blake 'what work he had in mind to execute next. The unsuspecting artist not only told him, but without the least reserve showed him the designs sketched out for a fresco picture; the subject Chaucer's "Pilgrimage to Canterbury"; with which Mr. Cromek appeared highly delighted.' Then, shortly afterwards, Blake discovered that Cromek had engaged Thomas Stothard, 'a brother-artist to whom

Canterbury Pilgrims

[Blake] had been extremely kind in early days',[27] to paint such a picture. Cromek, having seen Blake's sketch, supposedly gave instructions to Stothard for a design indebted to Blake, engaged William Bromley to do the engraving, and then switched to Schiavonetti.

Much later, Blake told John Linnell that Cromek 'employed or engaged him to finish the frescoe as he called it of the Canterbury Tales for him for 20 Guineas with the understanding that the remuneration for the whole would be made adequate by the price to be paid to Blake for the Engraving which [Blake] stipulated he should execute'.[28] By any reckoning, this is a strange, twisted tale. Up to this time, Blake had shown little or no interest in Chaucer. Also, Blake did not usually determine what authors he illustrated. In the case of Young, Gray and Blair, he had followed leads given by others.

Although Blake was capable of being mendacious, it is unlikely that he would have claimed that Cromek had seen a non-existent drawing by him, the content and arrangements of which were then passed on to Stothard. A more likely scenario is that Blake's fascination with Chaucer had been aroused by the portrait head of him which he

painted for Hayley's Turret gallery.* After that, he may have become intrigued by the pilgrims as an assortment of various types of persons undertaking a religious journey: this would have given him the opportunity to depict a wide range of responses to man's spiritual destiny, a theme which is clearly evident in the *Grave* illustrations. The topic was most suitable for a person with the desire to tackle history painting.

In the summer of 1805, Cromek, ecstatic about the Blair drawings, may understandably have wanted to discuss with Blake their next enterprise; Blake might have mentioned Chaucer and shown a sketch to Cromek, who approved it. Later, probably early in 1806, Cromek, infuriated with Blake over the *Death's Door* fiasco, approached Stothard about such a project, without informing him of the composition by Blake. If Cromek acted dishonestly, he did so because he was enraged at what he perceived to be Blake's ungrateful conduct. Of course, it could have been Cromek who mooted the Pilgrimage project to Blake. Or Blake could have become interested only after the Cromek–Stothard scheme had been launched.

The timetable of events which can be documented supports Cromek.

---

*In 1783, Blake had engraved a plate after Stothard for an edition of Chaucer.

In May 1807, Stothard exhibited his well-received oil painting of the pilgrims. Blake's 'fresco', dated 1808, was shown by him in 1809; his engraving of the picture was published in October 1810. Cromek's letter of May 1807 does not answer any charge by Blake that he 'stole' an idea from him, which he in turn passed on to Stothard. Curiously, Blake in his now-lost letter to Cromek seems perversely to have claimed that the subject itself was 'low' and 'contemptuously treated' by Stothard. Why, then, did Blake proceed to make a fresco and engrave it? This may well have been as a riposte to Cromek, Stothard and Schiavonetti: Blake's rendition of the pilgrims is done in a decidedly archaic manner, which allows him to juxtapose his primitive style with the oily smoothness favoured by his opponents. His pursuit of the project was also in large part motivated by revenge on the now, for him, infamous trio. Yet again, Blake completely misunderstood the demands of the marketplace, as Allan Cunningham pointed out in 1830: 'The picture is a failure. Blake was too great a visionary for dealing with such literal wantons as the Wife of Bath and her jolly companions. The natural flesh and blood of Chaucer prevailed against him. He gives grossness of body for grossness of mind, – tries to be merry and wicked – and in vain.'[29]

Meanwhile in 1808, if Blake, despite his bitter arguments with Cromek, had hoped for some sort of public acclaim for his *Grave* designs, he was rudely disappointed. In the *Examiner*, Robert Hunt, Leigh's brother, briefly complimented Phillips, Schiavonetti and Blair before launching into a detailed, rigorous examination of the designs. The November issue of the *Antijacobin Review* was also filled with invective against Blake: ' "The Soul hovering over the Body" ... has the same defect of giving *substantial* form to incorporeal substance, and arraying it in earthly habiliments.... Neither do we like the position of the soul, which is bending over the body, in a strained and awkward manner.'[30]

In 1805, Blake had been on the edge of a breakthrough – his name at long last would be brought before an appreciative public who could see his talents as a designer and engraver. Cromek, who worked assiduously to promote the Blair edition, did exactly that. But the financial rewards vanished and the reviews were castigating. Blake remained supremely isolated. In addition to losing the engraving fee for *The Grave*, to having his Chaucer 'idea' stolen, to being subjected to bad notices and to being branded as a difficult eccentric, Blake's dealings with Cromek cost him his friendship with Stothard and further damaged his relationship with Flaxman.

For a long time, Flaxman had turned a harsh eye in Blake's direction, feeling that he had to be purged of his excesses. He was not pleased when he saw how Blake had made use of yet another helping hand. Stothard was insulted by the accusation that he had lifted anything from Blake. In turn, Blake assumed that Flaxman had introduced him to Cromek in order to betray him; also, he was convinced that Stothard had acted treacherously. As young men, Blake, Flaxman, Stothard and Cumberland had been comrades-in-arms. Subsequently, Flaxman and Stothard had thrown work Blake's way and introduced him to potentially useful patrons. That fragile network collapsed in 1807.

Blake's paranoia was unleashed in his Notebook, which includes chilling accounts of his confrontation with his Spectre which 'Like a Wild beast guards my way'. His Emanation 'far within' wept 'incessantly' for his sins.[31] In such bitter moods, Blake jotted down his venomous hatred of those who had wronged him, as in this couplet about Flaxman's duplicity:

> I mock thee not, tho I by thee am Mocked.
> Thou callst me Madman but I call thee Blockhead.[32]

There are equally puerile attacks on Stothard and Cromek:

> S———— in childhood on the Nursery floor
> Was extreme old & most extremely poor.
> He is grown old & rich & what he will
> He is extreme old & extreme poor still.[33]
> Cr— loves artists as he loves his Meat
> He loves the Art but tis the Art to Cheat.[34]

After Cromek's death at the age of forty-two, Blake wrote an extended poem recapitulating his version of his publisher's perfidy:

> Not only in his Mouth his own Soul lay,
> But my Soul also would he bear away.
> Like as a Pedlar bears his weary Pack
> So Stewhard's Soul he buckled to his Back.
> But once alas! committing a Mistake
> He bore the wretched Soul of William Blake,
> That he might turn it into Eggs of Gold;
> But neither Back nor mouth those Eggs could hold.
> His under jaw dropd as those Eggs he laid,
> And Stewhard's Eggs are addled & decayd.

These animadversions are a combination of distorted history and wishful thinking. Here can also be found this sad, poignant outcry, when Blake describes Cromek's motivation in having hired him:

> That Blake would Etch for him & draw for me;
> For twas a kind of Bargain Screwmuch made,
> That Blake's designs should be by us displayed,
> Because he makes designs so very cheap.
> Then Screwmuch at Blake's Soul took a long leap –
> Twas not a Mouse, twas Death in a disguise.[35]

What Blake could not accept was that he had been a bitter disappointment to Cromek, who genuinely hoped to promote visionary art. The misalliance between these two men was not one which came into being because they had radically different ideas about commercial versus artistic integrity. Blake and Cromek were idealists, but Cromek became inflamed when he felt that Blake had betrayed him and the mercantile venture which they had supposedly launched in tandem. In reality, Cromek and Blake were very much alike, as Blake must have momentarily reflected when he read Cromek's obituary notice for Schiavonetti, who died in June 1810 at the age of forty-five. Therein, Cromek laments the crass commerciality 'which insinuates itself into our most refined and disinterested pursuits'. According to him, this was 'the great bar'[36] to the advancement of art in England.

13

A Hidden Life

1808–1818

THOMAS BUTTS's patronage remained an oasis in the desert of opportunities now open to Blake. From 1806 to 1811, he paid over £400 to Blake, who for that sum also gave engraving lessons to Tommy (Blake charged £26 5s 0d per annum for these), although a family legend insists that the father benefited more from these lessons than did the son. Prudently, Butts wanted Tommy to learn a trade that 'he might possess a manual art to serve him as a resource in case of any misfortune such as losing his situation'.[1] Blake, in gratitude, presented Butts with an intricate mahogany 'Apothecary's Cabinet' – $18\frac{1}{2}''$ by $16\frac{1}{8}''$ by $7\frac{1}{2}''$ – in which to hold his engraving tools. The Buttses and the Blakes continued to socialize and, when his parents were out of town in August 1809, Tommy visited the Blakes, who were 'very well'. Husband and wife dexterously and gently assured the self-conscious young man that he had become 'browner and taller'.[2]

Through Tommy, Blake in about 1809 met the twenty-one-year-old Seymour Stocker Kirkup, who lived in London at Leicester Place. In that year, Kirkup, with the assistance of Fuseli, was issued a ticket as one of the first 'Students Admitted to the Gallery of Antiquities' in the British Museum. Kirkup, also a student at the Royal Academy Schools, where he won a medal, had studied with Flaxman as well as Fuseli. He was surprised by Blake's praise of these two men, since he considered their work so different from his. He found Blake amiable and generous, although he was shocked at his disdain for the 'colourists', particularly Titian, whom Kirkup greatly admired. The callow young man thought Blake 'mad' although, later, he repented that rash judgement. Kirkup was moved by Catherine's devotion to her husband, recalling her observation, 'I have very little of Mr Blake's company; he is always in Paradise.'[3] Another pupil at that time was William Seguier, later the first Keeper of the National Gallery.[4]

In his series of tempera illustrations to the Bible, Blake had flirted with the possibility of turning in the direction of Venetian and Flemish art. Upon his return to London, he began for Butts a series of watercolour illustrations to the Bible. These new pictures – a return to Blake's rectilinear neo-classical style of the 1780s and 1790s – are far less domestic and homely than the earlier set. More radiantly coloured, these pictures – which were probably intended for an extra-illustrated Bible – have a freshness and vibrancy absent in the other series. Blake no longer felt constrained to limit himself to the tradition of biblical illustrations, the new pictures being more idiosyncratic.

Since he was adding to the tempera series, Blake felt freer in 1803–5 to concentrate on subjects which intrigued him: the life of Moses, the visions of Isaiah and Ezekiel, the Psalms, and additional scenes from the Acts of the Apostles and the Apocalypse. On the one hand, Moses is depicted as a messenger of a Urizenic God, but, on the other, Moses, the defiant opponent of Pharaoh, is shown as a prophet, whose courageous determination anticipates another outsider: Christ the revolutionary. From 1803 to 1805, Blake, in a similar manner, was trying to separate out conflicting notions within himself: did he want to serve Mammon in the form of Hayley and Cromek or did he want to pursue his own imaginative course which divorced him from the external world?

In the terrifying *The Great Red Dragon and the Women Clothed with the Sun*, Blake depicts Revelation 12: 1–4, wherein the monster waits to devour the infant who is just about to be born. The beast, a symbol of temporal force, is authorized by Satan to wage war against the saints. Here, Blake chillingly evokes a cannibalistic maniac, his own fear of becoming embroiled with materialism finding the perfect objective correlative.

Blake's deepest expression of the inner turmoil which beset him in the early 1800s can be seen in his watercolour illustrations to the Book of Job, a narrative which had been a source of fascination to him as early as 1785. In his earlier renditions, Blake had characterized the

The Great Red Dragon and the Woman Clothed with the Sun

Old Testament figure as a person whom God allows to be tormented in order to ascertain that he, even under terrible strife, will remain faithful. God does this because Satan has pointed out that Job persists in his loyalty only because he has enjoyed prosperity. Despite his increasing conviction that he has been unjustly punished, Job clings to his God, proving that he loves his creator under any and all circumstances.

When he made his series of watercolours for Butts, Blake transformed the story. In this rendition, Job is a prosperous merchant who, like his biblical counterpart, has never really examined his raison d'être. He has unquestioningly accepted the good fortune which has been bestowed upon him. When this Job suffers material deprivation, he gradually begins to realize that the God he has worshipped all his life is simply a narcissistic equivalent to himself. Moreover, he learns that this Urizenic God is really Satan. This gruelling truth is revealed in *Job's Evil Dream* – based on the 1795 colour print, *Elohim Creating Adam* – where the feet of God have metamorphosed into the cloven hoof of the devil.

Job comes to understand that he has – unknowingly – been the servant of corrupt materialism, symbolized by Behemoth and Leviathan. For example, Job had previously assisted the poor, but he had performed such actions solely out of obligation. As he comes to fathom the errors of his ways, he is able to accept a piece of money offered to him. The knowledge which Job painfully acquires separates him from his so-called 'comforters', who continue with an existence he must now renounce.

Like the Universal Man in *Vala*, Milton in the illuminated book of that name, and Albion in *Jerusalem*, Job realizes that he has simply slept through most of his existence, divorced from the things which should matter the most. In the very first illustration, Job and his family are seated in a pastoral setting. Husband and wife lead the assemblage in worship, their words of prayer derived from the books that nestle in their laps. The musical instruments – overhanging from the tree in the background – are neglected. In the final, companion illustration, the same group stands, many of them – including Job and his wife – playing the previously discarded instruments. Now, their prayers come from within their hearts. Some of the somnolent sheep of the earlier illustration have been awakened by the proclamation of a new dispensation.

In *Job and his Daughters*, the penultimate watercolour, a serene, calm Job tells his three children of the chaotic spiritual crisis in which he

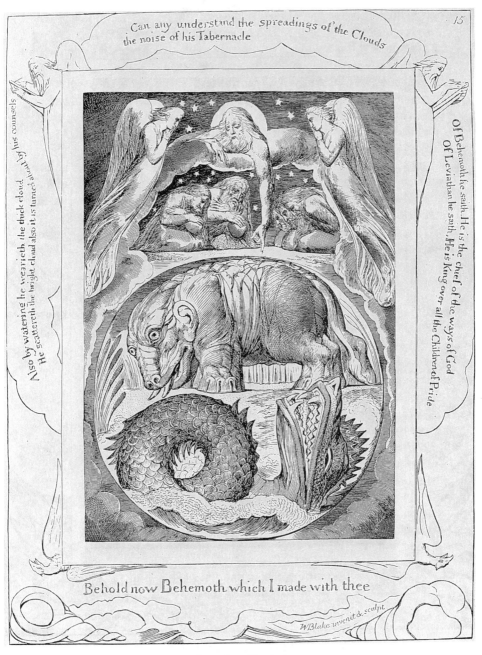

Behemoth and Leviathan

once existed and they – representing painting, poetry and music – will convert that experience into the order of art. Here, Blake is analysing his own dedication as an artist: an outsider, he endures the agony of exclusion. His suffering is worthwhile because it provides him with an awareness of the underlying sordidness of existence; most men are not in touch with this realm, and it is his responsibility to make works of art which will help to change them. Blake's messianic zeal is evident: the chaos he endures in the material world is bearable if he can point mankind in the right direction.

The Job watercolours are a stirring testimonial to Blake's inability to modify his inner world to the demands of London. Unlike the Old Testament Job, Blake does not see himself as the plaything of a whimsical God who makes a wager with Satan: he has been privileged to see into the real truths of life, and he is willing to pay the price for such wisdom.

A good friend in the early 1800s was Benjamin Heath Malkin, the headmaster of Bury Grammar School and twelve years Blake's junior, who was enamoured of picturesque scenery and radical politics. Malkin subscribed to *The Grave*, for which he offered to write a preface. In 1805, he bought a copy of *Songs of Innocence*, which he presented to a friend as a gift.

One bond shared by Malkin with Blake was an obsession with death. In 1802, Malkin's son, Thomas William, died at the age of six, and in 1805 Malkin was writing a memoir of that child, which was published in 1806 with a frontispiece designed by Blake and engraved by Cromek. So touched was Malkin by Blake, the 'Gothic monument',[5] that he wrote a biographical notice about him which he interpolated into *A Father's Memoirs of His Child* by way of an introductory letter to his friend Thomas Johnes of Hafod.

A profounder reason for Malkin's enthusiastic response to Blake was that he had seen a link between his own son as prodigy – linguist, historian, topographer, designer, copyist – and Blake's description of himself as a similarly endowed child. The still distraught father had been moved when Blake, after seeing the boy's drawings, admired their 'firm, determinate outline' and concluded that Thomas's 'efforts prove this little boy to have had that greatest of all blessings, a strong imagination, a clear idea, and a determinate vision of things in his own mind'.[6] Blake, whose design incorporates a portrait with a depiction of an angel guiding the child heavenward, had responded warmly to the child's creation of the imaginary land of Allestone with place names such as Bubblebop and Punchpeach.

Other friends tried to find employment for Blake. Early in 1808, the ever generous Ozias Humphry arranged for Blake to do a watercolour of the Last Judgement for the Countess of Egremont. Later, in endeavouring to find further work for him, Humphry asked Blake to provide him with a copy of a letter he had written explicating the painting. Humphry then sent this to another possible patron, David Steuart Erskine, eleventh Duke of Buchan. As their exchange of letters in December 1808 testifies, George Cumberland, in addition to arousing interest among friends and acquaintances in the illuminated books by showing them his own copies of *Thel, America, Visions, Song of Los* and *Songs of Innocence and Experience*, continually strove to befriend Blake by publicizing his 'new method of engraving'.[7]

However, Blake had abandoned that pursuit because he was putting his energies into 'a new channel', as he told Cumberland:

New Vanities, or rather new pleasures, occupy my thoughts. New profits seem to arise before me so tempting that I have already involved myself in engagements that preclude all possibility of promising any thing. I have, however, the satisfaction to inform you that I have Myself begun to print an account of my various Inventions in Art, for which I have procured a Publisher, & am determind to pursue the plan of publishing what I may get printed without disarranging my time, which in future must alone be devoted to Designing & Painting....[8]

This letter, which describes his attempt in the *Descriptive Catalogue* to present himself yet one more time to an unappreciative public, encapsulates Blake's increasing dissatisfaction with verbal expression. In the future, he wanted to focus on designing, painting and engraving.

With the single exception of Thomas Butts, Blake was fully aware by 1808 that his bids to find sponsorship had not met with any consistent response. As his letter to Cumberland also indicates, Blake realized that he had become involved in too wide a variety of activities. In order to achieve success, he would have to promote himself in a more precise, delineated manner. Blake's stratagem was to hold in 1809 a one-man show at his brother's house in Broad Street and to write a catalogue in which he explained and defended his seemingly idiosyncratic practices as an artist.*

* One indication of Blake's unwillingness to eschew public recognition was his submission of *Jacob's Dream* and *Christ in the Sepulchre* to the exhibition at the Royal Academy in May 1808. However, a year later, Blake felt that there was a prejudice there against watercolours, which led that institution and the British Institution to exclude him.

The sixteen items selected for display at James Blake's house included *Sir Jeffrey Chaucer and the Nine and Twenty Pilgrims on Their Journey to Canterbury*, a new *Bard, from Gray, A Subject from Shakespeare, Satan Calling Up His Legions, Angels Hovering Over the Body of Jesus in the Sepulchre* and *The Penance of Jane Shore*. This is a very concentrated exhibition, emphasizing as it does Blake's dedication to historical and literary topics in the tradition of West, Barry and Mortimer, thus laying claim to distinction in the highest calling to which an English artist could aspire. Blake could not be silent about the failings of 'official' art, wryly observing that the 'eye that can prefer the Colouring of Titian and Rubens to that of Michael Angelo and Rafael, ought to be modest and doubt its own powers'.[9] Blake's obsessive hatred of oil painting even leads him to pen a distorted history of Western art:

> All Frescos are as high finished as miniatures or enamels, and they are known to be unchangeable; but oil being a body itself, will drink or absorb very little colour, and changing yellow, and at length brown, destroys every colour it is mixed with, especially every delicate colour. . . . All the genuine old little Pictures, called Cabinet Pictures, are in fresco and not in oil. Oil was not used except by blundering ignorance, till after Vandyke's time, but the art of fresco painting being lost, oil became a fetter to genius, and a dungeon to art.[10]

This denigration of oil painting is based upon the assumption that it destroys outline in favour of rich, tonal values. According to Blake, this is a situation where meaning has been displaced by method.

> The Venetian and Flemish practice is broken lines, broken masses, and broken colours. Mr. B.'s practice is unbroken lines, unbroken masses, and unbroken colours. Their art is to lose form, his art is to find form, and to keep it. His arts are opposite to theirs in all things.[11]

Blake's new antipathy to Greek art can be discerned, this being a false art which merely imitates the true inspiration latent only in Hebrew art.

Blake also took the opportunity to launch invective against Cromek:

> The painter courts comparison with his competitors, who, having received fourteen hundred guineas and more from the profits of his designs, in that well-known work, Designs for Blair's Grave, have left him to shift for himself, while others, more obedient to an employer's opinions and directions, are employed, at a great expense, to produce works, in succession to his, by which they acquire public patronage.[12]

Blake's phrase – 'more obedient to an employer's opinions and directions' – is a precise delineation of the opposition between himself and
Cromek. Then, quite accurately and chillingly, Blake describes the
outcome of such disputes: 'This has hitherto been [the] lot [of an artist
such as Blake] – to get patronage for others and then to be left and
neglected, and his work, which gained that patronage, cried down as
eccentricity and madness; as unfinished and neglected by the artist's
violent temper. He is sure the works now exhibited will give the lie to
such aspersions.'[13]

Cromek's advertisement – included in the 1808 edition of *The Grave* –
for Stothard's engraving of his *Procession* de-emphasized both the
allegorical and visionary aspects of *The Canterbury Tales*. Blake accen-
tuates Chaucer's ability to create a narrative in which 'the characters
... compose all ages and nations: as one age falls, another rises,
different to mortal sight, but to immortals only the same.... Accident
ever varies, Substance can never suffer change nor decay.'[14] The
Catalogue and the exhibition poignantly closed with *Jane Shore*: 'This
Drawing was done above Thirty Years ago, and proves to the Author,
and he thinks will prove to any discerning eye, that the productions
of our youth and of our maturer age are equal in all essential points.'[15]
Having solicited public attention yet again, Blake ends on a disdainful –
but wistful – note:

> If a man is master of his profession, he cannot be ignorant that he is so;
> and if he is not employed by those who pretend to encourage art, he will
> employ himself, and laugh in secret at the pretences of the ignorant,
> while he has every night dropped into his shoe, as soon as he puts it off,
> and puts out the candle, and gets into bed, a reward for the labours of
> the day, such as the world cannot give, and patience and time await to
> give him all that the world can give.[16]

Although the exhibition of Blake's paintings at his brother's house
opened about the middle of May 1809 and was supposed to close that
September, the thirty-five-year-old gossip and journalist Henry Crabb
Robinson* made his way there the following May: 'The Entrance was
2/6, Catalogue included. I was deeply interested by the Catalogues as

---

* Robinson had become obsessed – through some casual words spoken by Elizabeth Iremonger,
a Unitarian 'literary lady' of Upper Grosvenor Street – with the 'insane poet, painter & engraver'
Blake (*BR*, p. 223). This led him to collect as much information about him as he could. Trained
as a lawyer, Robinson had travelled in Germany from 1800 to 1802 and had met, among others,
Goethe and Schiller. For ten years from 1803, Robinson worked as a journalist, his chief employer
being *The Times*. He was fascinated by writers and artists, particularly those of a highly imaginative

well as the pictures. I took four – telling the brother I hoped he would let me come in again – He said – "Oh! as often as you please" – I dare say such a thing had never happened before or did afterwards.'[17] In turn, Robinson persuaded Robert Southey to visit the exhibition. Southey was especially dismayed by *The Ancient Britons* (now missing): 'one of his worst pictures, – which is saying much; and he has illustrated it with one of the most curious commentaries in his very curious and very rare descriptive Catalogue of his own Pictures'.[18]

Robert Hunt, who had viciously attacked Blake's designs for *The Grave* in the *Examiner*, savaged him again in the 17 September 1809 issue of the same magazine, where he characterized the artist as 'an unfortunate lunatic, whose personal inoffensiveness secures him from confinement, and, consequently, of whom no public notice would have been taken, if he was not forced on the notice and animadversion of the EXAMINER, in having been held up to public admiration by many esteemed amateurs and professors as a genius in some respect original and legitimate'.[19] Added to vituperation was sarcasm in commenting on *The Ancient Britons*: 'This picture is a complete caricature: one of the bards is singing to his harp in the pangs of death; and though the colouring of the flesh is exactly like hung beef, the artist modestly observes – "The flush of health in flesh, exposed to the open air, nourished by the spirits of forests and floods, in that ancient happy period, which history has recorded, cannot be like the sickly daubs of Titian and Rubens."'[20] George Cumberland, who did not attend the exhibition, perused the *Catalogue* carefully and judiciously told his son: 'Blake's Cat is truly original – part vanity, part madness – part very good sense.'[21]

Blake's outrage at his exclusion from the art establishment is thunderously annunciated in his 'Public Address', written two or three years after the *Catalogue*. Blake's dispute with Cromek is rehearsed yet again, the emphasis this time being devoted to the public perception that Blake has a vivid imagination but cannot focus it in a satisfactory way:

> the Lavish praise I have recievd from all Quarters for Invention & Drawing has Generally been accompanied by this: 'he can concieve but he cannot Execute.' This Absurd assertion has done me, & may still do me, the greatest mischief. I call for Public protection against these Villains. I am like others, Just Equal in Invention & in Execution....[22]

turn, and his diary contains nuggets of information on Flaxman, Coleridge, Lamb, Wordsworth and Hazlitt.

However, Blake's deeply divided feelings about invention and execution are enshrined on the previous page in the Notebook, where he proclaims: 'I know my Execution is not like Any Body Else. . . . None but Blockheads Copy one another.'[23]*

By 1811, Blake's paranoia and surliness moved him even more to the edge of complete isolation. He was a Christ cast adrift in the wilderness of London. Thomas Butts, who had lent some of his acquisitions back to Blake for the 1809 exhibition, 'grew cool'. He found it increasingly difficult *not* to irritate the prickly artist 'ever the prouder for his poverty and neglect, always impracticable and extreme when ruffled or stroked the wrong way'. In turn, Butts took offence 'at

---

* Blake's marginalia to Reynolds (made 1801–2, 1808–9) are filled with sentiments similar in tone and belief to those espoused in the *Catalogue* and 'Public Address': 'To My Eye Rubens's Colouring is most Contemptible. His Shadows are of a Filthy Brown somewhat of the Colour of Excrement; these are filld with tints & messes of yellow & red' (*Writings*, p. 655). But Blake realizes that Reynolds, who genuinely understood the conflict between line and colouring, has placed Poussin in opposition to Rubens: 'but he ought to put All Men of Genius who ever Painted' there so that it would be fully recognized that 'Rubens & the Venetians are Opposite in every thing to True Art & they Meant to be so; they were hired for this Purpose' (ibid.).

In fact, Reynolds and Blake acquiesced on many things: they both espoused the grand historical style; they sought an art which embodied ideal beauty; they were both anxious to promote a distinctive English school. Ultimately, they agreed on ends – not means. For Blake, Reynolds was a Satanic figure who, knowing the right but difficult road, had chosen the path of ease. Blake envied Reynolds his adroit political sense which allowed him to balance opposing views in an attempt at synthesis. Blake, who had had an unsatisfactory stint as a portrait painter, despised the wealth such specialization had brought the older artist. For Blake, Reynolds's existence had been one of mediation and arbitration, and he satirizes the life of the portrait painter who must, of course, use oils:

> Some look to see the sweet Outlines
> And beauteous Forms that Love does wear;
> Some look to find out Patches, Paint,
> Bracelets & Stays & Powderd Hair. (ibid., p. 637)

Blake, very much in the manner of an envious pauper staring at a wealthy man's possessions, attacks Reynolds's ability to do something which he simply could not do: compromise.

> I consider Reynolds's Discourse to the Royal Academy as the Simulations of the Hypocrite who Smiles particularly where he means to Betray. His Praise of Rafael is like the Hysteric Smile of Revenge, His Softness & Candour, the hidden trap, & the poisoned feast. (ibid., p. 642)

Blake's fragile sense of himself as the wild, rebellious artist surfaces when Reynolds comments that the lives of the most eminent painters testify to the fact 'that no part of their time was spent in dissipation'.

> The Lives of Painters say that Rafael Died of Dissipation. Idleness is one Thing & Dissipation Another. He who has Nothing to Dissipate Cannot Dissipate; the Weak Man may be Virtuous Enough but will Never be an Artist.
> Painters are noted for being Dissipated & Wild. (ibid., pp. 643–4)

Here, Blake tenuously clings to the self-imposed notion of himself as an heroic figure who, of necessity, remains alienated from prevailing norms.

Christ in the Wilderness

Blake's quick resentment of well-meant, if blunt, advice and at the unmeasured violence of his speech when provoked by opposition'.[24]

Blake's resulting financial slump can be gleaned in his dealings with the young Charles Henry Bellenden Ker, later a prominent legal reformer, who, greatly admiring Blake's designs for *The Grave* but being unable to purchase a copy, innocently told Blake in 1808 that he expected a protracted legal case to be settled in his favour and, when that happened, wanted Blake 'at [his] leisure' to make two drawings which he then would be able to afford. After a hiatus of two years, the drawings arrived with a bill for twenty guineas. As Ker told George Cumberland, who had probably introduced him to Blake, he was startled: 'Now I was I assure you thunderstruck as you as well as he must know that in my present circumstances it is ludicrous to fancy I can or am able to pay 20Gs. for 2 Drawings not Knowing Where in the World [to] get any money.' Ker did not think the haphazard means he had used to commission these works required him to pay, but Blake had anticipated such a turn: 'now he desired in his note that the money was paid in a fortnight or part of it – intimating he should take hostile Mode if it was not'.

If he attempted to do so, Cumberland did not reconcile the disputants. First, Ker offered to pay fifteen guineas. This was refused. Then he proposed a number of compromises: the price should be determined by mutual friends; he would be willing to pay ten guineas and the remaining ten three months later. Both offers were declined. Finally, Blake had Ker arrested for the debt and defended the action, as the embarrassed young man recalled: 'now perhaps his obstinacy will never get a shilling of the 20L. he originally intended to defraud me of'. Ultimately, Ker was made to pay thirty guineas. As far as he was concerned, Blake had acted 'infamously'.[25*]

Blake stretched statute to its letter – not its spirit – in his dealings with Ker, clinging to the merest shred of a commission in a blatantly legalistic manner. He was desperate. For the next five years, Blake can be glimpsed only intermittently, as when Southey visited him in July 1811 and held him a 'decided madman'.[26] Blake submitted four entries to the 1812 exhibition of the Water Colour Society, including specimen pages from *Jerusalem*. In the following year, he was working on an engraving of Thomas Phillips's portrait of the Earl Spencer. When Cumberland called upon him in June 1814, he found him 'still poor, still Dirty'.[27]

Once, when a young artist called upon him and complained of bad health, Blake burst out: 'Oh! I never stop for anything; I work on, whether ill or not.'[28] This is no doubt a true story, but it makes Blake's life from 1808 to 1818 even more of a mystery. After *The Grave*, approximately sixty-five commercial engravings – most of this work being directed his way only because of the persistence and power of John Flaxman – by Blake were published until 1819. Little money would have been forthcoming for approximately six engravings per year, and there were few people, like Ker, whom Blake could dun. Occasional sales of the illuminated books and engravings augmented his slender income.

John Flaxman, in yet another attempt to help the destitute couple, asked Blake to make thirty-seven engravings from his Hesiod designs, which were published in 1816 and 1817. One day, when Flaxman was discussing history painting with the translator, Henry Francis Cary, the sculptor mentioned Blake. Cary responded: 'But Blake is a

---

*No document in the Public Record Office indicates that Blake had Ker arrested and that the case subsequently went to trial; the matter may have been settled out of court.

wild enthusiast, isn't he?' Affronted, the loyal friend drew himself up: 'Some think me an enthusiast.'[29]

Cumberland's sons, George and Sydney, calling upon William and Catherine in April 1816, found them 'drinking Tea, durtyer than ever'.[30] Blake showed them 'his large drawing in Water Colors of the last Judgement'. George informed his father: 'he has been labouring at it till it is nearly as black as your Hat – the only lights are those of a *Hellish Purple*.'[31] At about this time, William Sharp, renowned as an eccentric because of his devotion to Joanna Southcott and other millennial seers, tried to convert his fellow engraver, who was not 'fond of playing the second fiddle – Hence Blake himself a seer of visions & a dreamer of dreams would not do homage to a rival claimant of the privilege of prophecy.'[32] This anecdote was recorded by the sometimes gullible Crabb Robinson, whom Flaxman had told early in 1815 'that [Blake] had had a violent dispute with the Angels on some subject and had driven them away'.[33]

When Blake was invited in the spring of 1815 to engrave Laocoön for Flaxman's article on sculpture in Rees's *Cyclopaedia*, he visited the Royal Academy at Somerset House. While Blake was quietly sketching, Fuseli came upon him: 'What! you here, *Meesther Blake?* We ought to come and learn of you, not you of us.'[34] William Ensom, a young student at the Royal Academy, witnessing Blake's simple joy at the compliment, asked him to sit to him. The resulting, now lost pen-and-ink portrait won a silver medal in a competition sponsored in May 1815 by the Society for the Encouragement of Arts, Manufactures and Commerce. The young artist even gave the older man a much needed order for a coloured copy of the *Night Thoughts* volume.

Flaxman threw more work Blake's way in 1815 when he arranged for Josiah Wedgwood Jr. to employ Blake, to make engravings for the salesmen's pattern-books. Blake undertook eighteen designs and engravings, for which he received £30 in November 1816. There were other random sales. The Swedenborgian Charles Augustus Tulk purchased a copy of *Songs of Innocence and Experience*, which he gave to Coleridge.

Also in 1816, Blake aggravated another potential patron – possibly Tulk – to whom John and Nancy Flaxman had introduced him. As Nancy told her husband, Blake's conduct had yet again been unseemly:

It is true he did not give him anything, for he thought It would be wrong so to do after what pass'd between them, for, as I understand, B___ was very violent. Indeed beyond *all credence*, only that he has served you his *best friend* the *same trick some* time back, as you must well remember – but he *bought a drawing* of him. I have nothing to say in this affair. It is too tickilish, only I know what has happened both to yourself & me, & other people are not oblig'd to put up with B's odd humours – but let that pass.[35]

When John Gibson, a young sculptor from Liverpool, presented himself to Blake, the older artist, who showed him some designs, lamented 'the want of feeling in England for high art'.[36] Catherine supported her husband's contentions; not surprisingly, 'she was very bitter upon the subject'.[37]

By the late 1810s, Blake had become a legendary shadow, who could merit a rather full entry as an eccentric in *A Biographical Dictionary of the Living Authors of Great Britain and Ireland* (1816). In January 1818, Blake was even summoned to the table of Lady Caroline Lamb, Byron's sometime mistress and companion in masochism. Sir Thomas Lawrence was also there. According to the diarist Lady Charlotte Bury, the hostess had gathered together a 'strange party of artists and literati, and one or two fine folks, who were very ill assorted with the rest of the company'.[38]

If oddity had been Lady Caroline's aim, she succeeded admirably in the case of the 'little artist', who appeared to Lady Charlotte 'care-worn and subdued'. However, his 'countenance radiated' when he spoke of his commitment to his own brand of art. Next to the fashionably dressed Sir Thomas, Blake looked out of place. In fact, the diarist saw Lawrence's 'lips curl with a sneer, as if he despised me for conversing with so insignificant a person'. Despite this, Lady Charlotte remained impressed by Blake's imagination and genius, but she intuitively understood that he was 'unlearned in all that concerns the world'.[39] Later, Lawrence must have repented of his smirk: he commissioned two watercolours from his fellow artist.

Although they no longer saw each other, Butts probably directed money William's way through James Blake, who closed his shop in 1812.* Significantly, James's name appears in the *Imperial Calendar* in 1814, 1815 and 1816 as one of the clerks of the Commissary General of Musters, a post probably obtained by Butts.[40] In November 1802, James had been privy to Butts's displeasure at William's tardiness in delivering work, as the opening sentence of Blake's letter to his mentor

---

* Although no longer in touch with Blake, Butts purchased in the mid-1810s his sets of Blake's watercolour illustrations to Milton's *Comus, On the Morning of Christ's Nativity, L'Allegro* and *Il Penseroso.*

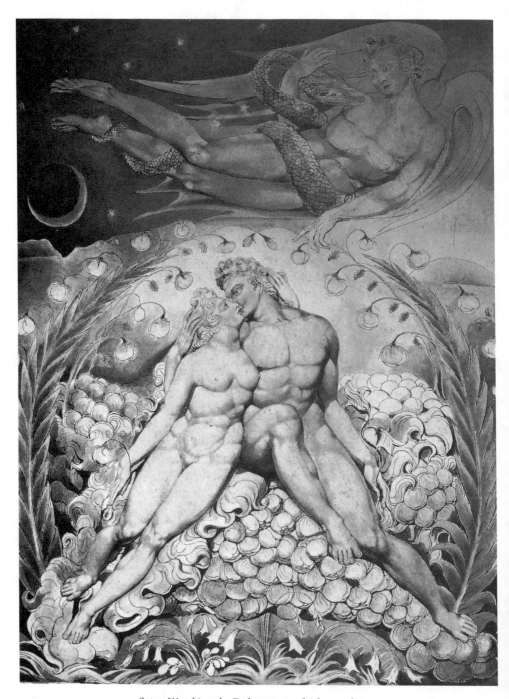

Satan Watching the Endearments of Adam and Eve

Milton in his Old Age

testifies: 'My Brother tells me that he fears you are offended with me.'[41] Butts no doubt hoped the elder brother would chastise his dilatory sibling; the letter also indicates that James Blake and Thomas Butts had forged some sort of alliance early in the 1800s. By the 1820s, the breach between William and James 'widened'. The brothers did not speak, James looking 'upon his erratic brother with pity and blame, as a wilful, misguided man, wholly in a wrong track'.[42]

In haphazard ways, the Blakes contrived to live uncomfortably on about a guinea a week. Constant, degrading penury had certainly taken its toll on Catherine, who now looked coarse and common, the dresses that she wore being often filthy. 'The traces of past beauty' – evident in her 'gleaming black eyes' – served to heighten the melancholy of her appearance. Unlike her husband, who treated his visions with a touch of irony, she maintained a *'literal* belief' in her husband's sighting of historical personages, such as King Alfred. Later, Alexander Gilchrist's investigations led him to some inescapable conclusions.

Not only was she wont to echo what he said, to talk as he talked, on religion and other matters – this may be accounted for by the fact that he had educated her; but she, too, learned to have visions; – to see processions of figures wending along the river, in broad daylight; and would give a start when they disappeared in the water.[43]

Like her husband, Catherine's sense of paranoia was easily aroused; this manifested itself as 'an exaggerated suspiciousness, for instance, and even jealousy of his friends'.[44] As they got older, the marriage of William and Catherine became more tranquil. In conversation, the elderly artist once asked a question he considered rhetorical: 'Do you think if I came home, and discovered my wife to be unfaithful, I should be so foolish as to take it ill?' His respondent was not quite so sure of stoical behaviour on Blake's part: 'I am inclined to think (despite the philosophic boast) it would have gone ill with the offenders.'[45]

In addition to the few engraving tasks that came his way, Blake sporadically worked on *Milton* and *Jerusalem* from 1808 to 1818. However, as he himself indicated, he was no longer interested in poetry. To a large extent, he had come to see that his ideas were best encapsulated visually. One task to which he did devote a great deal of attention in that hidden decade was his series of illustrations to Milton for Thomas Butts and Joseph Thomas, for whom he had illustrated *Comus* in 1801. These illustrations are rendered in a two-dimensional style in which the pictorial elements are blended in a much more richly coloured way than in any previous set of Blake watercolours.

In both sets of pictures to *Paradise Lost*, Christ is freely acknowledged to be the hero of Milton's epic poem. Blake is now much more suspicious of Satan than he was when he embedded his critique of *Paradise Lost* into *The Marriage of Heaven and Hell*. Although he remains distrustful of Eve, there is a serene sexual harmony in these pictures, as in *Satan Watching the Endearments of Adam and Eve*. Satan is now a voyeur, who pruriently observes the love-making of the beautiful couple.

A softer acceptance of the privations of human existence can also be glimpsed in these Milton illustrations. As he reached sixty, Blake finally let go of the envy and jealousy which had consumed much of the previous ten years. Why was he able to purge himself of these feelings? Part of the answer lies in his ability to concede that he was nearing the end of his life.

In *Milton in his Old Age*, the Job-like poet sits in his 'Mossy Cell Contemplating the Constellations, Surrounded by the Spirits of Herbs & Flowers' and 'bursts forth into' rhapsody. Blake is illustrating the lines from *Il Penseroso*: 'Till old Experience do attain / To somewhat like Prophetic Strain'. Like Job and Milton, Blake, having endured the hardships of this earth, can at long last look forward to a new, eternal existence.

14

An Antique Patriarch

1818–1827

IN 1818 Blake was regarded as a scrappy eccentric who had proved to be consistently difficult in all business dealings. As he himself knew, his designs were considered suspect and his 'execution' disgraceful. However, this recluse had gradually achieved – through his identification with Christ and through his attempt to redeem Milton – the inner peace which had eluded him since he had returned to London from Felpham.

That June, his interest aroused by Ozias Humphry, Dawson Turner, the banker, botanist, antiquary and collector, wrote to ask for a price list of the illuminated work. Blake provided this but went on to make two unrealistic claims:

> The few I have Printed & Sold are sufficient to have gained me great reputation as an Artist, which was the chief thing Intended. But I have never been able to produce a Sufficient number for a general Sale by means of a regular Publisher.[1]

Any 'reputation' that Blake had was not based on such books. If Joseph Johnson, Richard Edwards and Robert Cromek had been aware of the existence of such work, they had shown no interest in marketing it. Again, Blake's inability to come to terms with the way of the world is evident.

However, having largely abandoned hope for recognition, Blake was suddenly rediscovered in 1818 by thirty-five-year-old John Linnell, who adroitly helped the older man to garner some of the renown which had evaded him. In many respects, both men shared a common economic heritage. Linnell, born in Plumtree Street in Bloomsbury, was the son of a framemaker, picture-dealer and print-seller. Soon after his birth, John and his family moved to Streatham Street, also in Bloomsbury, where by the age of ten the future artist had developed into an adept copyist and portraitist. Like Blake years earlier, young Linnell haunted the auction houses. In 1805, he entered the Royal Academy Schools and two years later, at the age of fifteen, he was awarded a medal for his drawings from life. Three years later, this precocious young man was producing high-quality drawings and oils of landscape subjects.

Although Linnell's training was not the rigorous seven-year apprenticeship served by Blake, he was a much more proficient engraver than Blake. His handling of the minutiae of that calling was certainly more sophisticated and polished, particularly his agility in the use of 'fine lines and flick work, the multiple layering of patterns crossing at a variety of angles, and the use of white areas ... to define' surfaces.[2]

Why Linnell became fascinated with the outsider Blake is something of a mystery. When he was introduced to Blake in June 1818 by George Cumberland's son – also George – Linnell was well on his way to the commercial, popular success which would make him a rich man. Blake precariously lived on £50 a year; Linnell expected to earn five guineas a day. He would sometimes charge patrons £10 10s 0d for as much as he could paint of a portrait in two days.[3] There was a slight overlap in religious beliefs: Linnell was vigorously anticlerical and antisabbatarian; he also avowed the existence of a transcendental reality beyond the material. According to his eldest daughter, his was an 'angry, intolerant religion unattached to any sect ... revealed by God to him alone'.[4] However, Linnell, like Wordsworth, found traces of the supernatural in nature whereas Blake located such intimations in the self. Oil, Linnell's favourite medium, was abhorrent to Blake.

The young man was a brilliant entrepreneur, who could be predatory, as when he took Blake in April 1820 to the Old Water-Colour Society exhibition at the Great Room in Spring Gardens. There, Linnell espied the Duke of Argyll, who owed him money for a portrait of the Duchess. Without any trepidation, Linnell 'dunned him for money due',[5] the embarrassed peer appointing the next day for payment. Often Linnell engaged in shoddy business practices. Eager to clear space in his studio, he would pack an oil painting before it was completely dry – often in an old or mouldy case. Of course, such canvases arrived irretrievably damaged, but, since Linnell demanded full payment before delivery, little recourse was left to abused patrons.

Linnell's grasping temperament often concealed a bountiful heart, but, in the main, he was a rigid disciplinarian who craved financial stability. Blake had broken with Hayley because he could not replicate his haphazard but canny ability to market himself. Cromek was not as astute a businessman as Linnell. And yet those two relationships had been destroyed. By 1818, Blake's rage at his insolvent condition had lessened considerably, his ability to tolerate a friendship with a man such as Linnell being a barometer of this transformation.

Ultimately, Blake could develop a fast friendship with Linnell because they were such opposites. In the main, Hayley and Cromek had been sympathetic to Blake, anxious to promote a person whose concept of art varied from the standards of the world. Deeply at odds with the Blakean sublime, Linnell could nevertheless appreciate Blake's work and, he realized, he could do two things for him: he could show him how to sell himself in the marketplace, and he could prod him to compromise. Cromek had been unequal to this very task; Hayley had interfered with Blake's notion of himself as a painter. Now Blake welcomed such interference from Linnell.

What did Linnell gain from espousing Blake? At close quarters, this young businessman saw an artist who fervently clung to ideals disdained by his colleagues. The older man's commitment enthralled – and moved – Linnell. Nevertheless, he could not singlemindedly devote himself to such a pursuit. His ambivalence is captured in his description of one of his first meetings with Blake:

> I soon encountered Blake's peculiarities and [was] somewhat taken aback by the boldness of some of his assertions. I never saw anything the least like madness for I never opposed him spitefully as many did, but being really anxious to fathom if possible the amount of truth which might be in his most startling assertions, I generally met with a sufficiently rational explanation.[6]

By being a generous friend to Blake, he was able to keep in touch with alienated aspects of himself. In so doing, he could preserve his own visionary powers while still retaining his trust in the 'rational'.

A strong fraternal bond also held Blake and Linnell together. Since Robert's death in 1787, Blake had not experienced any kind of friendship which even in small part replicated that loss. Hayley had offered Blake the possibility of such a relationship, but he had been rebuffed.

The simple truth is that Blake could not have endured such a bond during the years when his feelings of envy were constantly being roused by Hayley, Flaxman and Stothard. At the age of sixty, he found a profound sense of renewal by acting as an elder brother to Linnell.

When he met Blake, the newly married Linnell, aware of Blake's impecunious state, immediately promised to get work for him: 'I employed him to help me with an engraving of my portrait of Mr Upton, a Baptist preacher, which he was glad to do, having scarcely enough employment to live by at the prices he could obtain....'[7] Linnell hired Blake to do the preliminary work on this plate, for which he paid him fifteen guineas. Blake's contribution was probably confined to the underlying etching; Linnell reportedly received a fee of fifty guineas, which suggests that he did 70 per cent of the work. Although Linnell's precise influence on Blake's graphic art is difficult to ascertain, Blake came to lament in the 1820s that he had been trained by Basire as a 'mere engraver, cross-hatching freely'. He became more concerned with precision of line, his handling of the graver having been 'advantageously modified' under Linnell's tutelage.[8]

Within a month of their first meeting, the two men went to Lord Suffolk's and Colnaghi's to view pictures. Linnell's diary for March and April 1821 records their attendance at Sheridan's *Pizarro* at Drury Lane, a watercolour exhibition, and a show at the Royal Academy. On 8 June 1821, they went again to Drury Lane to see a 'New Grand Serious Opera', *Dirce, or the Fatal Urn*. Earlier, in September 1818, Linnell introduced Blake to John Constable. That evening – or on a similar occasion – the elderly artist, while leafing through one of the forty-two-year-old painter's sketchbooks, came upon a drawing of an avenue of fir trees on Hampstead Heath and exclaimed: 'Why, this is not drawing, but *inspiration.*' Embarrassed, Constable rejoined: 'I never knew it before; I meant it for drawing.'[9]

In addition to being an enterprising taskmaster, Linnell was an impresario, eager, in a manner reminiscent of Flaxman, to find patrons for Blake; he presented Blake to the collector Sir Edward Denny and Anthony Stewart, who painted miniatures of the royal family. He also introduced him to the man with whom he had studied from the age of twelve: the bluff, oversized John Varley, who turned forty-one in 1819. A landscape painter who was mesmerized by Wales and the north of England, Varley exhibited regularly at the Royal Academy and the Water Colour Society and published treatises on art.

A man of profligate inclinations, Varley frequently landed himself in financial hot water because of his proclivity to aid down-and-out colleagues. Also, he was a supremely unlucky person: his house burned down three times. He had a good sense of humour, as when he lamented his lack of funds: 'all these troubles are necessary to me ... if it were not for my troubles I would burst with joy.'[10] Varley's enormous energy was released in a number of avocations, including boxing, palm reading and astrology.

Although it was obvious to Linnell that Blake 'claimed the possession of some powers only in a greater degree that all men possessed and which they undervalued in themselves & lost through love of sordid pursuits',[11] Varley believed in a spirit world which vouchsafed concrete manifestations, such ingenuousness arousing Blake's mischievous side. According to Linnell, it was Varley 'who excited Blake to see or fancy the portaits of historical personages'.[12]

> Among the heads which Blake drew was one of King Saul, who, as the artist related, appeared to him in armour, and wearing a helmet of peculiar form and construction, which he could not, owing to the position of the spectre, see to delineate satisfactorily. The portrait was therefore left unfinished, till some months after, when King Saul vouchsafed a second sitting, and enabled Blake to complete his helmet.[13]

Sometimes, the nocturnal visitors would be uncooperative, leading to explosions of anger from Blake: 'I can't go on, – it is gone! I must wait till it returns' or 'It has moved. The mouth is gone.' On occasion, the ghosts would show their displeasure at Blake's manner of rendering them. In the sober rays of daylight, the artist would maintain that the pictures were accurate representations: 'Oh, it's all right! It *must* be right: I saw it so.'[14]

Apparently, Blake and Varley, intent on seeing spirits, stayed up till three in the morning – or Blake, suffering from insomnia, passed the time with the gullible younger man. One night, Varley arrived at Blake's rooms to find the artist in a high state of excitement. 'He told me that he had seen a wonderful thing – the ghost of a flea!' Varley asked if he had made a drawing of it. No, Blake told him, but he would do so if the creature materialized again. Immediately thereafter, Blake asked Varley to fetch his pens and pencils while he kept his eyes on the flea, which had suddenly returned: 'There he comes! his eager tongue whisking out of his mouth, a cup in his hand to hold blood, and covered with a scaly skin of gold and green.' Blake's resulting drawing owes more to the engraving of a flea under a microscope in Robert Hooke's *Micrographia*, where the proboscis of the insect is

The Ghost of a Flea

described as 'slip[ping] in and out',[15] than to a visionary experience. Although Blake had a powerful eidetic imagination, the appearances of Achilles, Corinna, Laïs, Herod, Edward I and William Wallace smack more of tomfoolery on Blake's part than a serious interest in phantoms of the night.

Linnell probably told Thomas Griffiths Wainewright, a sometime pupil of Fuseli, of Blake. That young artist wrote, in his habitually facetious and sardonic manner, to the *London Magazine* in August 1820 of the *'eighty-eight pounder'* called *Jerusalem*, 'a tremendous piece of ordnance' which Dr Tobias Ruddicombe, MD (the pseudonym was presumably invented by Wainewright) was about to launch: 'The doctor assures me that the redemption of mankind hangs on the universal diffusion of the doctrines broached in this M.S.'[16] Waine-wright, who lived at 44 Great Marlborough Street and exhibited at the Royal Academy in the 1820s, bought an elaborately coloured copy of *Songs of Innocence and Experience* and a set of the Job engravings.

Wainewright's lasting fame is as a swindler and murderer. In 1830, he insured for £16,000 the life of a sister-in-law, whom he subsequently poisoned with strychnine. The insurance companies disputed the claim and after an arduous five-year 'delay' in Chancery and two trials at common law, Wainewright's claim was disallowed. The dissolute artist retreated to France, where he reputedly killed one or two others. Seven years later, in 1837, he was arrested for forging the signature of his trustees, pleaded guilty, and was transported to Australia, where he died in 1847.

Before, on 19 September 1818, Linnell had introduced Blake to Robert John Thornton, a physician who had studied at Cambridge and Guy's Hospital and had begun practising in London in 1797. However, Thornton's hobby – publishing botanical books, upon which he lost a great deal of money – preoccupied him. But some of his enterprises were commercially successful, including the tract *How to Be Rich and Respectable*. In 1812, he brought out a school edition of Virgil's *Pastorals*, the separately issued illustrations coming out in 1814. A second edition, with the woodcuts, was released in 1819. By September 1820, Thornton had engaged Blake to undertake twenty-six engravings, a small fraction of the 230 illustrations to the third edition of 1821. Blake drew and engraved on copper a set of six portrait busts of Theocritus, Virgil, Augustus Caesar, Agrippa, Julius Caesar and Epicurus; he also completed a drawing after Nicholas Poussin.*

Blake's major contribution to Thornton's Virgil was a series of twenty wood engravings to accompany Ambrose Philips's Imitation of the first eclogue. Earlier, Blake had run foul of Cromek because of the excessive use of white line in the engraving of *Death's Door*. There is a corresponding roughness in the use of white line in the Virgil illustrations, where Blake was drawn to the shepherd-piper Colinet's melancholia and abandonment of music. In many ways, the themes of *Experience* and the Book of Job are blended in Blake's reading of Virgil and Ambrose Philips.

In a manner similar to that of the opinionated Dr Trusler years earlier, Thornton was piqued. He wanted illustrations which followed the move towards smoothness and dexterity, which had become a standard part of the craft of wood engraving. On 15 September 1819, he alerted Linnell to his displeasure, hoping that Blake's designs would look better if they were transformed into lithographs. The portrait of Virgil was so altered, but on 9 October Blake and Linnell went to see Thornton, who had been assured by wood engravers that Blake's work would 'never do'.[17] Three of the woodcuts were 'redesigned' and the

* John Byfield engraved this drawing.

Illustrations for Thornton's *Virgil*

remaining seventeen would probably have met the same fate but for Thornton meeting several artists, including Thomas Lawrence, James Ward and Linnell, at the home of the collector Charles Aders: 'All present expressed warm admiration of Blake's art, and of those designs and woodcuts in particular.' The puzzled Dr Thornton shook his head in disbelief, but allowed the surviving wood engravings to appear untouched, although he penned this caveat: 'The Illustrations of this English Pastoral are by the famous BLAKE, the illustrator of *Young's Night Thoughts*, and *Blair's* Grave; who designed and engraved them himself. This is mentioned, as they display less of art then genius, and are much admired by some eminent painters.' Samuel Palmer's admiration for these 'models of the exquisitest pitch of intense poetry' was unbounded: 'Intense depth, solemnity, and vivid brilliancy only coldly and partially describe them. There is in all such a mystic and dreamy glimmer as penetrates and kindles the inmost soul.'[18]

In the summer of 1821, Blake ran into an old acquaintance, William Frend, the radical reformer, who was walking in the Strand with his eleven-year-old daughter Sophia. They came upon a man with a brown coat and 'uncommonly bright' eyes. Blake, who frequently dressed in a plain black suit, would have worn his '*rather* broad-brimmed, but not quakerish hat',[19] black knee breeches and buckles, black worsted stockings, tied shoes. Costumed in this slightly outré manner, he resembled an old-fashioned tradesman. The two men shook hands and Blake asked: 'Why don't you come and see me?' Then, he raised his hand and pointed to a street which led down to the river. Before parting, the two exchanged polite remarks about visiting each other. As soon as Blake went on his way, the curious little girl asked who he was.

'He is a strange man; he thinks he sees spirits.'

'Tell me his name.'

'William Blake.'[20]

Acquaintances who came upon Blake in the Strand were not always so kind, as when the Royal Academician William Collins espied him from a distance but cut him when he noticed that he was fetching porter for his evening meal. At about this time, another girl, who had been taken by her parents to a dinner party, was touched when Blake, after gazing at her awhile and stroking her head and ringlets, proclaimed: 'May God make this world to you, my child, as beautiful as it has been to me.' 'She thought it strange at the time, she said, that such a poor old man, dressed in such shabby clothes, could imagine the world had ever been so beautiful to him as it must be to her.'[21]

The directions given by Blake to Frend indicate that he had moved to 3 Fountain Court, a red-brick house, where he and Catherine rented a two-room first-floor flat. This was, according to Linnell, 'a private House Kept by Mr. Banes whose wife was a sister to Mrs. Blake'.[22] The Blakes' increasingly precarious financial straits are indicated by the necessity of relocating to a house owned by relatives, who presumably allowed them to live at a rent lower than that at South Molton Street. By employing the phrase 'a private House' Linnell was also distinguishing Blake's new residence from the grimy warehouses which filled most of Fountain Court. Although they had a view of the Thames, the rooms in which the Blakes lived were small, dank and dark.

These rooms were approached by a wainscoted staircase, lit by a window on the left which overlooked the back yard. Two doors faced the visitor on the landing. The first room – the 'show-room'[22] – looked out over Fountain Court and its panelled walls were adorned with various watercolours and temperas: this reception room was connected to the smaller back room used for sleeping, cooking and working. In one left-hand corner was a bed, in a right-hand corner a fireplace, in another Catherine's cooking utensils. Blake usually worked at the dining table which was by the side window. From there, he peered 'down a deep gap between the houses of Fountain Court and the parallel street; in this way commanding a peep of the Thames with its muddy banks, and of distant Surrey or Kent hills beyond'.[24] Blake 'often spoke of the beauty of the Thames, as seen from the window, the river resembling "a bar of gold"'.[25]

'I live in a hole here,' Blake said, 'but God has a beautiful mansion for me elsewhere.'[26] When Crabb Robinson visited him in 1825 he observed that nothing:

> could exceed the squalid air both of the apartment & his dress – but in spite of dirt – I might say, filth, an air of natural gentility is diffused over him, and his wife notwithstanding the same offensive character of her dress & appearance has a good expression of countenance.[27]

At home, the clothes that Blake wore were 'threadbare, and his grey trousers had worn black and shiny in front, like a mechanic's'.[28] Since his eyesight had begun to fail slightly, he sometimes wore glasses when working. Once, Catherine, to excuse 'the general lack of soap and water', told a young friend *You see, Mr. Blake's skin don't dirt!*[29]

Blake's drop in fortune in 1821 was signalled by his sale of his print collection to Colnaghi. Nevertheless, Blake was – or claimed to be – oblivious of finances, as when, reduced to a few shillings, he purchased a camel-hair brush. Often, Catherine's patience reached breaking point: 'The money is going, Mr Blake.' Her husband, somewhat petulantly, rejoined: 'Oh, d— the money! It's always the money!' Since verbal assaults were no use, Catherine resorted to setting before her husband 'at dinner just what there was in the house, without any comment until, finally, the empty platter had to make its appearance'.[30]

The wily Linnell knew that the only way of helping Blake would be to find him, much in the manner of Richard Edwards and Robert Cromek, large-scale projects which could be promoted and distributed to a large audience. At some point, Linnell, who had obviously introduced himself to Butts, visited Blake's old patron and saw Blake's set of watercolour drawings to the Book of Job. By 7 September 1821, he and Blake decided to collaborate on reproducing those pictures. Tracings of the set were completed four days later; Linnell also commissioned Blake to make 'copies of his Drawings from Milton's P.L.'.[31] Once again, Butts was an understanding supporter of the impoverished artist. When Butts called on Blake in April of 1826, he insisted upon paying three guineas (the normal price was five guineas) for a set of the engravings. He refused to accept them gratis. As Blake said, 'this is his own decision quite in Character'.[32]

In June 1822, Linnell used his connections to force the Royal Academy Council to give Blake 'an able Designer & Engraver laboring under great distress' twenty-five pounds.[33] Indefatigable and enterprising, Linnell sought other means to augment Blake's income. In April 1822, he introduced him to James Vine, who purchased copies of *Thel*, *Milton* and the Job engravings. Three months later, he accompanied Blake to Sir Thomas Lawrence's. Varley also attempted to assist him by taking him to Lady Blessington's house in St James's Square. At that salon, although Blake was attired in 'the simplest form of attire as then worn, which included thick shoes and worsted stockings, nobody complained of the strange guest's lack of refinement and gentle manliness'.[34]

Not until 25 March 1823 did Blake and Linnell reach a 'Memorandum of Agreement' concerning the Job engravings. Linnell paid Blake five pounds for each engraving 'part before and the remainder when the Plates are finished, as Mr Blake may require it'; he also agreed to give Blake one hundred pounds out of the 'Profits of the work as the receipts will admit of it'.[35] On that same day, Linnell gave him five pounds. The 'implicit understanding'[36] of this contract was that Linnell should pay Blake about a pound a week. He gave Blake £54 in 1823, £46 7s 9d in 1824, and £49 6s 6d in 1825.

In August 1823, the phrenologist James S. Deville asked if he could make a cast of Blake's head as 'representative of the imaginative faculty'. When the plaster was removed, Blake felt tremendous pain, especially when some of his hair was pulled out. The resulting mask gives a severe look to the face. Catherine disliked Deville's efforts, 'perhaps the reason being that she was familiar with varying expressions of her husband's fine face, from daily observation: indeed it was difficult to please her with any portrait'.[37]

Even closed, Blake's eyes are the centre of attention in this portrait, as if the eyelids are concealing an enormous vitality and almost as if the subject resents the fact that his eyes cannot be depicted. The austerity of Blake's countenance also comes from the taut, harsh lines of the mouth, which suggests his often choleric disposition. In sum, the life mask reveals that the haughty, troubled side of his personality was still intact. However, the young men – the Antients – who gathered around Blake in his last four years saw only what they wanted to see – or what Blake wanted them to discern: the gentle sweetness which had now become the dominating part of his character.

When Blake was sixty-seven in 1824, the persistently helpful Linnell introduced him to a group of young artists: Henry Waller, then thirty-four, Edward Calvert, twenty-five, Francis Oliver Finch, twenty-two, Samuel Palmer and Frederick Tatham, nineteen, George Richmond, fifteen, and the fourteen-year-old John Giles, who gave the circle its name because of his repeated claim that ancient man was superior to modern man. Blake, who had long held that English art, in its pursuit of cosy fashionableness, had lost touch with its heroic heritage, could thus become their 'Interpreter'. The young men were thinking of the moment when Christian in *Pilgrim's Progress* arrives at the house of the Interpreter and beseeches him: 'I am a man that am come from the City of DESTRUCTION, and am going to Mount ZION; and I was told. . . that if I called here, you would shew me excellent things, such as would be a help to me in my journey.'[38]

Quickly, these young men were awed by the grandeur of Blake's commitment to his profession, with the simple fact that he had carried on his visionary tasks largely in isolation. Richmond 'confessed long years afterwards that never did he enter Blake's house without imprinting a reverent kiss upon the bell-handle which the seer had touched;

nor was he alone in this homage, which was practised by all the band of friends'.[39]

The Antients responded to Blake as an artist, not as a poet. Frederick Tatham remarked that the 'poetry ... was mostly unintelligible'.[40] Like Hayley twenty-five years earlier, they were shocked by the sheer unconventionality of the illuminated verse. Palmer in particular was priggish. He urged Gilchrist not to include in his biography any 'passage ... in which the word Bible, or those of the persons of the blessed Trinity, or the Messiah were irreverently connected'. He also urged the exclusion of any indecent or coarse word from *The Marriage*.[41] Ultimately, Tatham became convinced that 'Blake was inspired; but quite from a wrong quarter – by Satan himself.'[42] Some of these sentiments show the onset of Victorian prudery. Blake's influence upon the work of these artists was largely confined to the pastoral landscapes in *Innocence, Experience, America* and the Virgil woodcuts.

Previously, Blake had been deeply suspicious of parents, but – having established a strong fraternal bond with John Linnell – he could tolerate the idea of being a father to these young men, who craved his approval. Such a turn made Blake more profoundly aware of his own, long-suppressed love for his own father. One of his young artist sons witnessed such an epiphanic moment, when the elderly man burst into tears as he recited the parable of the Prodigal Son.

Since he had long been a friend of his architect father Charles Heathcote Tatham, Blake probably knew Frederick Tatham from his birth in 1805. In 1824, C. H. Tatham, who had been invited with his son to dine with Linnell, wrote to his host: 'Can you engage Michael Angelo *Blake* to meet us at your Study, & go up with us? – Such a Party of Connoisseurs is worthy Apollo & the muses.'[43] Once, George Richmond met Blake at the architect's house and walked home with him, the older man talking of his youthful aspirations. 'Never', Richmond claimed, 'have I known an artist so spiritual, so devoted, so single-minded, or cherishing imagination as he did.' One day, while he was taking tea with William and Catherine, he lamented how awful it was when inspiration flagged. Blake turned to his wife, 'It is just so with us, is it not, for weeks together, when the visions forsake us? What do we do then, Kate?' Matter-of-factly, she replied: 'We kneel down and pray, Mr Blake.'[44]

Palmer must have been taken by Linnell to meet Blake in 1824. That evening, the sensitive nineteen-year-old observed that Blake fastened his grey eyes on him immediately. Then he enquired: 'Do you work with fear and trembling?' When the youngster assured him that he did, Blake said: 'You'll do.'[45] On that occasion, the precocious teenager noticed 'the copper of the first plate [of Job] ... was lying on the table where he had been working on it. How lovely it looked by the lamplight, strained through the tissue paper.'[46] On that occasion and many others, Blake spoke of his devotion to Fra Angelico and, especially, Michelangelo, who had dedicated his life 'without earthly reward, and solely for the love of God, in the building of St Peter's'. Palmer was transfixed by the older man's unflaggingly bright eyes: 'brilliant, but not roving, clear and intent, yet susceptible. [They] flashed with genius, or melted in tenderness.'[47]

In May 1824, Palmer and Blake went to the Royal Academy, where Blake singled out a work by Wainewright for praise. He also admired Fuseli's *Satan Building the Bridge over Chaos* and remarked of the Apostles in a copy of Leonardo's *Last Supper* that each of the men assembled, except Judas, looked 'as if he had conquered the natural man'. Palmer's overwhelming impression that day was of the contrast between Blake's prosaic clothing and the 'dressed-up, rustling, swelling people'. He reflected: 'How little you know *who* is among you!'[48] The following autumn he and Linnell called upon Blake, who, having scalded his foot or leg, was lying in bed lame. Nevertheless, he was busy working, his bed covered with books. Blake seemed 'like one of the Antique patriarchs, or a dying Michael Angelo'.[49]

Linnell's move to Hampstead in March 1824 prompted Blake to walk out there regularly on Sundays, although he was convinced that the air of the north of London was unhealthy. Once, when Mrs Linnell asserted that Hampstead air was perfectly wholesome, he retorted: 'It is a lie! It is no such thing!'[50] He recalled previous walks to the north of the city: 'When I was young, Hampstead, Highgate, Hornsea, Muswell Hill, & even Islington & all places North of London, always laid me up the day after, & sometimes two or three days, with precisely the same Complaint & the same torment of the Stomach.'

Little Hannah Linnell would await Blake as he came over the brow of the nearby hill, watch for his special signal, and, soon after his arrival, climb on his knee to hear stories. Despite his prejudice against Hampstead, Blake 'would often stand at the door, gazing in tranquil reverie across the garden toward the gorse-clad hill'. He also liked sitting in the arbour, at the bottom of the long garden, 'or walking up and down the same at dusk, while the cows, munching their evening meal, were audible from the farmyard on the other side of the hedge'. Often, later in the evening, he would burst into tears when Mrs Linnell, accompanying herself on the pianoforte, sang the Border Melody. As he had done many years before at the Mathews' salon, Blake would also sing, 'in a voice tremulous with age, sometimes old ballads, sometimes his own songs, to melodies of his own'.[51]

In the summer of 1824, as Blake's work on the Job series was winding down, Linnell commissioned a similar series of designs for Dante's *Commedia*. The agreement was that Linnell should go on paying Blake '2l. or 3l. a week, as he wanted money, Blake doing as little or as much as he liked in return'.[52] Excited at the prospect of yet another major series of illustrations, Blake set himself to learn Italian.

Blake's friendship with Thomas Butts remained in disarray, so the artist never kept his promise to take Palmer to see the collection of his work held by his old patron. In the summer of 1825, Blake again took to his bed with shivering fits,* but he was well enough to accompany Linnell to a gathering at the Euston Square home of Charles and Elizabeth Aders on Saturday, 6 August 1825. There the reception rooms, bedrooms, the staircase – 'as much a picture gallery as a house'[53] – were filled to overflowing with early Italian and especially Flemish and German paintings. Blake's health had so improved a month later that he made a twenty-mile expedition in a carrier's wagon to Shoreham, Kent with Palmer and Mr and Mrs Calvert.

Shortly before, Palmer, who suffered from asthma and bronchitis, had discovered this remote village and welcomed it as a refuge from urban pollution. In part inspired by Blake's Virgil woodcuts, he responded in a deeply mystical way to the pastoral landscape which confronted him. Palmer's first home there was an old dilapidated cottage, which he dubbed 'Rat Abbey'. During Blake's stay, Samuel Palmer's father was also visiting from Bloomsbury; he and the Calverts remained at the cottage, Blake went to a neighbour, and Palmer had a 'shake-down at the village bakery'. The day after their arrival, Blake and the older Palmer 'talked of the divine gift of Art and Letters, and of spiritual vision and inspiration'. This 'elicited from old Palmer the story of the ghost which was said to haunt a half-ruined mansion close by'. Since 'Calvert believed in adventure, and Blake believed in ghosts, and the younger Palmer believed in Blake', Calvert's suggestion that they investigate the place was greeted enthusiastically.

---

* Today, a 'shivering fit' is sometimes referred to as a shaking chill or rigor. This is a nonspecific sign of infection. It could be the result of an ascending biliary tract infection, but it could equally indicate a urinary infection, possibly due to an enlarged prostate. Blake's condition was also described as 'gall mixing with his blood'. In addition to confirming the likelihood of a biliary tract infection, this supports the possibility of jaundice and gall stones.

That night, the wind moaned and the moon was down. The mansion had partly dismantled windows and 'weird shadows crossed each other on the broken walls'. Then the group heard a clattering sound, which quickly became a tapping, grating noise. Palmer was transfixed; Blake's reaction is not recorded. Finally, Palmer and Calvert followed the sound to an oriel window: 'Here they discovered a large snail crawling up the mullion, while his shell oscillated on some casement glass with strange significance.'

The following day, Blake, Palmer Senior and Calvert were sitting in the cottage's large room. More than an hour before, Samuel had taken his departure in a coach for London. Blake put his hand to his forehead and quietly stated: 'Palmer is coming; he is walking up the road.' Someone in the group contradicted him: 'Oh, Mr Blake, he's gone to London; we saw him off in the coach.' A little while later, Blake, pointing to the closed door, said: 'He is coming through the wicket – there!' A minute later, Samuel – his coach having broken down – raised the latch and rejoined the group.[54]

Blake's last great project – his illustrations to Dante – was yet another attempt to correct a writer who had seriously erred. From 1824, Blake completed over 100 large drawings (approximately seventy for the *Inferno*, nineteen for *Purgatorio* and only nine for *Paradiso*) as well as a handful of smaller ones. He engraved only seven, including the *Whirlwind of Lovers*. In particular, Blake objected to Dante's orthodox Roman Catholicism. On 10 December 1825, he told Crabb Robinson: '*Dante* saw devils where I see none – I see only good.'[55] On the back of one of his drawings he wrote, 'Every thing in Dante's Comedia shews That for Tyrannical Purposes he has made This World the Foundation of All; & the Goddess ... Nature is his Inspirer & not Imagination, the Holy Ghost.'[56] On another of the drawings, he condemned Dante's idea of Hell as 'originally Formed by the devil Himself', adding, 'Whatever Book is for Vengeance for Sin & Whatever Book is Against Forgiveness of Sin is not of the Father but of Satan the Accuser & Father of Hell.'[57] In a particularly petulant moment, he commented on his own design showing the Goddess Fortune in a hole: 'The hole of a Shit house: The Goddess Fortune is the devil's servant, ready to Kiss any one's Arse.'[58] However, Blake had conflicting notions about Dante, for on 17 December 1825 he characterized Milton 'as being at one time – A sort of classical Atheist – And of Dante as being now with God.'[59]

Dante's obsession with Beatrice had been, as far as Blake was

Beatrice Addressing Dante from the Car

concerned, the stumbling block in the Italian poet's existence. For Blake, Beatrice – whom he identified with the Catholic Church – was a form of Vala, a woman who led men to their damnation.

On 12 May 1826, Blake attended a party given by Crabb Robinson, at which the Flaxmans were also present. Blake asserted that 'the oldest painters poets were the best'. A fellow guest responded, 'Do you deny all progression?' Blake rejoined: 'Oh, yes.'[60] That evening, the host discerned hostility to Blake emanating from Flaxman. Robinson, who tried to interest Blake in Wordsworth, subsequently sent him a copy of *Descriptive Sketches*, in an attempt to convince Blake that his fellow poet was a true Christian.

Earlier, in late March, Blake was in a 'tottering state'.[61] Later, in May, Blake 'had another desperate Shivring Fit; it came on yesterday afternoon after as good a morning as I ever experienced. It began by a gnawing Pain in the Stomach & soon spread. A deathly feel all over the limbs which brings on the shivring fit, when I am forced to go to bed where I contrive to get into a little Perspiration, which takes it quite away.'[62] The 'deathly feel' had now taken hold, and in July the unexpected cold weather had 'cut all' his hopes of visiting Linnell. A few days later, Blake was sure that a sound dietary regimen 'if the Machine is capable of it' would allow him to become 'an old man yet'.[63] He was also upset that the new Linnell son was going to be named William after him rather than Thomas after his paternal grandfather. He pleaded (successfully) for Linnell to reconsider 'if it is not too late. It very much troubles Me, as a Crime in which I shall be The Principal.'[64]

To his pervasive feeling of weakness and recurring stomach problems were added piles later that July. Under these trying circumstances, he did not know when he 'could start for Hampstead like a young Lark without feathers'.[65] In February, Linnell, worried about Blake's increasing debility, wanted William and Catherine to move to Hampstead, where he could mind them, but Blake resisted the tempting offer, in a poignant letter of gratitude which contains a dash of self-irony:

I have Thought & Thought of the Removal & cannot get my Mind out of a State of terrible fear at such a step; the more I think, the more I feel terror at what I wishd at first & thought it a thing of benefit & Good hope; you will attribute it to its right Cause – Intellectual Peculiarity. That must be Myself alone shut up in Myself, or Reduced to Nothing. I could tell you of Visions & dreams upon the Subject. I have asked & intreated Divine help, but fear continues upon me, & I must relinquish the step that I had wished to take, & still wish, but in vain.[66]

Throughout 1826 and into 1827 'that Sickness to which there is no name'[67] continued unabated, Blake forcing himself to work on the Dante illustrations. When he was informed in December 1826 of Flaxman's death, he simply remarked: 'I thought I should have gone first.' Then he paused: 'I cannot consider death as any thing but a removing from one room to another.'[68] By April 1827, he had been very 'near the Gates of Death & have returned very weak & an Old Man feeble & tottering, but not in Spirit & Life, not in The Real Man: The Imagination which Liveth for Ever. In that I am stronger & stronger as this Foolish Body decays.'[69] That month he began printing a set of *Innocence and Experience* which he could not do 'under Six Months consistent with' other work;[70] also, he was 'too much attachd to Dante to think much'[71] of any other of the small projects upon which he was still busy. A visit to Hampstead in July 'brought on a relapse'. He realized that he could no longer 'go on in a youthful Style'.[72]

By 10 August, Blake was completely bedridden. On that day, Linnell sketched him wearing a black skull cap. Blake's strength had deserted him, and he was not expected to last much longer. Catherine asked him where he wanted to be buried, 'and whether he would have the Dissenting Minister, or the Clergyman of the Church of England, to read the service: his answers were, that as far as his own feelings were concerned, they might bury him where she pleased, adding, that as his father, mother, aunt, and brother, were buried in Bunhill-row, perhaps it would be better to lie there, but as to service, he should wish for that of the Church of England'.[73]

Even on his last days, Blake worked, one 'of the very last shillings spent was in sending out for a pencil'.[74] Two days later, Linnell wrote in his Journal: 'Sunday 12. Mr Blake died.'[75] Death came early that Sunday evening. At first, Blake had felt better and asked for the coloured print of the Ancient of Days (the frontispiece to *Europe*) he was preparing for Tatham. After he had worked on it, he burst out: 'There, I have done all I can; it is the best I have ever finished; I hope Mr Tatham will like it.' Then he threw the picture down and turned to his wife: 'Kate, you have been a good Wife. I will draw your portrait.' She sat by the bed, and her husband sketched. Later, he flung the paper to the ground and began to sing 'Hallelujahs & songs of joy & Triumph. . . . He sang loudly & with true extatic energy and seemed, too, happy that he had finished his course, that he had ran his race, & that he was shortly to arrive at the Goal.'[76]

George Richmond, who reached Fountain Court just after Blake died, 'kissed William Blake in death'[77] and closed his eyes in order to 'keep the vision in'.[78] Three days later, he wrote to Samuel Palmer, who was out of London, to tell him that Blake was going to be buried on Friday the 17th:

He said He was going to that Country he had all His life wished to see & expressed Himself Happy, hoping for Salvation through Jesus Christ – Just before he died his countenance became fair. His eyes Brighten'd and He burst out into Singing of the things he saw in Heaven.[79]

Richmond, Calvert and Tatham were among those who accompanied the body to Bunhill Fields. Catherine's only inheritance was the stock of illuminated books, engravings, copper-plates, water-colours and manuscripts left by her husband. Various collectors – including Lord Egremont – bought pieces of his work from Catherine, who avoided 'as a good saleswoman should, the display of too large a choice to her customers'.[80] Eventually, she became estranged from

Linnell, whom she increasingly perceived as rapacious. (She left all her remaining stock of Blake's work to Tatham.)

Shortly after Williams death, George III's sister, Princess Sophia, sent Catherine a gift of £100. The virtually destitute widow promptly returned the money, 'not liking to take or keep what (as it seemed to her) she could dispense with, while many to whom no chance or choice was given might have been kept alive by the gift'.[81] To the end, she remained, like her husband, deeply divided about the comforts, esteem and pity of the world.

In September 1827, Catherine became John Linnell's housekeeper at Cirencester Place. When he moved nine months later, she took up the same position at Frederick Tatham's. Finally, she moved to No 17 Upper Charlotte Street, Fitzroy Square, where she died on 18 October 1831. In the last hours of her life she called 'continually to her William, as if he were in the next room, to say she was coming to him, and would not be long now'.[82]

Notes

A Note on Sources

Virtually all citations from Blake are taken from *The Complete Poetry and Prose of William Blake*, ed. David V. Erdman (Berkeley and Los Angeles: University of California Press, 1982). I have followed Erdman's replication of Blake's inconsistent spelling, but I have frequently inserted punctuation so that Blake's lack of same does not unduly distract the reader.

G. E. Bentley's *Blake Records* (Oxford: The Clarendon Press, 1969) and its *Supplement* (Oxford: The Clarendon Press, 1989) contain the most accurate pieces of factual information about Blake's existence. In particular, Bentley points out inconsistencies and errors in the early biographical accounts of Benjamin Heath Malkin (1806), Henry Crabb Robinson (1811; 1852), John Thomas Smith (1828), Allan Cunningham (1830) and Frederick Tatham (c.1832); he also isolates the distinct, important contributions made by each man. In addition Bentley carefully weighs the study of Blake's life by Alexander Gilchrist, the compassionate, investigative reporter to whom we owe much of our scanty knowledge of Blake's life. In citing *Blake Records*, I have occasionally, for the sake of clarity, inserted punctuation and modernized odd spellings.

Short Titles and Abbreviations

WB   William Blake
BR   G. E. Bentley Jr, *Blake Records* (Oxford: The Clarendon Press, 1969)
BR II   G. E. Bentley Jr, *Blake Records Supplement* (Oxford: The Clarendon Press, 1989)
Gilchrist   Alexander Gilchrist, *Life of William Blake* (London: J. M. Dent, 1945)
Wilson   Mona Wilson, *The Life of William Blake*, revised by Geoffrey Keynes (London: Oxford University Press, 1971)
Writings   *The Complete Poetry and Prose of William Blake*, ed. David V. Erdman (Berkeley and Los Angeles: University of California Press, 1982)

Chapter 1: Infant Joy and Sorrow 1757–1767

1. As cited by George Rudé, *Hanoverian London* (Berkeley: University of California Press, 1971), p. 86.
2. As cited by ibid., p. 91.
3. As cited by M. Dorothy George, *London Life in the Eighteenth Century* (Chicago: Academy Chicago), p. 47.
4. *Survey of London: St James Westminster*, ed. F.W. Sheppard (London: London County Council, 1963), p. 67.
5. Rudé, op. cit., p. 194.
6. *BR*, pp. 7–8.
7. E.P. Thompson, *The Making of the English Working Class* (Harmondsworth: Penguin Books, 1980), p. 52. His source: E.D. Andrews, *The People Called Shakers* (New York, 1953), p. 6.
8. *BR*, p. 508.
9. WB to Thomas Butts, 22 November 1802. *Writings*, p. 721.
10. *BR*, p. 508.
11. Ibid., p. 422.
12. Ibid., p. 510.
13. Ibid.
14. Ibid.
15. Ibid., p. 7.
16. Ibid.
17. Ibid.
18. Cited by Wilson, p. 3.
19. *BR*, p. 456.
20. Ibid., p. 477.
21. Ibid., p. 456.
22. *Writings*, p. 31.
23. Ibid.
24. Ibid., p. 11.
25. Ibid., p. 17.
26. Ibid., pp. 21–2.
27. Ibid., p. 28.
28. Ibid., pp. 276, 283.
29. Ibid., p. 30.
30. Ibid., p. 223.
31. Ibid., p. 502.
32. *BR*, p. 509.

Chapter 2: The Young Antiquarian 1768–1778

1. *BR*, p. 508.
2. George Rudé, *Hanoverian London* (Berkeley: University of California Press, 1971), p. 202.
3. Ibid.
4. As cited by ibid., p. 216. His source is the *Annual Register*.

5. Rudé, op. cit., p. 199.

6. *BR*, p. 25.

7. *Writings*, pp. 412–13.

8. WB to George Cumberland, 2 July 1800. *Writings*, p. 706.

9. Annotation to the Works of Reynolds. *Writings*, p. 660.

10. See E.P. Thompson, *The Making of the English Working Class* (Harmondsworth: Penguin Books, 1980), p. 34.

11. Cited by ibid., p. 35.

12. WB to Hayley, 4 December 1804. *Writings*, p. 758.

13. *BR*, p. 510.

14. Ibid., p. 477.

15. Annotations to Reynolds. *Writings*, p. 637.

16. *BR*, p. 510.

17. 'Memoirs of Thomas Jones', *Walpole Society* XXXII, p. 21. Cited by David Bindman, *Blake as an Artist* (Oxford: Phaidon, 1977), p. 226.

18. *BR*, pp. 510–11.

19. Ibid., p. 511, n. 1.

20. 'Public Address'. *Writings*, p. 571.

21. *A Dictionary of Artists of the English School*, 2nd edn (London, 1878), p. 31. Cited by Robert N. Essick, *William Blake: Printmaker* (Princeton: Princeton University Press, 1980), p. 35.

22. Annotation to Reynolds. *Writings*, p. 647.

23. Gilchrist, p. 13.

24. *BR*, p. 422.

25. Ibid.

26. Ibid.

27. Ibid.

28. Geoffrey Keynes, *Blake Studies*, 2nd edn (Oxford: The Clarendon Press, 1971), p. 22.

29. *Writings*, p. 411.

30. As cited by Robert N. Essick and Morton D. Paley in 'Introduction: The Poet in the Graveyard', in their facsimile edition of *The Grave* illustrated by William Blake (London: Scolar Press, 1982), p. 8.

31. *BR*, p. 13.

32. Ibid.

33. Ibid.

34. Ibid., p. 301.

35. *Writings*, p. 29.

36. Ibid., p. 340.

37. Ibid., p. 341.

38. *BR*, p. 283.

39. Ibid., p. 672.

40. Ibid., p. 671.

41. Ibid., p. 439.

Chapter 3: Conservative Revolutionary 1778–1784

1. Washington to G.W. Fairfax in London, 31 May 1775. Cited by David V. Erdman, *Blake: Prophet against Empire* (Garden City: Doubleday, 1969), p. 15.
2. *Writings*, p. 671.
3. If Blake executed any or all of these engravings, they do not seem to have survived. See Robert N. Essick, *William Blake: Printmaker* (Princeton: Princeton University Press, 1980), p. 42.
4. Cited by Butlin in *The Paintings and Drawings of William Blake* (New Haven and London: Yale University Press, 1981), p. 23. Source is Rapin, 1732 edn, vol. I, p. 635, n. 7.
5. Butlin, op. cit., p. 20. Source Rapin, 1732 edn, vol. I, p. 134.
6. Ibid.
7. *Writings*, p. 440.
8. Ibid., p. 417.
9. Ibid., p. 567.
10. Ibid., p. 568.
11. RA Council Minutes, vol. I, pp. 4–6; as cited by Sidney C. Hutchison, *The History of the Royal Academy 1768–1968* (London: Chapman & Hall, 1968), p. 49.
12. J. Elmes, *Annals of Fine Arts* ii (1818) 359. Cited by Bentley, *BR*, p. 17.
13. W.G. Constable, *Richard Wilson* (London, 1953), p. 55. Cited by Hutchison, op. cit., p. 61.
14. RA General Assembly Minutes, vol. I, p. 102. As cited by Hutchison, op. cit., p. 61.
15. Blake's *Marginalia* to Reynolds's *Works*. Cited by Bentley, *BR*, p. 17.
16. *BR*, p. 31.
17. Ibid., p. 423.
18. As cited by William L. Pressly in *James Barry: The Artist as Hero* (London: Tate Gallery, 1983), p. 21.
19. Reynolds, *Marginalia*. *Writings*, p. 636.
20. Ibid.
21. *BR*, p. 17.
22. Ibid., p. 362.
23. Ibid., p. 332.
24. BM Add MS 36494, f. 81.
25. Information is from the Introduction to G.E. Bentley Jr, *A Bibliography of George Cumberland* (New York: Garland, 1975), pp. xvii–xxiii.
26. A.E. Bray, *Life of Thomas Stothard, R.A.* (London: John Murray, 1851), p. 9.
27. Ibid., p. 22.
28. As cited by David Irwin, *John Flaxman 1755–1826* (London: Studio Vista, 1979), p. 4.
29. As cited by Irwin, p. 6.
30. *Writings*, p. 508.
31. *BR*, p. 18.
32. Ibid.
33. Bray, op. cit., pp. 20–1.
34. Ibid.

35. *Writings*, p. 414.
36. *BR*, p. 281.
37. Ibid., p. 518.
38. Gilchrist, p. 314.
39. Ibid., p. 21.
40. Ibid., p. 517.
41. *Writings*, pp. 496–8.
42. Ibid., p. 488.
43. *BR*, p. 518.
44. Cited by Bentley in *BR*, p. 557.
45. Ibid., p. 30.
46. See Essick, op. cit., p. 12.
47. *Writings*, p. 572.
48. *BR*, p. 27.
49. I am grateful to Professor G.E. Bentley Jr for calling my attention to this recently discovered information, which is forthcoming in his article 'Blake and Wedgwood' in *Blake/An Illustrated Quarterly*.
50. WB to Hayley, 23 October 1804. *Writings*, p. 756.
51. 'Public Address'. *Writings*, p. 572.
52. Ibid.
53. Flaxman to Nancy Denman. Cited by Bentley in 'A.S. Mathew, Patron of Blake and Flaxman', *Notes and Queries* 203 (1958) 171.
54. Ibid., p. 170.
55. Ibid.
56. Ibid., p. 169.
57. *BR*, p. 457.
58. Ibid., p. 518.
59. Peter Tomory, *The Life and Art of Henry Fuseli* (London: Thames & Hudson, 1972), p. 24.
60. *Writings*, p. 457.
61. Ibid.
62. Erdman, op. cit., p. 110.
63. Ibid.
64. *Writings*, p. 452.
65. Ibid., pp. 452–3.
66. Ibid., p. 455.
67. Ibid., p. 458.
68. Ibid., p. 465.
69. Ibid., p. 460.
70. See Martha W. England, 'Apprenticeship at the Haymarket?', in *Visionary Forms Dramatic*, ed. David V. Erdman and John E. Grant (Princeton: Princeton University Press, 1970), pp. 3–29.
71. *William Blake's Writings*, ed. G.E. Bentley Jr (Oxford: The Clarendon Press, 1978), p. 749.
72. *Writings*, p. 417.
73. Ibid., p. 410.

74. Ibid., p. 443.
75. Ibid., pp. 410–11.

Chapter 4: Brothers of Eternity 1784–1787

1. WB to George Cumberland, 2 July 1800. *Writings*, p. 706.
2. Sven H.A. Bruntjen, *John Boydell, 1719–1804: A Study of Art Patronage and Publishing in Georgian London* (New York: Garland, 1985), pp. 29–30.
3. *BR*, p. 29.
4. Robert N. Essick, *William Blake: Printmaker* (Princeton: Princeton University Press, 1980), p. 58.
5. *BR*, p. 509.
6. Ibid., p. 559.
7. Ibid., p. 31.
8. Ibid., p. 457.
9. Ibid., p. 31.
10. Ibid., p. 526.
11 *Writings*, p. 589.
12. 'Public Address'. *Writings*, p. 573.
13. Ibid., p. 574.
14. *BR*, pp. 31–2.
15. Ibid., p. 32.
16. Ibid.
17. WB to Hayley, 6 May 1800. *Writings*, p. 705.

Chapter 5: A Rural Pen 1787–1789

1. As cited by Morton D. Paley, ' "A New Heaven is Begun": Blake and Swedenborgianism', in *Blake and Swedenborg* (New York: Swedenborg Foundation, 1985), p. 18.
2. Ibid., p. 21.
3. Quoted by Morton D. Paley in *The Continuing City: William Blake's Jerusalem* (Oxford: The Clarendon Press, 1983), p. 128.
4. *BR*, p. 35.
5. *An Island in the Moon*. *Writings*, p. 465.
6. See n. 58, p. 116 in Robert N. Essick, *William Blake: Printmaker* (Princeton: Princeton University Press, 1980).
7. Ibid., p. 115.
8. *BR*, p. 32.
9. Ibid., p. 460.
10. *Jerusalem*. *Writings*, p. 153.
11. WB to Thomas Butts, 10 January 180[3]. *Writings*, p. 724.
12. Jean H. Hagstrum, *William Blake: Poet and Painter* (Chicago: University of Chicago Press, 1964), p. 31.
13. Essick, op. cit., pp. 121–5.
14. *BR II*, p. 2.

15. *Writings*, p. 2.
16. Ibid.
17. Ibid., p. 3.
18. Ibid., p. 1.
19. Ibid., p. 7.
20. Ibid., p. 11.
21. Ibid., p. 15.
22. Ibid., p. 31.
23. Ibid., p. 10.
24. Ibid., p. 9.
25. Ibid., p. 31.
26. Ibid., p. 3.
27. Ibid., pp. 4–5.
28. Ibid., p. 6.

Chapter 6: Prophet from Albion 1789–1791

1. Gilchrist, p. 85.
2. Warwick Wroth, *The London Pleasure Gardens* (London, 1896), pp. 268–70.
3. David V. Erdman, *Prophet against Empire* (Garden City: Doubleday, 1969), p. 290.
4. As cited by Wilson, p. 81.
5. *BR*, p. 54.
6. Ibid.
7. Ibid., pp. 521–2.
8. Ibid., p. 52.
9. Ibid., p. 522.
10. Ibid., pp. 523–4.
11. Ibid., pp. 38–9.
12. WB to John Flaxman, 12 September 1800. *Writings*, p. 707.
13. *BR*, p. 39.
14. Ibid.
15. Ibid.
16. Ibid., p. 53.
17. Ibid., p. 39.
18. As cited by Peter Tomory, *The Life and Art of Henry Fuseli* (London: Thames & Hudson, 1972), p. 20.
19. *Writings*, p. 599.
20. *BR*, p. 40.
21. See Erdman, op. cit., p. 157.
22. *BR*, p. 43.
23. *BR II*, pp. 94–5.
24. *BR*, p. 40.
25. Ibid., p. 530.
26. Ibid., pp. 530–1
27. Ibid., pp. 43–4.

28. Ibid., p. 45.
29. *Writings*, p. 286.
30. Ibid.
31. Ibid., pp. 289–90.
32. Ibid., pp. 287–8.
33. Ibid., p. 58.
34. Ibid., p. 66.
35. Annotation to Swedenborg's *Divine Love and Divine Wisdom*. *Writings*, p. 602.
36. *Writings*, p. 34.
37. Ibid., p. 33.
38. Ibid., p. 34.
39. Ibid.
40. Ibid., p. 36.
41. Ibid., pp. 38–9.
42. Ibid., p. 41.
43. Ibid., p. 42.
44. Ibid.
45. Ibid., pp. 43–4.

Chapter 7: Fearful Symmetry 1792–1795

1. *Writings*, p. 694.
2. *BR*, p. 24.
3. WB to William Hayley, 11 December 1805. *Writings*, p. 767.
4. 20 January 1807. *Writings*, p. 694.
5. *Writings*, p. 32.
6. *The Journal of John Gabriel Stedman 1744–1797* ..., ed. Stanbury Thompson (London, 1962), p. 20.
7. Ibid., p. 125.
8. *Narrative of a Five Years' Expedition Against the Revolted Slaves of Surinam* ..., 2 vols (Barre, Massachusetts: The Imprint Society), vol. I, p. 61.
9. Ibid., vol. II, p. 382.
10. Ibid.
11. *Journal*, op. cit., p. 375.
12. Ibid., p. 337.
13. G.E. Bentley Jr, *Blake Books* (Oxford: The Clarendon Press, 1977), p. 622.
14. Ibid.
15. *BR*, pp. 50–1.
16. Ibid., p. 49.
17. *Journal*, op. cit., p. 390.
18. *Writings*, p. 46.
19. Ibid.
20. Ibid.
21. Ibid., p. 48.
22. Ibid., p. 50.
23. Ibid., p. 51.

24. Writings., p. 46.
25. Ibid., p. 51.
26. Ibid., p. 50.
27. Annotation (1827) to Thornton's *The Lord's Prayer. Writings*, p. 668.
28. *Writings*, p. 19.
29. Ibid., p. 23.
30. Ibid., p. 28.
31. Ibid., p. 471.
32. Ibid., pp. 692–3.
33. Ibid., pp. 24–5.
34. Ibid., p. 77.

Chapter 8: To Fame Unknown 1795–1798

1. *BR*, p. 50.
2. Ibid., p. 55.
3. Ibid., pp. 54–5.
4. Ibid., p. 50.
5. Ibid., p. 52.
6. Ibid.
7. Ibid., pp. 57–8.
8. Ibid., pp. 524–5.
9. *Milton. Writings*, p. 122.
10. *BR*, p. 52.
11. G.E. Bentley Jr in 'Richard Edwards, Publisher of Church-and-King Pamphlets and of William Blake', *Studies in Bibliography* 41 (1988) 300.
12. *BR*, p. 57.
13. Ibid., p. 56.
14. Ibid., p. 59.
15. *Writings*, p. 23.
16. See Morton D. Paley, 'Blake's *Night Thoughts*: An Exploration of the Fallen World', in *William Blake: Essays for S. Foster Damon* (Providence: Brown University Press, 1969), p. 134.
17. *Night Thoughts*, ed. Stephen Cornford (Cambridge: Cambridge University Press, 1989), p. 293. IX, 1422–3.
18. Ibid., p. 108. IV, 683–90.
19. *BR II*, p. 11.
20. Ibid., p. 14.
21. As cited by Irene Tayler, *Blake's Illustrations to the Poems of Gray* (Princeton: Princeton University Press, 1971), p. 15.
22. Ibid.
23. *Writings*, p. 482.
24. WB to Dawson Turner, 9 June 1818. *Writings*, p. 771.

Chapter 9: The Female Will 1798–1800

1. *Writings*, p. 417.
2. Ibid., p. 355.
3. Ibid., p. 320.
4. Ibid., pp. 360–1.
5. Ibid., pp. 328–9.
6. Ibid., p. 328.
7. Ibid., p. 391.
8. Ibid., p. 398.
9. Ibid., p. 406.
10. WB to William Hayley, 19 October 1801. *Writings*, p. 717.
11. *Writings*, pp. 467–8.
12. Ibid., p. 516.
13. Ibid., p. 474.
14. Ibid., pp. 488–9.
15. Ibid., pp. 483–6.
16. Ibid., p. 324.
17. *Jerusalem. Writings*, p. 250.
18. *BR*, p. 459.
19. Ibid., p. 534.
20. Ibid., p. 106.
21. Gilchrist, p. 314.
22. *BR II*, p. 81.

Chapter 10: The Perils and Pleasures of Patronage 1799–1803

1. WB to Trusler, 16 August 1799. *Writings*, p. 701.
2. Ibid.
3. WB quotes Trusler in his letter to George Cumberland of 26 August 1799. *Writings*, p. 704.
4. WB to Trusler, 23 August 1799. *Writings*, p. 702.
5. Ibid.
6. Ibid.
7. Ibid., p. 703.
8. WB to Cumberland, 26 August 1799. *Writings*, p. 703.
9. Ibid., p. 704.
10. Cited by G.E. Bentley Jr. in 'Thomas Butts, White Collar Maecenas', *Publications of the Modern Language Association of America* 71 (1956) 1054.
11. Ibid., p. 1056.
12. *BR*, pp. 67, 73.
13. As cited in *The Letters of William Blake*, ed. Geoffrey Keynes (London: Rupert Hart-Davis, 1968), p. 43.
14. Ibid., p. 44.
15. WB to Cumberland, 2 July 1800. *Writings*, p. 706.
16. WB to Cumberland, 26 August 1799. *Writings*, p. 704.
17. David Bindman, *Blake as an Artist* (Oxford: Phaidon, 1977), p. 126.

18. *Horace Walpole Correspondence*, ed. W.S. Lewis and others (New Haven: Yale University Press, 1955), vol. 25, pp. 255–7.

19. Cowper cites Hayley in his letter to Lady Hesketh of 5 May 1792. *The Letters and Prose Writings of William Cowper*, ed. James King and Charles Ryskamp (Oxford: The Clarendon Press, 1984), vol. IV, p. 72.

20. As cited by Morchard Bishop, *Blake's Hayley* (London: Gollancz, 1951), p. 128.

21. 26 May 1792. *Letters*, vol. IV, p. 82.

22. Cowper to Hayley, 14 June 1792. *Letters*, vol. IV, p. 117.

23. Cowper to Lady Hesketh, 21 June 1792. *Letters*, vol. IV, p. 125.

24. *BR*, p. 27.

25. Ibid., p. 51.

26. Ibid., p. 63.

27. WB to Hayley, 1 April 1800. *Writings*, p. 705.

28. *BR*, p. 64.

29. Ibid., p. 65.

30. 6 May 1800. *Writings*, p. 705.

31. Bishop, op. cit., p. 129.

32. Ibid., p. 262.

33. *BR*, p. 72.

34. Ibid.

35. Bishop, op. cit., p. 251.

36. *BR*, p. 71.

37. 12 September 1800. *Writings*, p. 707.

38. 14 September 1800. *Writings*, p. 709.

39. WB to Hayley, 16 September 1800. *Writings*, p. 709.

40. WB to Flaxman, 21 September 1800. *Writings*, p. 710.

41. WB to Thomas Butts, 23 September 1800. *Writings*, p. 711.

42. WB to Hayley, 18 December 1804. *Writings*, p. 759.

43. WB to Thomas Butts, 2 October 1800. *Writings*, p. 712.

44. *BR*, p. 77.

45. WB to William Hayley, 26 November 1800. *Writings*, p. 714.

46. WB to Thomas Butts, 11 September 1801. *Writings*, p. 716.

47. *BR*, p. 80.

48. Ibid., p. 109.

49. Ibid., p. 97.

50. Ibid., p. 101.

51. Ibid., pp. 104–5.

52. Annotations to Spurzheim's *Observations on Insanity* (1817). *Writings*, p. 663.

53. *BR*, p. 79.

54. Ibid.

55. WB to Thomas Butts, 10 May 1801. *Writings*, p. 715.

56. WB to William Hayley, 28 September 1804. *Writings*, p. 755.

57. *BR*, p. 100.

58. Ibid., p. 83.

59. Ibid.

60. WB to John Flaxman, 19 October 1801. *Writings*, p. 718.

61. *BR*, p. 95.
62. Ibid., p. 106.
63. Ibid., p. 111.
64. Ibid., p. 112.
65. WB to Thomas Butts, 10 January 1803. *Writings*, p. 724.
66. Ibid., p. 723.
67. *BR*, p. 524.
68. WB to Thomas Butts, 11 September 1801. *Writings*, p. 716.
69. WB to Thomas Butts, 19 January 1803. *Writings*, p. 724.
70. WB to Thomas Butts, 22 November 1802. *Writings*, p. 720.
71. 30 January 1803. *Writings*, p. 726.
72. *Writings*, p. 725.
73. Ibid., p. 726.
74. WB to Thomas Butts, 25 April 1803. *Writings*, p. 728.
75. Ibid.
76. Ibid.
77. *BR*, p. 114.
78. Ibid., p. 117.
79. Ibid., p. 118.
80. Ibid., p. 120.
81. 6 July 1803. *Writings*, p. 730.
82. *Writings*, p. 731.
83. Ibid., p. 730.
84. As cited by Jack Lindsay, *William Blake: His Life and Work* (London: Constable, 1978), p. 157.
85. WB to Thomas Butts, 16 August 1803. *Writings*, p. 732.
86. *BR*, pp. 124–5.
87. Ibid., p. 236.
88. Ibid., p. 126.

Chapter 11: Further Hazards of Patronage 1803–1805

1. WB to William Hayley, 26 October 1803. *Writings*, p. 738.
2. WB to William Hayley, 22 March 1805. *Writings*, p. 764.
3. WB to William Hayley, 7 October 1803. *Writings*, p. 736.
4. *BR*, p. 135.
5. Ibid., p. 144.
6. Ibid., p. 145.
7. Ibid., p. 146.
8. Ibid., p. 145.
9. Ibid., p. 146.
10. Ibid., p. 145.
11. WB to William Hayley, 14 January 1804. *Writings*, p. 704.
12. WB to William Hayley, 7 October 1803. *Writings*, p. 736.
13. Ibid., pp. 736–7.
14. Ibid., p. 737.

15. WB to William Hayley, 4 December 1804. *Writings*, p. 758.
16. WB to William Hayley, 23 February 1804. *Writings*, p. 742.
17. 7 April 1804. *Writings*, p. 746.
18. Ibid., p. 747.
19. 27 April 1804. *Writings*, p. 747.
20. *Writings*, p. 741.
21. WB to William Hayley, 22 June 1804. *Writings*, pp. 752–3.
22. Ibid., p. 753.
23. 28 September 1804. *Writings*, p. 755.
24. 28 December 1804. *Writings*, p. 760.
25. 19 January 1805. *Writings*, p. 762.
26. 22 January 1805. *Writings*, p. 763.
27. 22 March 1805. *Writings*, p. 765.
28. 4 June 1805. *Writings*, p. 765.
29. 4 May 1804. *Writings*, p. 749.
30. Ibid.
31. 28 May 1804. *Writings*, p. 751.
32. Ibid.
33. Ibid.
34. 23 October 1804. *Writings*, p. 756.
35. William Hayley, *Life of George Romney* (London, 1809), p. 123.
36. WB to William Hayley, 23 October 1804. *Writings*, pp. 756–7.
37. Joseph Farington, *Diary*, ed. James Grieg (London: Hutchinson, 1923), vol. II, pp. 137–8.
38. *Notebook*, K. 547.
39. WB to William Hayley, 23 October 1804. *Writings*, p. 756.
40. 31 July 1805. *BR*, p. 163.
41. 3 August 1805. *BR*, p. 164.
42. *BR*, p. 154.
43. 22 March 1805. *Writings*, p. 764.
44. *Writings*, p. 506.
45. Ibid.
46. WB to William Hayley, 28 December 1804. *Writings*, p. 759.
47. WB to William Hayley, 28 May 1804. *Writings*, p. 750.
48. *Writings*, pp. 95–6.
49. Ibid., p. 100.
50. Ibid., pp. 100–1.
51. Ibid., pp. 107–8.
52. Ibid., p. 108.
53. Ibid., p. 142.
54. Ibid., p. 115.
55. 22 November 1802. *Writings*, p. 721.
56. *Writings*, p. 258.
57. *BR*, p. 229.

Chapter 12: 'Bob Screwmuch' and the Infamy of Patronage 1805–1808

1. 27 November 1805. *Writings*, p. 766.
2. *BR*, p. 48.
3. Gilchrist, p. 218.
4. Ibid.
5. As cited by Dennis M. Read, 'The Rival *Canterbury Pilgrims* of Blake and Cromek: Herculean Figures in the Carpet', *Modern Philology* 86 (2) (November 1988) 171.
6. Ibid., p. 172.
7. *BR*, p. 209, n. 2.
8. 27 November 1805. *Writings*, p. 766.
9. *The Life of Samuel Johnson*, 4th edn (London, 1804), vol. III, p. 45.
10. *The Grave* (London: Cromek, 1808), p. 3.
11. Ibid., p. 33.
12. *BR II*, p. 47.
13. Ibid., p. 31.
14. Ibid., p. 35.
15. Ibid., p. 32.
16. *BR*, p. 172.
17. Ibid., p. 167.
18. *BR II*, p. 30.
19. *BR*, p. 468.
20. *BR II*, p. 45.
21. *BR*, pp. 182–3.
22. *Writings*, p. 480.
23. *BR*, p. 184.
24. Ibid., pp. 184–6.
25. See Aileen Ward, 'Canterbury Revisited: The Blake Cromek Controversy', *Blake/An Illustrated Quarterly* 22 (1988–9) 83 and nn. 18–20.
26. *The Grave*, p. 37.
27. *BR.*, pp. 464–5.
28. Ibid., p. 464.
29. Ibid., p. 492.
30. Ibid., p. 205.
31. *Writings*, p. 475.
32. Ibid., p. 507.
33. Ibid., p. 508.
34. Ibid., p. 509.
35. Ibid., pp. 503–4.
36. The *Examiner* for 1 July 1810, as cited by Essick and Paley in their study with facsimile of the Blake–Cromek edition of *The Grave* (London: Scolar Press, 1982), p. 29.

Chapter 13: A Hidden Life 1808–1818

1. *BR*, p. 220.
2. Ibid., p. 215.
3. Ibid., p. 221.
4. Ibid., p. 222.
5. Ibid., p. 424.
6. Wilson, p. 218.
7. 18 December 1808. As presented in *The Letters of William Blake*, ed. Geoffrey Keynes (London: Rupert Hart-Davis, 1968), p. 134.
8. 19 December 1808. *Writings*, p. 770.
9. *Writings*, p. 529.
10. Ibid., p. 531.
11. Ibid., p. 538.
12. Ibid., p. 537.
13. Ibid., pp. 537–8.
14. Ibid., p. 532.
15. Ibid., p. 550.
16. Ibid.
17. *BR*, pp. 225.
18. Ibid., p. 226.
19. Ibid., p. 216.
20. Ibid., pp. 217–18.
21. Ibid., p. 219.
22. *Writings*, p. 582.
23. Ibid.
24. Gilchrist, p. 287.
25. *BR*, pp. 227–8.
26. Ibid., p. 229.
27. Ibid., p. 232.
28. Ibid., p. 233.
29. Ibid., pp. 232–3.
30. Ibid., p. 235.
31. Ibid.
32. Ibid.
33. Ibid.
34. Ibid., p. 238.
35. Ibid., pp. 241–2.
36. Ibid., p. 245.
37. Ibid.
38. Ibid., p.249.
39. Ibid., pp. 249–50.
40. G.E. Bentley Jr, 'Thomas Butts, White Collar Maecenas', *Publications of the Modern Language Association of America* 71 (1956) 1058–9.
41. *Writings*, p. 718.
42. Gilchrist, p. 243.
43. *BR*, p. 237.

44. Gilchrist, p. 316.
45. *BR*, p. 238.

Chapter 14: An Antique Patriarch 1818–1827

1. 8 June 1818. *Writings*, p. 771.
2. Robert N. Essick, 'John Linnell, William Blake, and the Printmaker's Craft', *Huntington Library Quarterly* 46 (1983) 25.
3. G.E. Bentley Jr, 'Blake and the Antients: A Prophet with Honour Among the Sons of God', *Huntington Library Quarterly* 46 (1983) 3.
4. A.H.P., as cited in Raymond Lister, *Samuel Palmer: His Life and Art* (Cambridge: Cambridge University Press, 1987), p. 17.
5. *BR*, p. 264.
6. Ibid., p. 257.
7. Ibid.
8. Essick, op. cit., p. 25. He is quoting Gilchrist.
9. *BR*, p. 258.
10. Bentley, op. cit., p. 4.
11. *BR*, p. 257.
12. Ibid., p. 263.
13. Ibid., pp. 260, 271.
14. Ibid.
15. As cited by Geoffrey Keynes, *Blake Studies*, 2nd edn (Oxford: The Clarendon Press, 1971), p. 135.
16. *BR*, pp. 265–6.
17. Ibid., p. 267.
18. Ibid., p. 271.
19. Gilchrist, p. 283.
20. *BR*, p. 273.
21. Ibid., pp. 274–5.
22. Ibid., p. 564.
23. Ibid., p. 566.
24. Ibid., p. 565.
25. Ibid., p. 566.
26. Ibid., p. 567.
27. Ibid., p. 315.
28. Ibid., p. 281.
29. Ibid., p. 294.
30. Ibid., p. 276.
31. Ibid.
32. WB to Linnell, [April 1826]. *Writings*, p. 777.
33. *BR*, p. 276.
34. Ibid., p. 277.
35. Ibid.
36. Ibid., p. 278.

37. *BR*, p. 278.
38. As cited in ibid., p. 295.
39. Ibid., p. 293.
40. Ibid., p. 531.
41. See Bentley, op. cit., p. 6.
42. *BR*, p. 418.
43. Ibid., p. 288.
44. Ibid., pp. 293–4.
45. Ibid., p. 291.
46. Ibid., p. 282.
47. Ibid., p. 283.
48. Ibid., pp. 280, 281.
49. Ibid., p. 291.
50. Ibid., p. 306.
51. Ibid., p. 305.
52. Ibid., p. 290.
53. Gilchrist, p. 331.
54. *BR*, pp. 302–3.
55. Ibid., p. 313.
56. *William Blake's Writings*, ed. G.E. Bentley Jr (Oxford: The Clarendon Press, 1978). p. 1340.
57. Ibid., p. 1344.
58. Ibid., p. 1341.
59. *BR*, p. 317.
60. Ibid., p. 331.
61. WB to Linnell, 31 March 1826. *Writings*, p. 776.
62. WB to Linnell, 19 May 1826. *Writings*, p. 777.
63. WB to Linnell, 5 July 1826. *Writings*, p. 778.
64. WB to Linnell, 16 July 1826. *Writings*, p. 780.
65. WB to Linnell, 29 July 1826. *Writings*, p. 780.
66. WB to Linnell, February 1827. *Writings*, p. 782.
67. WB to Linnell, 1 August 1826. *Writings*, p. 781.
68. *BR*, p. 337.
69. WB to Cumberland, 12 April 1827. *Writings*, p. 783.
70. Ibid., p. 784.
71. WB to Linnell, 25 April 1827. *Writings*, p. 784.
72. WB to Linnell, 3 July 1827. *Writings*, p. 785.
73. *BR*, pp. 475–6.
74. Ibid., p. 341.
75. Ibid., p. 342.
76. Ibid., pp. 527–8.
77. Ibid., p. 342.
78. *Blake Newsletter* 6 (1972) 24, as told by Richmond's grandson to Ruthven Todd.
79. *The Letters of William Blake*, ed. Geoffrey Keynes (London: Rupert Hart-Davis, 1968), p. 165.

80. Wilson, p. 366.
81. *BR*, p. 345.
82. Ibid., p. 410.

Select Bibliography

G. E. Bentley Jr's magisterial *Blake Books* (Oxford: The Clarendon Press, 1977) is an authoritative guide to Blake scholarship up to 1974. Work published after that date is reviewed annually in *Blake/An Illustrated Quarterly* (previously called *Blake Newsletter*). Listed below are those books and articles which I found especially useful in the writing of this book.

Bellin, Harvey F. and Darrell Ruhl, ed. *Blake and Swedenborg*. New York: Swedenborg Foundation, 1985.

Bentley, Gerald E., Jr. 'Blake and Swedenborg', *Notes and Queries* 199 (1954) 264–5.

——'Thomas Butts, White Collar Maecenas', *Publications of the Modern Language Association* 71 (1956) 1052–66.

——'A. S. Mathew, Patron of Blake and Flaxman', *Notes and Queries* 203 (1958) 168–78.

——'The Promotion of Blake's *Grave* Designs', *University of Toronto Quarterly* 31 (1962) 340–53.

——'Blake and Cromek: The Wheat and the Tares', *Modern Philology* 71 (1974) 366–79.

——*A Bibliography of George Cumberland*. New York: Garland, 1975.

——'Blake and the Antients: A Prophet with Honour Among the Sons of God', *Huntington Library Quarterly* 46 (1983) 1–17.

——'Richard Edwards, Publisher of Church-and-King Pamphlets and of William Blake', *Studies in Bibliography* 41 (1988) 283–315.

Bindman, David. *Blake as an Artist*. Oxford: Phaidon, 1977.

——*William Blake: His Art and Times*. New Haven and Toronto: The Yale Center for British Art and the Art Gallery of Ontario, 1982.

Bishop, Morchard [Oliver Stonor]. *Blake's Hayley*. London: Gollancz, 1951.

Bogen, Nancy. 'The Problem of William Blake's Early Religion', *Personalist* 49 (1968) 509–22.

Bray, A. E. *Life of Thomas Stothard, R. A.* London: John Murray, 1851.

Bronowski, Jacob. *William Blake: A Man Without a Mask.* Harmondsworth: Penguin Books, 1954.

Bruntjen, Sven. *John Boydell: A Study of Art Patronage and Printselling in Georgian London.* New York: Garland, 1985.

Burke, Joseph. *English Art 1714–1800.* Oxford: The Clarendon Press, 1976.

Butlin, Martin. *William Blake.* London: Tate Gallery, 1978.

——*The Paintings and Drawings of William Blake.* New Haven and London: Yale University Press, 1981.

Damon, S. Foster. *A Blake Dictionary.* New York: Dutton, 1971.

Damrosch, Leopold, Jr. *Symbol and Truth in Blake's Myth.* Princeton: Princeton University Press, 1980.

Dorfman, Deborah. *Blake in the Nineteenth Century: His Reputation as a Poet from Gilchrist to Yeats.* New Haven and London: Yale University Press, 1969.

Eaves, Morris, ed. 'Inside the Blake Industry: Past, Present, and Future', *Studies in Romanticism* 21 (1982) 389–443.

Erdman, David V. 'Lambeth and Bethlehem in Blake's Jerusalem', *Modern Philology* 48 (1951) 184–92.

——'"Blake" Entries in Godwin's Diary', *Notes and Queries* 198 (1953) 354–6.

——*Blake: Prophet against Empire.* Revised edition. Garden City: Doubleday, 1969.

——and John E. Grant, eds. *Blake's Visionary Forms Dramatic.* Princeton: Princeton University Press, 1970.

Essick, Robert N. *William Blake: Printmaker.* Princeton: Princeton University Press, 1980.

——*The Separate Plates of William Blake: A Catalogue.* Princeton: Princeton University Press, 1983.

——'John Linnell, William Blake, and the Printmaker's Craft', *Huntington Library Quarterly* 46 (1983) 18–32.

Ferber, Michael. '"London" and Its Politics', *English Literary History* 48 (1981) 310–38.

——*The Social Vision of William Blake.* Princeton: Princeton University Press, 1985.

Frye, Northrop. *Fearful Symmetry.* Princeton: Princeton University Press, 1947.

Gardner, Stanley. *Blake's Innocence and Experience Retraced.* London and New York: Athlone Press and St Martin's Press, 1986.

George, M. Dorothy. *London Life in the Eighteenth Century.* Chicago: Academy Chicago, 1984.

Hagstrum, Jean H. *William Blake: Poet and Painter.* Chicago: University of Chicago Press, 1964.

Keynes, Geoffrey, *Blake Studies.* 2nd edition. Oxford: The Clarendon Press, 1971.

King, James. 'The Meredith Family, Thomas Taylor, and William Blake', *Studies in Romanticism* 11 (1972) 153–7.

——*William Cowper: A Biography.* Durham: Duke University Press, 1986.

Larrissy, Edward. *William Blake.* Oxford: Basil Blackwell, 1985.

Lindberg, Bo. *William Blake's Illustrations to the Book of Job.* Abo: Abo Akademi, 1973.

Lindsay, Jack. *William Blake: His Life and Work.* London: Constable, 1978.

Lister, Raymond. *The Paintings of William Blake.* Cambridge: Cambridge University Press, 1986.

——*Samuel Palmer: His Life and Art.* Cambridge: Cambridge University Press, 1987.

Miner, Paul. 'William Blake's "Divine Analogy"', *Criticism* 3 (1961) 46–61.

Mitchell, W. J. T. *Blake's Composite Art.* Princeton: Princeton University Press, 1978.

Paley, Morton D. *Energy and the Imagination: A Study of the Development of Blake's Thought.* Oxford: The Clarendon Press, 1970.

——'The Truchsessian Gallery Revisited', *Studies in Romanticism* 16 (1977) 165–77.

——*The Continuing City: William Blake's Jerusalem.* Oxford: The Clarendon Press, 1983.

——and Michael Phillips, eds. *William Blake: Essays in Honour of Sir Geoffrey Keynes.* Oxford: The Clarendon Press, 1973.

Porter, Roy. *English Society in the Eighteenth Century.* Harmondsworth: Penguin Books, 1984.

Pressly, Nancy L. *Fuseli Circle in Rome.* New Haven: Yale Center for British Art, 1979.

Pressly, William L. *James Barry: The Artist as Hero.* London: Tate Gallery, 1983.

Read, Dennis M. 'The Context of Blake's "Public Address": Cromek and The Chalcographic Society', *Philological Quarterly* 60 (1981) 69–86.

——'The Rival *Canterbury Pilgrims* of Blake and Cromek: Herculean Figures in the Carpet', *Modern Philology* 86 (1988) 171–90.

Roe, Albert S. *Blake's Illustrations to the Divine Comedy*. Princeton: Princeton University Press, 1967.

Rudé, George. *Hanoverian London*. Berkeley: University of California Press, 1971.

Stone, Lawrence. *The Family, Sex and Marriage in England 1500–1800*. London: Weidenfeld & Nicolson, 1977.

Sutherland, John. 'Blake: A Crisis of Love and Jealousy', *Publications of the Modern Language Association* 87 (1972) 424–31.

Tayler, Irene. *Blake's Illustrations to the Poems of Gray*. Princeton: Princeton University Press, 1971.

Thompson, E. P. *The Making of the English Working Class*. Harmondsworth: Penguin Books, 1980.

Todd, Ruthven. *William Blake the Artist*. London and New York: Studio Vista and Dutton, 1971.

Viscomi, Joseph. 'The Myth of Commissioned Illuminated Books: George Romney, Isaac D'Israeli, and "ONE HUNDRED AND SIXTY designs ... of Blake's"', *Blake/An Illustrated Quarterly* 23 (1989) 48–66.

Ward, Aileen. 'Canterbury Revisited: The Blake–Cromek Controversy', *Blake/An Illustrated Quarterly* 22 (1988–9) 80–92.

——'"Sir Joshua and His Gang": William Blake and the Royal Academy', *Huntington Library Quarterly* 52 (1989) 75–95.

Index